Modular Programming in Java 9

Write reusable, maintainable code with the Java Platform Module System

Koushik Kothagal

BIRMINGHAM - MUMBAI

Modular Programming in Java 9

First published: August 2017

Production reference: 1240817

Published by Packt Publishing Ltd.
Livery Place
35 Livery Street
Birmingham
B3 2PB, UK.

ISBN 978-1-78712-690-9

www.packtpub.com

Credits

Author
Koushik Kothagal

Reviewers
Mozart Brocchini
Mandar Jog

Commissioning Editor
Aaron Lazar

Acquisition Editor
Alok Dhuri

Content Development Editor
Siddhi Chavan

Technical Editor
Abhishek Sharma

Copy Editor
Safis Editing

Project Coordinator
Prajakta Naik

Proofreader
Safis Editing

Indexer
Francy Puthiry

Graphics
Abhinash Sahu

Production Coordinator
Nilesh Mohite

About the Author

Koushik Kothagal is the founder of Java Brains, an online training website that offers courses on various enterprise Java and JavaScript technologies entirely for free. He works as a Senior Staff Engineer at Financial Engines. He has over 14 years of professional experience working on full-stack web applications and has worked extensively with technologies such as Java, Spring, Java EE, JavaScript, and Angular. He loves teaching, and when he's not coding Java and JavaScript, he's probably teaching it! He currently lives in the Bay Area.

About the Reviewers

Mozart Brocchini is a software architect who loves to code. Currently, he is helping the largest food distributor in the world adopt modern application architectures, platforms, and practices, such as microservices, cloud, PaaS, APIs, and DevOps.

Previously, he designed and implemented distributed real-time systems in the Oil and Gas sector. He has also built scientific applications that perform high throughput DNA sequencing at Human Genome Sequence Lab with Baylor College of Medicine. Mozart codes in many programming languages and has extensive experience in building software for a variety of other industries including legal, eDiscovery, construction, and GIS.

Mandar Jog is an expert IT trainer with over 15 years of training experience. He is an expert in technologies such as Java, J2EE, and Android. He also holds SCJP and SCWCD certifications. He is also an occasional blogger, where he makes the readers feel "I can" for the complex concepts in Java and J2EE. He is a regular speaker at many engineering colleges for technical seminars and workshops.

I would like to thank Packt for giving me the opportunity to review relatively new technology updates. And, of course, my wife, Tejaswini, for her ever-lasting support--she is a real source of inspiration and motivation for the growth of my career.

www.PacktPub.com

For support files and downloads related to your book, please visit www.PacktPub.com.

Did you know that Packt offers eBook versions of every book published, with PDF and ePub files available? You can upgrade to the eBook version at www.PacktPub.com and as a print book customer, you are entitled to a discount on the eBook copy. Get in touch with us at service@packtpub.com for more details.

At www.PacktPub.com, you can also read a collection of free technical articles, sign up for a range of free newsletters and receive exclusive discounts and offers on Packt books and eBooks.

www.packtpub.com/mapt

Get the most in-demand software skills with Mapt. Mapt gives you full access to all Packt books and video courses, as well as industry-leading tools to help you plan your personal development and advance your career.

Why subscribe?

- Fully searchable across every book published by Packt
- Copy and paste, print, and bookmark content
- On demand and accessible via a web browser

Customer Feedback

Thanks for purchasing this Packt book. At Packt, quality is at the heart of our editorial process. To help us improve, please leave us an honest review on this book's Amazon page at `https://www.amazon.com/dp/1787126900`.

If you'd like to join our team of regular reviewers, you can e-mail us at `customerreviews@packtpub.com`. We award our regular reviewers with free eBooks and videos in exchange for their valuable feedback. Help us be relentless in improving our products!

Table of Contents

Preface

Modularity is coming to Java with Java 9, and it's a big deal! Unlike other Java releases that come with added features to the language that you can optionally use in your code, the Java Platform Modular System is a complete change in the way we think about, design, and write Java applications.

This book is a detailed guide and a hands-on companion to help you learn about and write modular code in Java. After reading and working through the code in this book, you'll have a deep understanding of Java 9 modularity, its features, the impact on the platform, and how you can use this new paradigm to build modular applications yourself.

This book has been carefully designed to provide a gentle introduction to the topics, while gradually ramping up the scope and complexity of the topics covered. This is not a reference book. For example, when I introduce a concept or a feature, I don't provide all possible details or syntax combinations in an attempt to be comprehensive. My primary goal while writing this book is to help you grasp the concepts and gain a deep understanding of Java modularity. The ordering of topics and discussions in this book has been carefully crafted to make sure you always have the necessary knowledge to understand the topic being covered. Thus, this book benefits greatly from being read sequentially. Having said that, if you are already aware of some of the topics and you want to jump to a specific topic, you should be able to do that too. A handy index is provided at the end of the book for this purpose.

What this book covers

Chapter 1, *Introducing Java 9 Modularity*, covers the status quo of code structuring and management in Java 8 and before. It outlines the challenges and pitfalls in maintaining and organizing large code bases over time, with the example of a large Java code base everyone is familiar with--the JDK. It then introduces Project Jigsaw and explains how the concept of modularity attempts to solve the challenges outlined in the previous chapter. It discusses the module-based changes to the JDK structure as well as the ability to create modules in application code.

Chapter 2, *Creating Your First Java Module*, gets you started on a sample code project that is written without using the module construct. It then guides you step-by-step through creating your first Java 9 module. It introduces you to the module keyword, the module-info.java class and how to define a custom Java module. It then covers compiling and running a module. It explains the structure of the .class files and how the runtime uses the same module definition to infer the module structure.

Chapter 3, *Handling Inter-Module Dependencies*, shows how modules can hardly work well in isolation. They are designed to be parts of a bigger unit and are meant to work with each other. This chapter covers creating a second module and having the modules depend on each other. You'll learn how to define such a relationship in Java 9, as well as how to compile and run a multi-module application.

Chapter 4, *Introducing the Modular JDK*, switches our attention to the Java platform, specifically the JDK. You'll learn about the important changes to the JDK that has resulted from the modularization of the platform. You'll learn about the modules that come out of the box with the JDK. You'll also learn about the tools and techniques to browse and get more information about any of those modules.

Chapter 5, *Using Platform APIs*, teaches you how to use the platform modules in the sample application through a hands-on step-by-step guide. You'll understand some of the challenges that you may typically face when depending on platform modules and how to solve them.

Chapter 6, *Module Resolution, Readability, and Accessibility*, delves deep into inter-module dependencies and how you can control the level of encapsulation for their modules and libraries. It continues the module resolution discussion of the previous chapter by adding two new criteria that influences the encapsulation and availability of Java elements-- accessibility and readability.

Chapter 7, *Introducing Services*, looks at a vital element of coupling that exists between two modules in the sample application and how that prevents the extensibility and "plugging-in" of new modules. It explains the new Java 9 services, provides step-by-step instructions to encapsulate implementation classes, and uses ServiceLoader to look them up.

Chapter 8, *Understanding Linking and Using jlink*, introduces the static linking step in the Java 9 development process and what happens during it. It explains how linking plays an important part when developing modules in Java 9. It then provides step-by-step instructions to create a runtime image for the sample project, how to optimize it, and how to execute the image.

Chapter 9, *Module Design Patterns and Strategies*, covers several best practices when it comes to building modular applications in Java. Now that you have a good understanding of the Java module system features and how it works, the next question is when and how to use them? You'll learn how to establish module scopes and boundaries, how to define good module interfaces, and how to tackle some common challenges when building a modular application.

Chapter 10, *Preparing Your Code for Java 9*, walks you through getting an old sample code base (written in Java 7) ready to be migrated to Java 9. It illustrates the optional nature of Java modules and how a classpath-based code is automatically assigned to an "unnamed" module. It then provides step-by-step instructions to get legacy code to compile and run in Java 9. It also shows you how to handle issues with usage of encapsulated types, and how to work around them.

Chapter 11, *Migrating Your Code to Java 9*, walks you through upgrading legacy code to use the new modularity features of Java 9. You'll learn how to form a migration strategy for your code, as well as how to deal with dependencies that are not compatible with Java 9. You'll learn how to use Java 9 features that are designed to assist such migration, such as automatic modules and command-line overrides.

Chapter 12, *Using Build Tools and Testing Java Modules*, covers two important aspects of Java programming--build tool integration and unit testing. You'll learn to use Maven to structure your projects and align Maven's multi-module project concepts with Java 9 modular applications. You'll also learn how to test Java modules using JUnit.

What you need for this book

To follow the example code in this book, you'll need a computer running a reasonably recent version of Windows, macOS, or Linux. You'll also need a text editor to edit the code. I highly recommend using a text editor that allows you to open multiple files at a time and switch between them easily.

Who this book is for

If you are a Java developer who has been coding Java applications, and you want to learn about the new modularity features in Java 9, you are the perfect audience for this book. You may working on a Java 9 modular project, or may be tasked with the effort to migrate an existing Java code base to Java 9, or you may have found the buzz around modularity in Java intriguing and want to learn more; either way, this is the right book for you!

This book assumes you are familiar with the Java programming language and have written some Java code before. It also assumes you are comfortable with the command-line interface in your operating system of choice. The commands you need to run will be provided in the book.

Conventions

In this book, you will find a number of text styles that distinguish between different kinds of information. Here are some examples of these styles and an explanation of their meaning.

Code words in text, database table names, folder names, filenames, file extensions, pathnames, dummy URLs, user input, and Twitter handles are shown as follows: "We'll first call the getContacts() method on an instance of ContactUtil to get the hardcoded Contact list."

A block of code is set as follows:

```
module packt.addressbook {
    requires packt.sortutil;
}
```

Any command-line input or output is written as follows. Lines beginning with $ indicate an input command. The input command might be broken into several lines to aid readability, but needs to be entered as one continuous line at prompt:

```
$ export JAVA_HOME=$(/usr/libexec/java_home -v 1.8)
```

New terms and **important words** are shown in bold. Words that you see on the screen, for example, in menus or dialog boxes, appear in the text like this: "Click on **File | New Project**, you'll see a **New Project** overlay with a new option in the Java category--**Java Modular Project**."

Warnings or important notes appear like this.

Tips and tricks appear like this.

Reader feedback

Feedback from our readers is always welcome. Let us know what you think about this book--what you liked or disliked. Reader feedback is important for us as it helps us develop titles that you will really get the most out of.

To send us general feedback, simply email `feedback@packtpub.com`, and mention the book's title in the subject of your message.

If there is a topic that you have expertise in and you are interested in either writing or contributing to a book, see our author guide at `www.packtpub.com/authors`.

Customer support

Now that you are the proud owner of a Packt book, we have a number of things to help you to get the most from your purchase.

Downloading the example code

You can download the example code files for this book from your account at `http://www.packtpub.com`. If you purchased this book elsewhere, you can visit `http://www.packtpub.com/support` and register to have the files emailed directly to you.

You can download the code files by following these steps:

1. Log in or register to our website using your email address and password.
2. Hover the mouse pointer on the **SUPPORT** tab at the top.
3. Click on **Code Downloads & Errata**.
4. Enter the name of the book in the **Search** box.
5. Select the book for which you're looking to download the code files.
6. Choose from the drop-down menu where you purchased this book from.
7. Click on **Code Download**.

Once the file is downloaded, please make sure that you unzip or extract the folder using the latest version of:

- WinRAR / 7-Zip for Windows
- Zipeg / iZip / UnRarX for macOS
- 7-Zip / PeaZip for Linux

The code bundle for the book is also hosted on GitHub at
`https://github.com/koushikkothagal/Modular-Programming-in-Java-9`. We also have
other code bundles from our rich catalog of books and videos available at
`https://github.com/PacktPublishing/`. Check them out!

Errata

Although we have taken every care to ensure the accuracy of our content, mistakes do
happen. If you find a mistake in one of our books--maybe a mistake in the text or the code--
we would be grateful if you could report this to us. By doing so, you can save other readers
from frustration and help us improve subsequent versions of this book. If you find any
errata, please report them by visiting `http://www.packtpub.com/submit-errata`, selecting
your book, clicking on the **Errata Submission Form** link, and entering the details of your
errata. Once your errata are verified, your submission will be accepted and the errata will
be uploaded to our website or added to any list of existing errata under the Errata section of
that title.

To view the previously submitted errata, go to
`https://www.packtpub.com/books/content/support` and enter the name of the book in the
search field. The required information will appear under the **Errata** section.

Piracy

Piracy of copyrighted material on the internet is an ongoing problem across all media. At
Packt, we take the protection of our copyright and licenses very seriously. If you come
across any illegal copies of our works in any form on the internet, please provide us with
the location address or website name immediately so that we can pursue a remedy.

Please contact us at `copyright@packtpub.com` with a link to the suspected pirated
material.

We appreciate your help in protecting our authors and our ability to bring you valuable
content.

Questions

If you have a problem with any aspect of this book, you can contact us at
`questions@packtpub.com`, and we will do our best to address the problem.

1
Introducing Java 9 Modularity

This book covers modularity features in Java 9--an important new change to the Java programming language. We'll look at its impact on Java development and how you can use it to build powerful modular applications. The Java 9 release also comes with a few other changes, such as support for HTTP 2.0 and a shell called `jshell` that lets you run Java code snippets in a **Read-Eval-Print-Loop** (**REPL**). While these are exciting new changes, they are not the focus of this book. We will be primarily focusing on the modularity features, which are arguably the most important and powerful among all the new changes with the Java 9 release.

This chapter provides an introduction to the new module features in Java 9 by covering the following topics:

- Examining two important structural and organizational problems when building Java applications today, and their implications
- Why does Java even need modularity features? What are we missing right now? And what do we gain from modularity?
- Introducing the **Java Platform Module System** (**JPMS**)
- Understanding the benefits that the Java modular system aims to provide

Modularity in Java

If you've been a developer for any length of time, you'll have very likely realized that the word **module** is perhaps one of the most overused terms in software development. A module can mean anything ranging from a group of code entities, components, or UI types, to framework elements to complete reusable libraries. Sometimes, we use the word to imply multiple meanings in the same context!

There is a good reason for that. When writing code, we typically try to break the code base down into smaller units in order to manage complexity. For anything more than very simple programs, having a monolithic code base is not a good idea. That's why *modular programming* is a generally favored software design approach. There are two important goals that modularity in software development usually achieves, which are as follows:

- Divide and conquer approach

  What do you do when you need to solve a large and seemingly insurmountable problem? *You break it down!* You'll very likely split it into smaller problems and solve them individually.

  The principles of modularity encourages separating large code bases into smaller encapsulated units of functionality that are then composed to work together as a bigger unit. This aligns well with the approach we humans usually take to solve large problems. Also, once you've got a bunch of smaller modules with specialized concerns, you can use those to solve various other problems. Thus, we also achieve *reusability!*

- Achieving encapsulation and well-defined interfaces

  When you build modules, you have the ability to hide the internal implementation from the consumers of your module. The hidden implementation details are usually referred to as being *encapsulated*, and what you expose to the consumers of your module is usually called the *interface* of your module.

Although Java developers have leveraged many different patterns and best practices over the years in order to write and structure modular and maintainable code, the language has never had native support to create modular units and build modular applications, until Java 9. With Java 9, Java developers now have the ability to create smaller units of code with a new construct called **Java modules** that they can group together like building blocks in order to compose larger applications. In addition to introducing this feature to the language, Java 9 also comes with what is probably the biggest overhaul to the core Java code base itself. The **Java Runtime Environment** (**JRE**) and the **Java Development Kit** (**JDK**) have been rewritten to use the concepts of modularity so that the core Java Platform itself is modularized.

When learning about Java 9 module features, it's important to understand what those new features add to the language when compared to the other features the language already has. Can't we write well organized code in Java 8? In fact, one of the benefits of object-oriented programming is indeed the idea of breaking down functionality into sub-units called *objects* or *classes*. We've been writing code like this in Java since version 1. Every Java class contains a portion of the overall application functionality that happens to belongs together. We have the ability to *encapsulate* some functionalities as internal to a class (as `private`) and some others as external (or `public`).

And then there's something in between with `protected`, thanks to the concept of packages.

Rethinking Java development with packages

Think about why we use packages in Java. We could very well write entire Java applications without creating any packages and, thereby, using just the default *unnamed* package. It would work! However, unless it's a simple or throwaway application, that's not a good idea. The idea of packages is to group your Java types into namespaces that signify the relationship, or perhaps a common *theme* among those types. It makes code easier to read, understand, and navigate.

The following diagram shows an example of classes organized in packages. Adding all classes to a single package (left) is not good practice. We typically group related classes into well-named packages that describe the nature of the classes in them (right):

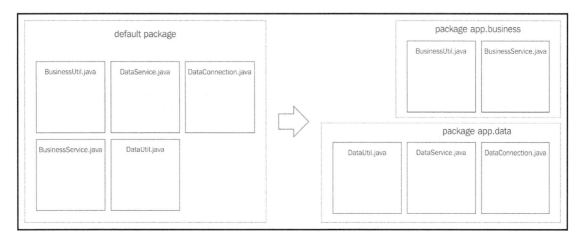

There's really no *rule* about what types belong together in a package. However, it's generally understood that when you create a package and put a bunch of Java types in it, the types are usually related in some way. You could very well write any random set of types in the same package and the compiler wouldn't care. However, anyone else who ends up working on your code could potentially hate you forever, so this is not a wise thing to do! Having related types in common packages also has the benefit of those types being able to access the protected members of each other. This is another level of *encapsulation*--any protected members or methods are encapsulated within types of a package. (Although, there's an exception to this, as inherited classes are able to access private members across packages.)

So, if the idea of modular programming is to break code and functionality into encapsulated units, there's a sense in which you can do *some* kind of modular programming in Java well before Java 9.

The following table shows the various ways in which you can encapsulate code in Java before Java 9:

What to encapsulate	How to encapsulate	Encapsulation boundary
Member variables and methods	`private` modifier	Class
Member variables and methods	`protected` modifier	Package
Member variables, methods, and types	No modifier (default package - protected)	Package

Isn't that good enough? Well, not really. The preceding table is where a limitation in the modular ability of the language becomes apparent. Notice the *What to encapsulate* column. Most of the encapsulation features provided by these modifiers focus on controlling access to member variables and methods. The only way you can really protect access to a type is by making it package-protected. That, unfortunately, ends up making access difficult for even your own library code to access the type, and you are forced to move all the code that accesses that type into the same package. What if you want more?

Why, you ask? There are a couple of problems with approaching modularity with just the preceding paradigm available in Java 8 and earlier. Let me explain both those problems with two stories.

The unfortunate tale of a library developer

Meet Jack. He's a Java developer at a medium-sized enterprise organization. He's a part of a team that writes code to do data processing. One day, Jack wrote some Java code to sort a list of usernames in alphabetical order. His code worked well without any errors and Jack was proud of his work. Since this was something that could be used by other developers in the organization, he decided to build it as a reusable library and share it with his colleagues as a packaged JAR file. Here's the structure of Jack's library:

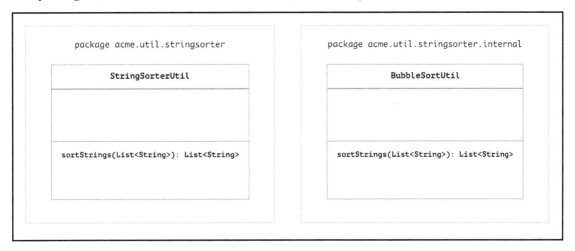

His code belonged to two packages--acme.util.stringsorter and acme.util.stringsorter.internal. The main utility class was StringSorterUtil with one method--sortStrings. The method in turn internally called and delegated the sorting responsibility to the BubbleSortUtil.sortStrings() class from a class in the acme.util.stringsorter.internal package. The BubbleSortUtil class used the popular Bubble Sort algorithm to sort a given list of Strings.

All that any developer had to do was to drop the jar in the classpath and call the StringSorterUtil.sortStrings() method by passing in an list of strings they needed sorting. And they did! Jack's little library became a hit! His colleagues loved the convenience that his library provided and they started using it to sort many things, such as names, tokens, addresses, and so on.

A few months later, Jack happened to talk to Daryl at the water cooler, and as usual, their conversation veered towards a discussion about their current favorite sorting algorithms. Daryl couldn't stop talking about his new-found love for hash sort. He said he found it performs much better than bubble sort, and it was unabashedly his new favorite algorithm! Jack was intrigued. He went to his desk and ran a few tests. Daryl was right! Hash sort outperformed bubble sort in most of his tests. Jack knew right then that he had to update his sorting utility to use hash sort. He added a new class, HashSortUtil in the acme.util.stringsorter.internal package and removed BubbleSortUtil.

The following is the structure of Jack's library after the change:

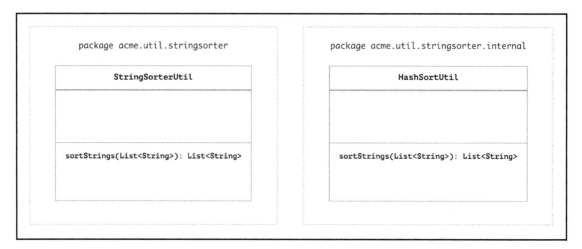

Thankfully, he had a separate internal class that did the sorting, so the process to invoke the StringSorterUtil.sortStrings() utility wouldn't change. Everyone could just drop in the newer version of the JAR and everything would work just fine.

But it didn't! A few of the code builds in his company started failing. It turned out the culprit was the newer version of Jack's library. Jack couldn't believe it. He didn't miss anything, did he? Well, no. All the projects that used just the StringSorterUtil class worked just fine. However, it turned out that some of the developers ended up using the BubbleSortUtil class in the internal package directly. It was available in the classpath, so they had just imported and used it. Now, since that class didn't exist in the new jar anymore, their code couldn't compile!

Jack sent out an email instructing everyone using `BubbleSortUtil` to update their code to use `StringSorterUtil` instead. However, it turned out the `BubbleSortUtil` class was being used in multiple places by that time, and it wasn't an easy task to change them all. "Couldn't Jack just put the `BubbleSortUtil` class back?" they asked. Jack yielded to their requests and the next version of the library had both the `SortUtil` classes (and would possibly do so well into the foreseeable future), even though it internally used only one of those two classes.

After the dust settled, Jack sat at his desk and wondered what had gone wrong. What could he have done to prevent this problem? Clearly, naming the package as internal did not prevent developers from using it. One solution would have been to write that internal bubble sort type as package-protected and move the external type to the same package. This way, he could leverage the third mechanism in the preceding encapsulation table. However, he liked the idea of separating the bubble sort class into its own type and package. Also, imagine if this were a bigger library and there was a common shared class that was supposed to be internal. In that case, pretty much all types in that library that need the internal type have to exist in the same package as that internal type! Wasn't there a better way to encapsulate the internal types?

The impossible task of a deployment engineer

Meet Amit, a deployment engineer at yet another enterprise technology firm. His job is to make sure that during every product release, the organization's code base is compiled and deployed properly in the production environment. During every release, he pulls in the application code and all the necessary jar files and places them in the classpath. He then starts the application that results in the **Java Virtual Machine** (**JVM**) loading all the classes and initializing execution.

One night, there was a major product feature release. There were a lot of changes to the code that were all supposed to be deployed and launched together. Amit made sure that all the new code was compiled properly and he had all the necessary jars in the classpath. He then had to start the application. Before he clicked on the button to launch the build, Amit wondered if there was some way he could make sure everything was good and that the application would work without any runtime class errors.

One thing that could potentially go wrong was if he had missed adding a certain class or jar in the classpath. Was there a way he could statically verify whether all the classes were available without actually running the application?

Each JAR bundled a set of types in a set of packages. Each type therein could potentially import other types, either from the same JAR or from other jars. To make sure he has all the classes in the classpath, he has to go to each class and verify that all its imports are in the classpath. Considering that the number of classes in his application run to thousands, it's a Herculean task.

The following diagram is a simplified version of what a sample deployed Java application looks like:

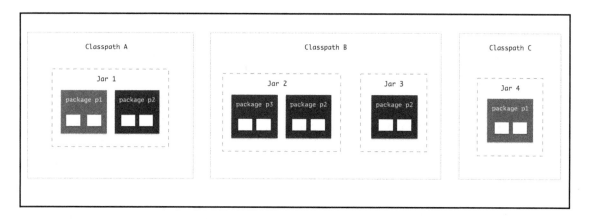

There are four jar files in the picture above, each of which contains packages and classes within them. **Jar 1** is deployed in **Classpath A**, **Jar 2** and **Jar 3** in **Classpath B**, and **Jar 4** in **Classpath C**. Let's assume each jar has two classes as indicated by the smaller white boxes. The three paths are configured as classpaths for the Java runtime, so the runtime knows to look at all three paths to scan and pick up classes.

After scanning all the classpaths, this is what the structure looks like to the Java runtime:

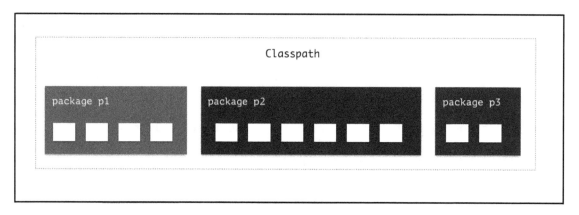

Notice that the runtime doesn't care which directory or classpath the package/type is in. It also doesn't care which jar the package/type is bundled in. As far as the Java runtime is concerned, it's just a flattened list of types in packages!

In Java, a classpath is a just set of paths. Any of those locations could have the jars and classes that the application needs to work. You can immediately see how easy it is for things to break! There's always a possibility that some of the classes that the application uses are *not* available in the classpath. Perhaps a missing jar or library. If the runtime doesn't have a specific class it needs, the application could start running fine, but throw a `NoClassDefFoundError` much later. That too, only when the execution hits a point where a missing class is actually needed.

This is a huge and very real problem in large Java applications today. There is a whole ecosystem of solutions that have sprung up to address this. For example, tools and build utilities, such as Maven or Gradle, standardize the process of specifying and acquiring external dependencies. Process-based solutions such as continuous integration aim to solve the unpredictable nature of builds across various development environments. However, all that such tools can do is make the process *predictable*. They cannot verify the *validity* or *accuracy* of the result that they help assemble. Once the dependencies are fetched, there's nothing that those tools can do to detect missing or duplicate types in the classpath.

Back to Amit's story. Having no way to verify whether all the classes are available up front, Amit hopes for the best and deploys the application. The application starts up fine and runs for a couple of hours without any errors. However, there's still no saying if he's got it right. Maybe there's a class in there that hasn't been executed yet, but when it has, the JVM might realize that it cannot find one of its imports. Or, maybe, there are duplicate versions of the same class in the classpath and the JVM picks up the first copy it finds. Wasn't there a better way to ensure that any given Java application will work *reliably* in advance?

The classpath problem

We've seen two problems in Jack's and Amit's stories. Jack needed an effective way to *encapsulate* portions of his library, but couldn't. Amit needed a way to *ensure reliable execution* of his application without actually executing it. Both Jack and Amit didn't really have a solution to their problems because of the way classpath resolution works in Java. We may sometimes mistakenly think of a JAR file as a way to build a reusable module in Java, but that's unfortunately not the case. A JAR file is just a convenient bundle of classes. Nothing more! Once in the classpath, the JVM treats classes in a JAR no differently from separate class files all in the same root directory. At runtime, as far as the JVM is concerned, an application is just a set of classes in a flat list of packages.

What's worse is, once a class is in the classpath, it's free for all. It's incredibly easy for any developer to use a type they are not supposed to, or a type that might be available for them during compile time, but not at deployment/runtime. Or there could be multiple copies or even multiple versions of the same class in two different classpath locations, making it unpredictable which version the runtime will actually pick up during execution. There's a problem commonly called **JAR hell**, which refers to several issues resulting from mismatched and incorrect classes and versions in JAR files.

This problem is exacerbated in huge code bases with hundreds of thousands of classes. Imagine all those classes in your application as a flat list with no structure! It's a nightmare to maintain and organize. The bigger the code base, the bigger the problem. To illustrate this, let's take the classic example of a code base that's written in Java, that's incredibly large and complex, and has lasted for many years now. It is perhaps one of the oldest Java code bases ever, and still it continues to grow and change at a fairly rapid pace. Any guesses? Well, it's the Java platform itself!

Java - the 20-year-old code base

Talk about a monolith! Java has come a long way since its first release in 1996. The first major release of the JDK had a little over 500 public classes. A far cry indeed from JDK 8 released in 2014, which counts upwards of 4,200 public classes and over 20,000 total files.

The following commands extract the rt.jar file, a library JAR file bundled in JDK 8, and count the number of classes in it. With the Java 8 version I have installed on my machine, the count is 20651:

```
~ $ cd $JAVA_HOME/jre/lib
/Library/Java/JavaVirtualMachines/jdk1.8.0_66.jdk/Contents/Home/jre/lib $ unzip -l rt.jar | grep \.class | wc -l
    20651
```

The JDK and the runtime, the JRE, have continued to grow over the years. There are a lot of features that have been added to the language, so this growth is understandable. However, the Java language is also notorious for going to great lengths to maintain backward compatibility and for its reluctance to deprecate features unless it is absolutely necessary. So, in a way, the current size of the runtime is a little over what it could have ideally been.

Normally, most application developers wouldn't need to worry about the JDK code base. They just focus on their application code. However, the contents of the runtime *does* matter for application execution because of the way it is bundled. Traditionally, every JRE has had all the classes necessary for runtime bundled into a single JAR that resides in the lib directory called rt.jar. The name rt, as you might have guessed, stands for **runtime**.

Not only is this huge monolith of classes unnecessarily bulky in size, it also adds performance overheads for the Java Virtual Machine to manage. And that's a price the execution environment of all your applications have to pay, irrespective of whether all of those classes are being used or not.

Legacy classes

A good example of classes that you don't need is the set of classes in the JRE related to CORBA. Ever heard of CORBA? If you haven't, don't despair. It's for a reason! It's an old technology that was introduced to the Java runtime back in version 1.4. It has mostly fallen out of popular use since then. Considering most applications don't use the CORBA technology anymore, wouldn't it be great if apps could be bundled with JREs that do not contain the unnecessary CORBA classes?

That's unfortunately not possible, again, because of rt.jar. Since everything gets bundled into a single runtime JAR, you cannot pick and choose what features you need. Everybody gets everything. And since the runtime has been increasing in size, so has the standalone deployable application. This is a more significant challenge when the runtime needs to be used on smaller devices with limited resources. If you are bundling the runtime with a simple *Hello World* application that uses just a handful of classes from the runtime, you have no option but to bundle a whole lot of unused classes in rt.jar with it. And, yes, even those old CORBA classes join in for the ride!

Java 8 introduced the concept of profiles, and with that, you can technically deploy smaller runtimes. But they do have some drawbacks. Also, this feature was just an initial step in the introduction of modularity features in Java 9 anyway. We'll examine compact profiles in detail in Chapter 4, *Introducing the Modular JDK.*

Internal APIs

Remember the problem that Jack had with his BubbleSortUtil class? It was a Java class he wrote with the intention of it being private to his library. However, even though it started out as a private *internal* class, it ended up being a *public* class because other developers just decided to use it.

That was just a small library. Now, think about a library as big and as widely used as the Java runtime. The Java runtime obviously bundles in internal classes that are required for its functioning and aren't meant to be used by application developers. However, considering the magnitude of its usage, it isn't surprising that some of the internal classes are inadvertently used by developers anyway.

A classic example of this is a class called `Unsafe` in the `sun.misc` package. This ominous sounding class has been a part of every major JDK release for a while now. Can you guess what it does? It contains a collection of methods that perform, according to the author of the class, *low-level unsafe operations*. Yes, it actually says that in the comments in the class! For instance, it has a method that gets a value from a memory address. Not a typical day's work for a Java application developer! You wouldn't, and ideally shouldn't, do something like that as an application developer. This is why the class has been marked as an internal API. Want to look up its Javadoc to use it? You won't find it in there. Want to create a new instance of the class? Its constructors are marked as private. If you do somehow use it and compile your code, every Java compiler since Java 6 will give you a nasty warning, discouraging the usage of the class. And, if you still need more reasons to avoid using it, you'd be best served to just look at the name of the class!

You must have guessed what's coming by now. The `sun.misc.Unsafe` class has now been used in multiple projects by many developers to perform those very low-level operations, in spite of all those preventive measures that the Java runtime authors have put in place. One could argue that it implements functionality that isn't commonly available elsewhere, and for a developer who needs to do something like that, nothing beats just picking it up while it's available in the classpath and ready to use. `Unsafe` isn't the only internal API that is being used this way, of course. There are a few more internal classes, many in the `sun.*` packages, that developers have used over the years even though they shouldn't. Moreover, as long as developers continue to use these APIs, it becomes harder to remove them from the runtime. This has ended up continuing the existence of these classes in subsequent versions of the runtime, thereby allowing more developers to use them!

These limitations of the Java runtime and library system have been felt for a while now. All the problems I've outlined so far exist because of the lack of ability to create modular units of code in Java. Such a construct simply hasn't existed in the language so far. The need for it has been strongly felt in the community.

Multiple proposals for a module system for Java have been made over the years, including JSR-277 way back in 2005 (`https://jcp.org/en/jsr/detail?id=277`) and JSR-294 (`https://jcp.org/en/jsr/detail?id=294`) in 2006. After facing several hurdles, modularity is finally coming to Java with the 2017 release of Java 9 with JSR-376 (`https://jcp.org/en/jsr/detail?id=376`), the spec titled Java Platform Module System, as well as Project Jigsaw.

Acronym alert: JCP and JSR

JCP: The Java language specification has, for a long time, been a community-owned asset. There is no one central authority that has complete control and the decision-making power in how the language evolves. Each of us, as Java developers, can have a say in how we want the language to change and grow. The **Java Community Process (JCP)** is a mechanism, introduced in 1998, that allows anyone interested in the future of the language specification to register, provide input, and take part in the technical specifications process. Go to `https://jcp.org` to learn more.

JSR: Let's say you are a part of the Java Community Process, and you have a great idea for a change in the language specification. What you do is create a **Java Specification Request (JSR)**--a formal document that describes the proposed changes. JSRs are reviewed and voted upon as a part of the community process before they become final. Once a JSR does become final, it is worked on and eventually becomes a part of the language specification.

Fun fact: The Java Community Process itself is an important part of the language, and so changes to it are also handled just like any other changes to the language--by submitting a Java Specification Request for it. Yes, there's the JSR that describes the JCP!

Java Platform Module System

The modularity features in Java 9 are together referred to by the name **Java Platform Module System (JPMS)**. It introduces a new language construct to create reusable components called *modules*. The Java Platform Module System makes it easy for developers to create contained units or components that have clearly established dependencies on other modules. With Java 9 modules, you can group certain types and packages into a module and provide it with the following information:

- **Its name**: This is a unique name for the module
- **Its inputs**: What does the module need and use? What's required for the given module to be compiled and run?
- **Its outputs**: What does this module output or export out to other modules?

I'll explain the input and output configuration shortly, but at a very high level, these three pieces of information are what you typically supply when you create a new module. Whenever developers need to create any components that are meant to be reusable, they can create new Java modules and provide this information to create a unit of code with a clear interface. Since a module can contain both its inputs and outputs specified formally, it adds a whole set of advantages compared to the classpath approach that we've critiqued so far.

Let's now look at the process of creating a module step by step. We'll look at it at a conceptual level now, and we'll cover the syntax in Chapter 2, *Creating Your First Java Module*. Let's say you want to create a reusable library and you've decided to put your code in a Java 9 module. Here are the steps you need to follow:

1. **Create a module and give it a name**: Every module has a name associated with it, for the obvious purpose of referring to it. You can give a module any name that you'd traditionally give to types. All the rules you are already familiar with regarding Java package names apply here (so certain characters like '/' or '-' aren't allowed, but '_' or '.' are okay). The recommended way to name a module is to use the *reverse domain name* convention, similar to the way you name your packages. So, for example, if someone in Acme Corp wrote an analytics module, they'd probably name the module com.acme.analytics.

2. **Define the module inputs**: Not many modules can realistically be self-sufficient. You'll often need to import types that aren't in your module. This is where the module input configuration comes into play. When you create a module, you explicitly need to declare which *other modules* you need for your code to work. You do that specifying which modules your module *requires*.

3. **Define the module outputs**: We've seen that in a traditional JAR file system, placing Java types in a JAR file doesn't really mean anything and every public type is accessible to every other type in the classpath, irrespective of which JAR it is in. A module behaves differently. By default, every Java type you place in a module is accessible only to other types in the same module. Even if the type is marked public! In order to expose types outside the module, you need to explicitly specify which *packages* you want to *export*. From any module, you can only export packages that are in that module. Once you've exported a package, all types in that package are potentially accessible outside the module. This enables every Java module to clearly separate and hide *internal* packages that are to be used only inside the module and expose only types that are intended to be used externally. If a Java type is in a package that isn't exported, then no other type outside the module can import it, even if the type is public!

Note the difference between the things you export from a module (which are packages) and the things you import or require (which are other modules). Since we are exporting types from a module at a package level, why not require packages too? The reason is simple. When a module requires another module, it automatically gets access to all the packages that that module exports. This way, you don't have to specify every package that your module needs. Just the name of the module you depend on will suffice. We'll look at the access mechanisms in much more detail in Chapter 3, *Handling Inter-Module Dependencies*.

The following diagram illustrates the input and output definitions of a typical module:

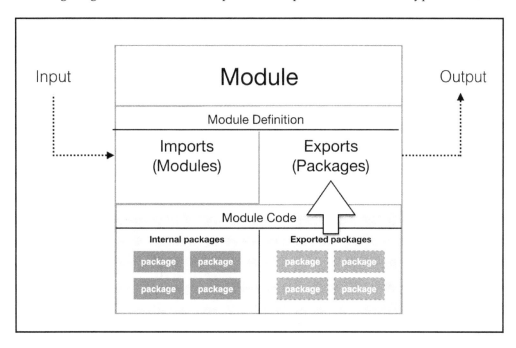

JPMS was designed with two primary goals in mind:

- **Strong encapsulation**: We've seen the dangers of having every public class accessible to every other class in the classpath. Since every module declares which packages are public and isolates those which are internal, the Java compiler and runtime can now enforce these rules to make sure that none of the internal classes are being used outside the module.
- **Reliable configuration**: Since every module declares what it needs, the runtime can check whether every module has what it needs well before the application is up and running. No more wishing and hoping that all the required classes are available in the classpath.

You can guess how happy Jack and Amit would be to hear this! Thanks to **strong encapsulation**, Jack would just need to put all of his `StringSorter` code in a module and export just his public package. Thus, his *internal* package would be hidden and not accessible by default. And, thanks to **reliable configuration**, Amit can always confidently say whether a given set of modules have all their dependencies met before running the application.

In addition to these two core goals, there has been another important goal that the module system was designed for--to be scalable and easy to use even on huge monolithic libraries. As a validation of that, the Java 9 team went ahead and modularized what's pretty much the oldest and biggest Java code base they could get their hands on--the Java Platform itself. This task, something that ended up involving significant effort, was performed under the name *Project Jigsaw*.

Project Jigsaw

Alan Bateman, a member of the Java Platform Group at Oracle said this is in his talk in Java One in September 2016:

> *Modular development starts with a modular platform.*

No matter what the application is about, there's one set of libraries that every Java program is guaranteed to use without a doubt--the Java Platform. For Java developers to be writing modular Java code, it's essential for the core Java platform and the JDK library to be modular as well. Before Java 9, all the classes and types in the JDK had such complicated inter-dependencies that they resembled a big bowl of spaghetti.

Not only is the final `rt.jar` bundle unnecessarily large, it makes the JDK code base itself harder to change and evolve. Considering how any type in such a huge code base could be used by any of the other thousands of types in the platform, I wouldn't want to go in there and make any major changes to that code. Another problem with the platform is that it has always lacked ways to hide and encapsulate internal platform APIs such as `sun.misc.Unsafe`. The platform itself could very well use the same strong encapsulation and reliable configuration benefits that JPMS gives us.

With Java 9, we've finally got a modular JDK to build on top of. Various different sets of related JDK classes are bundled into separate modules, each with its own imports and exports. For example, SQL related types are in a module called `java.sql`. XML functionality has gone into the `java.xml` module, and so on. We'll be looking at these out-of-the-box modules in more detail in Chapter 3, *Handling Inter-Module Dependencies*.

The following is an illustration of a subset of the new Java 9 platform modules. Don't worry about the individual names. We'll cover platform modules in detail in Chapter 4, *Introducing the Modular JDK*:

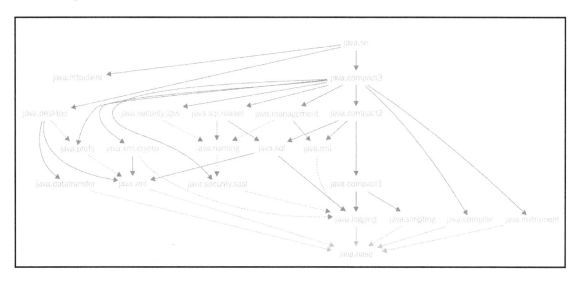

Project Jigsaw claims the following as its primary goals. It's important to keep this in mind as you learn about the impact of the modularization of the platform:

- **Scalable platform**: Moving away from a monolithic runtime and enabling the ability to scale the platform down to smaller computing devices.
- **Security and maintainability**: Better organization of the platform code to make it more maintainable. Hiding internal APIs and better modular interfaces to improve platform security.
- **Improved application performance**: Smaller platform with only the necessary runtimes, resulting in faster performance.
- **Easier developer experience**: The combination of the module system and the modular platform to make it easier for developers to create applications and libraries.

What does this mean for application developers? The most immediate difference is that not all types in the JDK are now accessible in your code. The same mechanisms we saw apply to our modules work with the Java modules too. Any time you depend on a platform class, you'll have to import into your module the right platform module that contains that class. And, even then, you'll be able to use the class only if it has been exported from the module and is public.

This way, the JDK code base also gets all the advantages of the strong encapsulation and reliable configuration that the JPMS promises. There are potential backward compatibility issues though. What if you used a JDK class in JDK 8 or earlier that's now an encapsulated class in a module? That code wouldn't work in Java 9! The platform uses the encapsulation features to protect certain internal JDK classes from external use. So, any code that depends on such classes in Java 8 or earlier cannot be migrated to Java 9 without removing that dependency first. There are a few challenges associated with moving code from Java 8 or earlier to Java 9. We'll look at Java 9 migration-related challenges and best practices in Chapter 9, *Module Design Patterns and Strategies*.

Another important aspect of modularity that most modular platforms have to deal with, and we haven't covered so far, is *versioning*. Are modules versionable? Can you declare dependencies between modules that specify which versions of the modules need to work together? You cannot! Java Platform Module System does not support versioning today. We'll briefly examine the reasons why in Chapter 3, *Handling Inter-Module Dependencies*.

Summary

In this chapter, we looked, at a high level, at some limitations of the traditional way of building reusable components in Java using JAR files. We saw how packaging libraries in JAR files doesn't allow developers to encapsulate inner APIs and types. There's also no way to reliably figure out whether a given application has all the necessary classes in the classpath. We learned how these problems that developers face in their code are not only present in the JDK code base itself, but are actually an issue on a much bigger scale. We understood the Java Platform Module System and the two primary goals that it set to achieve--strong encapsulation and reliable configuration. We learned about *Project Jigsaw* and the effort to modularize the core JDK using the same modular paradigm that's available to developers to use in their code.

At this time, you are probably wondering how the concept of modularity manifests in the Java language. What does a Java module look like?

In the next chapter, we'll answer these questions by creating our first Java 9 module, and get started on our sample application project which we'll be working on throughout this book.

2
Creating Your First Java Module

In the previous chapter, we took a detailed look at the problems associated with modularizing Java code pre-Java 9, as well as the new module construct in Java 9 and *Project Jigsaw*. Before we examine how Java modularity solves these problems, you'll need to first understand what a Java module looks like. In this chapter, you'll create your first Java 9 module and learn what it takes to build and execute code in a Java module. Here are the top-level topics you'll be learning in this chapter:

- Setting up the JDK with Java 9
- Creating a new Java 9 module
- Defining a module (using `module-info.java`)
- Compiling and executing a module
- Handling possible errors

You'll be building a sample Java 9 application throughout this book as you learn the different concepts related to modularity. The application you'll build is an address book viewer application that displays some contacts sorted by last name. We'll start simple and enhance this application as we go. When you are done with this chapter, you'll have built your first Java 9 module and learned how to compile and execute it. Let's start by first installing the JDK.

Setting up the JDK

In order to write Java 9 code, you'll first need to download and install the Java 9 SDK (referred to as the Java Development Kit or JDK). In this book, we'll be using the **OpenJDK** build available at `http://jdk.java.net/9/`. When you navigate to the URL, you'll see a list of available downloads based on the platform you are using, as shown here:

Platforms		JRE	JDK
Windows	**32-bit**	exe (md5) 84.81 MB	exe (md5) 307.73 MB
	64-bit	exe (md5) 91.19 MB	exe (md5) 320.01 MB
Mac OS X	**64-bit**	dmg(md5) 65.25 MB	dmg (md5) 309.20 MB
Linux	**32-bit**	tar.gz (md5) 77.49 MB	tar.gz (md5) 280.41 MB
	64-bit	tar.gz (md5) 76.05 MB	tar.gz (md5) 288.85 MB
Linux ARM	**32-bit**		tar.gz(md5) 175.20 MB
	64-bit		tar.gz(md5) 175.10# MB
Solaris SPARC	**64-bit**	tar.gz (md5) 51.79 MB	tar.gz (md5) 216.16 MB
Solaris x86	**64-bit**	tar.gz (md5) 51.45 MB	tar.gz (md5) 215.20 MB

Make sure you choose the download for your platform in the **JDK** column, not the **JRE** column. After accepting the license agreement, you should be able to download an installer for your platform. Run the installer and choose the defaults; after this, you should have JDK 9 installed in your machine:

After the installation is complete, it's a good idea to verify that the JDK installation and configuration process completed successfully. You do that by opening a **Command Prompt** or terminal window. Type the command java -version to output the version of the java command currently in the PATH:

 Note that the installer adds the location of the installed Java binaries to your system PATH variable, which is why this command works.

```
$ java -version
java version "9"
Java(TM) SE Runtime Environment (build 9+181)
Java HotSpot(TM) 64-Bit Server VM (build 9+181, mixed mode)
```

Additionally, you can also make sure that the JAVA_HOME value is set.

On macOS/Linux, type the command `echo $JAVA_HOME` and make sure the path to the JDK 9 installation is returned:

```
$ echo $JAVA_HOME
/Library/Java/JavaVirtualMachines/jdk-9.jdk/Contents/Home
```

On Windows, right-click on **My Computer**, click **Properties**, and switch to the **Advanced** tab. Here, click **Environment Variables** and view the value for the variable `JAVA_HOME`. It should point to the location you've chosen to install the JDK. For example, the location could be something like `C:\Program Files\Java\jdk9`.

With this, you've now successfully installed JDK 9 and you are all set to start coding in Java 9!

Switching between JDKs

Once you've installed a newer version of the JDK with an earlier version already installed, it is possible to switch what the currently selected version is.

On macOS and Linux, you do this by switching the value of `JAVA_HOME`

The following command switches the current Java platform to Java 8:

```
$ export JAVA_HOME=$(/usr/libexec/java_home -v 1.8)
```

To switch to Java 9, use the following command:

```
$ export JAVA_HOME=$(/usr/libexec/java_home -v 9)
```

With this command, you are passing the Java version of choice to the `-v` parameter. But, note that the format is different between Java 8 and 9. With Java 8, the version string is `1.8`. With Java 9, the version string is just `9`. Traditionally, Java has been using the `1.X` version format, for example, Java version 7 had the version string `1.7`. This is being changed from Java 9 onward. The idea is that subsequent releases of Java will drop the `1.X` format and just use a single number to denote the format. So it's Java 9, not Java 1.9.

It's about time this was changed! Imagine the confusion Java 10 would have caused!

On Windows, you switch JDK versions by changing the `JAVA_HOME` and `PATH` variables. Follow the same steps as earlier to get to the **Environment Variables** section. Update the value of `JAVA_HOME` to point to the location where the version you need is installed. Also, make sure the `PATH` is updated to point to the corresponding folder for the Java version you'd like to switch to.

Setting up the NetBeans IDE

In order to write and follow the code in this book, you don't *have* to use any **integrated development environments** (**IDEs**). This book will cover writing, compiling, and executing code manually using the command line. You can write code using a text editor of your choice. The code samples accompanying this book also work with the steps and commands showcased in this book.

You could also follow along with an IDE. At the time of writing, NetBeans and IntelliJ Idea has growing support for Java modular projects, with Eclipse support under development. This chapter outlines the steps to create a modular project in NetBeans, should you choose to use the NetBeans IDE. To set it up, in addition to following the steps to set up Java, make sure you install the latest version of NetBeans with Java 9 module support by going to `https://netbeans.org/downloads/` and choosing either the Java SE or the Java EE version to download:

			NetBeans IDE Download Bundles			
Supported technologies *	Java SE	Java EE	HTML5/JavaScript	PHP	C/C++	All
NetBeans Platform SDK	●	●				●
Java SE	●	●				●
Java FX	●	●				●
Java EE		●				●
Java ME						—
HTML5/JavaScript		●	●	●		●
PHP			●	●		●
C/C++					●	●
Groovy						●
Java Card™ 3 Connected						—
Bundled servers						
GlassFish Server Open Source Edition 4.1.1		●				●
Apache Tomcat 8.0.27		●				●
	Download	Download	Download	Download	Download	Download
	Free, 116 MB	Free, 242 MB	Free, 142 MB	Free, 142 MB	Free, 147 MB	Free, 277 MB

Note that if the release version of NetBeans does not yet support Java 9 when you read this, you might have to download an early access copy here: `http://bits.netbeans.org/download/trunk/nightly/latest/`. Once you download the installer and execute it, you should have a shiny new copy of NetBeans on your computer ready for you to use.

Most veteran Java programmers would acknowledge that it has been a while since they have created folder structures by hand for their Java projects. The Java language has benefitted from incredibly useful tooling support over the years. IDEs such as Eclipse, NetBeans, and IntelliJ IDEA make it such a breeze to create source and package folders that developers don't even tend to think about those aspects of code organization too often. However, in this chapter, and in fact in the rest of the book, we will learn how to build folders and files by hand, as well as compile and run the code by executing commands manually from the command line. This is because IDEs, as convenient as they might be, tend to hide the details and workings around the process of structuring and compiling code. We intend to examine how Java 9 modules work, and the fundamental workings of the code structure, as well as compiling and linking commands, are essential to mastering these concepts.

While the prospect of writing Java code without an IDE might seem daunting, let me assure you that this is something you'll likely get used to very quickly. You'll learn the steps to build and execute modular Java 9 code in this chapter, and then it's just a matter of applying the same steps independent of the complexity of the code base itself.

Java 9 modules

When writing an application in Java 9, you are ideally creating a modular application. It's important to note that a modular Java application isn't just a regular Java application (like those we've been building all these years) with just an extra module feature thrown in. It actually calls for a completely new way of thinking about writing and structuring your code base. Before we get into creating Java 9 modules, let's do a quick recap of the traditional Java code structure pre-Java 9.

Traditional Java code structure

Traditionally, writing a Java application starts with creating one or more source directories. These are special directories that serve two purposes--firstly, they act as root locations of your Java source code and secondly, the contents of these directories are added to the class path. So, the steps to organize source code have typically been:

1. Create one or more source folders.
2. In a source folder, create package folders to mirror the package name.
3. Place the .java files in the right package folders:

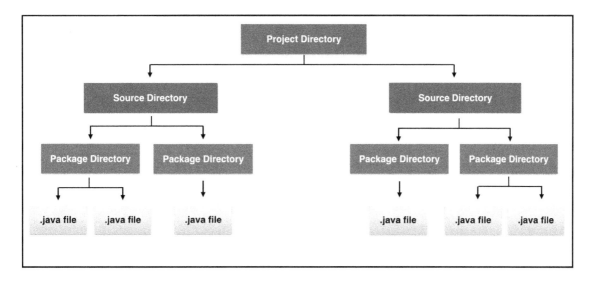

Many Java developers use the directory structure `src/main/java` for the source directory. So, for example, a class `Main.java` in the package `com.acme.app` would have the overall path `src/main/java/com/acme/app/Main.java`:

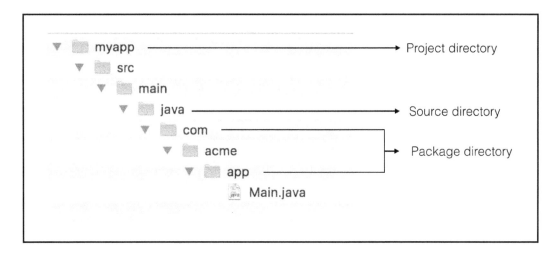

This is how source code in Java has typically been organized by developers for many years now. With Java 9 modules, there's a change in the way we approach structuring and writing code. Let's switch gears and examine what a module in Java 9 looks like.

What is a module?

The *module* is a new construct that has been introduced into the Java 9 programming language. Think of modules as first-class citizens and as new program components in the language, just like classes or packages. A Java 9 module is a named, self-describing collection of code and data that you can create and use in Java applications. A module can contain any number of Java packages that in turn contain Java code elements, such as classes or interfaces. A Java module can also contain files such as resource files or property files. An application is built by bringing together a collection of these modules. The analogy of building blocks applies well here--a module is a building block that exists on its own, but can be a part of a bigger whole.

With Java 9 modular programming, we move away from building applications as monolithic code bases and instead look to break down the problem into modules. In other words, rather than having one big Java project, you create several modular units that work together to form an application.

This significantly influences how you design and code your application. In Java 8 and earlier, your design process involved breaking down the problem into classes and packages. In Java 9, you first break the problem down into modules. These modules are ideally components that are reusable with a clear interface (inputs and outputs) and solve a specific part of the problem. Inside each module, however, the process of designing and writing code is, more or less, business as usual with packages, classes, interfaces, and so on.

Creating a module

Here are the steps to create a module in Java 9. Before you start with *step 1*, I should mention an obvious starting point--*step 0*: Know what the module's purpose is. Before you begin creating a module, you should have a clear idea of what the module is for. Remember the important tenet of modular development here! Rather than having one large code base for your application, you instead break the problem down into reusable subprojects. Think *reusable libraries*. The main difference is that rather than the libraries just being separate JARs that are nothing more than a collection of Java packages and types, we are leveraging the concept of Java modules to group those packages and types:

1. **Assign a module name**: The first step to creating a module is to come up with a unique name for the module. The name should ideally describe what the module is about and the problem it solves. A Java module name should be a valid Java identifier, so you cannot use certain characters, such as hyphens and slashes. A valid package name is also a valid module name. But apart from that, any name will do as long as it is unique in an application. However, to avoid clashing names, you don't want to call a module something very generic, such as `util`.

   The recommended practice is to use the same convention that has worked well all these years for package names in Java--using the reverse domain name pattern. It's also recommended that you use all lowercase naming for modules, just like packages. So, for example, if you are writing a String utilities module for Acme Corp, the name of the module could be something such as `com.acme.stringutil`.

2. **Create a module root folder**: Every Java module resides in its own folder, which acts as the top-level folder for the module and contains all the assets of the module. This folder is called the **module root** folder. The module root folder has the same name as the module. So, the root folder for the aforementioned example module has the name `com.acme.stringutil`. It is named exactly the same as the module name, including the periods, if any.

3. **Add the module code**: Inside the module root folder goes the code that belongs to the module. This begins with packages, so you start your package folders from the module root folder onward. So, if your module com.acme.stringutil has the class StringUtil.java in the package com.acme.util, the folder structure should look like this:

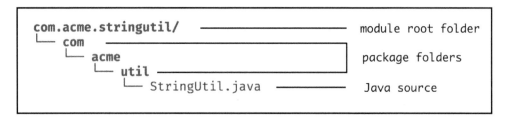

Note the difference in the file structure from the pre-Java 9 structure that we looked at before. What used to go directly into the source folders in earlier versions of Java now goes into the module root folder. As you can see from the following table, with Java 9 there's just an additional folder level with the module root folders. From the module root folder onward, there's nothing new in the way Java types are organized:

The Java 8 (and earlier) way	The Java 9 way
1. Create one or more source folders. 2. In a source folder, create package folders to mirror the package name. 3. Place the .java files in the right package folders.	1. Create one or more source folders. 2. In a source folder, create a module folder for each module. 3. In the module folders, create package folders to mirror the package name. 4. Place the .java files in the right package folders.

Here's a diagram representing the code structure with the modules:

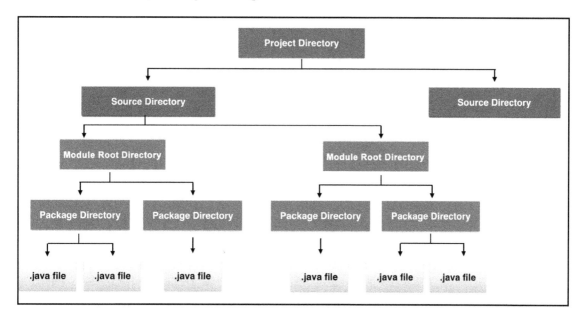

4. **Create and configure the module descriptor**: Here's the final step! Every module comes with a file that describes it and contains metadata about the module. This file is called the module descriptor. This file contains information about the module, such as what it requires (the inputs to the module) and what the module exports (the outputs from the module). The module descriptor is always located directly at the module root folder, and it is always given the name `module-info.java`. That's right! A module descriptor file is actually a `.java` file. What do the contents of this module descriptor file look like?

Here is a barebones and minimal module descriptor for the example module-- `com.acme.stringutil`:

```
module com.acme.stringutil {

}
```

The file starts with the `module` keyword followed by the module name and curly braces. The curly brace structure resembles other Java type declarations you should be familiar with. Note that the name of the module (following the `module` keyword) should exactly match the name of the module root folder.

Within the curly braces, you can optionally specify the metadata (the inputs and outputs) of the module. In the preceding example, the module descriptor is essentially *empty*, with nothing between the curly braces. For any real-world module you create, you will more than likely add some metadata here to configure the behavior of the module. We'll cover this metadata in more detail in `Chapter 3`, *Handling Inter-Module Dependencies*, but what you can see in the example is the bare minimum *necessary and sufficient* content needed for the module descriptor.

With the module descriptor file in the **module root**, this is the folder and file structure for our simple module:

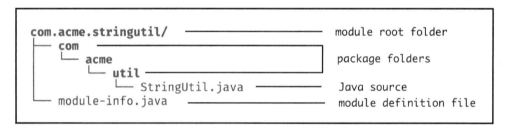

For someone used to writing Java classes, the name of the `module-info.java` file might seem a bit odd at first. This is because of a couple of reasons:

- The – character here isn't a valid identifier to be used in a Java type name, and nor is it valid for the name of a `.java` file
- The name of the `.java` file usually matches the name of the public type contained in the file, but in this case, it doesn't

However, some Java developers might also find this familiar, having used a similar-looking file name that has been used in Java since Java 1.5--`package-info.java`. The `package-info.java` file is used to specify package-level configuration and annotations, and has been used for many years now, although not very widely. Both `module-info.java` and `package-info.java` files have intentionally been given *invalid* Java type names in order to convey their special meaning and purpose, and to separate them from the other Java types and files you'd normally create in the process of building your application.

Steps **1** to **4** in the preceding method are the four necessary steps required to create a module. Let's put these steps into action by creating an addressbook viewer application using the Java 9 modular application approach. This is a simple application that helps you view a set of contact information. Nothing too complex, but just enough for us to put all the Java modularity concepts we learn in this book into practice!

Creating your first Java module

Let's start by creating our first Java 9 module and walk through the process of coding, compiling, and executing a module. Ideally, any application should consist of multiple modules, but in this chapter, we'll start small. In this chapter, we'll create just **one** module called `packt.addressbook`. This will be our first Java module. Over the next few chapters, we'll break this down into multiple modules.

We'll obviously need to start with the folder where all our code resides. In the screenshots in this book, I've chosen the path `<home>/code/java9`, but you can feel free to use any path of your preference. I'll be referring to this folder as the project root folder throughout this book.

We've just learned the four steps required to create any Java module. Let's run through those four steps for the `addressbook` module now:

1. **Name the module**: We've already done this! The name of our `addressbook` module is `packt.addressbook`.

2. **Create a module root folder**: You'll now need to create one module folder for each module you intend to write. Since we are creating only one module called `packt.addressbook`, we create a folder with the same name. I recommend keeping all your Java source files in a separate folder called `src` in the project root folder. You'll then create all your module root folders in the `src` folder. Since my project root is `~/code/java9`, the module root folder resides at `~/code/java9/src/packt.addressbook`. This `packt.addressbook` folder is where all the packages and Java files of the module reside.

3. **Add code to the module**: This step is business as usual for Java developers. From the module root folder onward, your folder structure reflects your package. For our first attempt, let's write a simple *Hello World* application. Create a Java file called `Main.java` in the package `packt.addressbook`. The complete path for `Main.java` is `~/code/java9/src/packt.addressbook/packt/addressbook/Main.java`. Let's add a main method that just prints a message to the console:

```
package packt.addressbook;
public class Main {
  public static void main(String[] args) {
    System.out.println("Hello World!");
  }
}
```

 Note that the actual difference from the previous Java 8 directory structure is the introduction of the module root folder. It's helpful to think about each module as a *subproject* of sorts. The package structure begins from the module root folder onward.

4. **Create a module descriptor**: Create a file called `module-info.java` and place it directly in the module root folder. We'll go over the details of what can be configured in this file in Chapter 3, *Handling Inter-Module Dependencies*, but for now, create this file with the following contents:

```
module packt.addressbook {

}
```

The keyword `module` is followed by the name of the module, which in our case is `packt.addressbook`. There's nothing between the curly braces for now because we are not specifying any details about the module in this file yet, except for the module name. However, adding this file to the module directory is essential for the Java compiler to treat this as a module.

With this, you are done! These four steps are what it takes to create a simple Java 9 module. Here's how the folder structure should look when you are done:

```
src
└── packt.addressbook
    ├── module-info.java
    └── packt
        └── addressbook
            └── Main.java
```

Now, let's move on to compiling and executing this module.

Compiling your module

Compiling code in a Java 9 module requires the use of the `javac` command as always, but with a few different options this time. To compile modules in Java 9, you need to provide the `javac` command with the following information:

1. The location of your modules. This is the directory that contains the module root folders for all the modules in your application. In our case, this is the `src` folder. In it, we just have one module root folder.
2. The paths and names of the Java files that need to be compiled. In our case, it's just one file--`Main.java`.
3. The destination location where the compiler needs to output the compiled `.class` files. This can be any location, but I recommend choosing a folder named `out` directly below the project root folder.

To compile the module you've written, go to the project root (in our example, it's
~/code/java9) and run the following command:

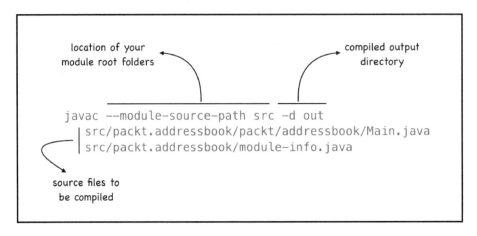

Here, you are specifying the module source path (**1**) using the --module-
source-path command option, the output directory for compiled classes (**2**)
using the -d command option, and the list of Java source files (**3**) by specifying
them directly in the command (in this case, Main.java and module-info.java).

If the compiler is successful, there is no output to the console. The out directory
should contain the compiled classes:

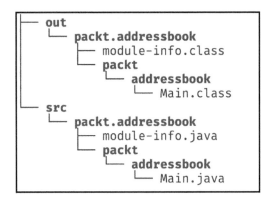

Note that there is a one-to-one mapping between the source and compiled classes. Even the module descriptor `module-info.java` has been compiled to a `.class` file--`module-info.class`. This is for a very important reason. The module configuration provides metadata information about the module not just to the compiler during compile time, but also to the JVM during runtime. Thanks to the `module-info.class`, the JVM also has all the information about every Java module, thus enabling the runtime to tap into many of the benefits of the module system during execution.

Executing your module

Executing your compiled code again uses the familiar `java` command, but with some new options. Here is the information you need to tell the `java` command in this case:

1. The location of the compiled modules--also called the **module path**.
2. The module that contains the class with the `main` method that needs to start the execution.
3. The class with the `main` method in the preceding module that needs to start the execution.

To execute the code you just compiled in the previous step, you'd need to run the following command in the same directory:

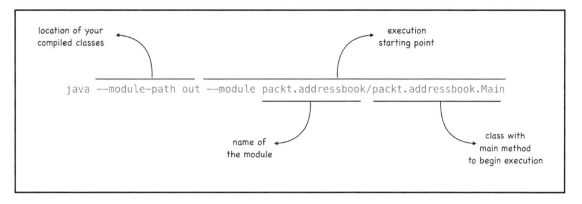

Here, you are specifying the location of the compiled modules (**1**) using the `--module-path` flag. We've told the compiler in the previous step to place our compiled code in the `out` folder, and so that's the value we need to provide here. You specify the module (**2**) and the class with the main method (**3**) using the `--module` option. Note the format of the value--it's `<module-name>/<fully-qualified-classname>`. Here, our code consists of just one class, so it feels unnecessary to specify this, but you can imagine a code base with multiple modules and classes, many of which might have main methods. It's important for the runtime to know which main method of which class of which module it needs to start the execution on.

There are alternative option names for many of these options. For example, instead of using `--module-path`, you can simply use `-p`, and `--module` can be replaced with `-m`.

If the execution completed successfully, you should see the message `Hello World!` printed on the console.

> You've learned about two new arguments, `--module-source-path` and `--module-path`. They roughly correspond to the `-sourcepath` and `-classpath` options that we've been using in Java for a while now.
>
> **Java 8 and earlier:**
>
> `sourcepath`: Tells the compiler where the source files are that need to be compiled.
>
>
> `classpath`: Tells the compiler/runtime where the compiled types are that need to be included in the `classpath` for compiling/running code.
>
> **Java 9:**
>
> `module-source-path`: Tells the compiler where the source files for the modules are.
>
> `module-path`: Tells the compiler/runtime where the compiled modules are that need to be considered for compiling/running code your code.

Creating a module using NetBeans

Now that you've learned how to create, compile, and execute a module using the **Command Prompt**, let's see how to do the same thing using the NetBeans IDE:

1. Create a new project in the NetBeans IDE by clicking 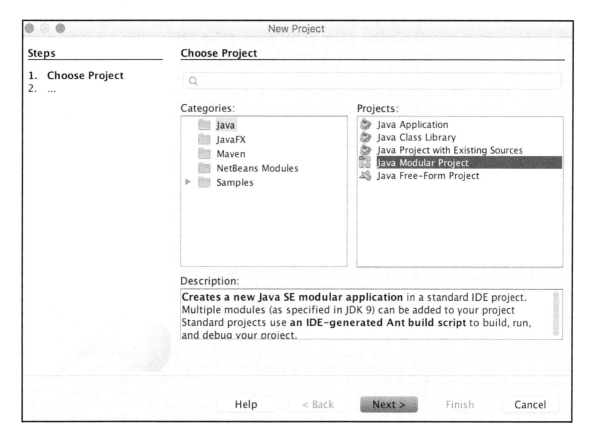 in the toolbar or, through the menu **File | New Project**, you'll see a **New Project** overlay with a new option in the Java category--**Java Modular Project**:

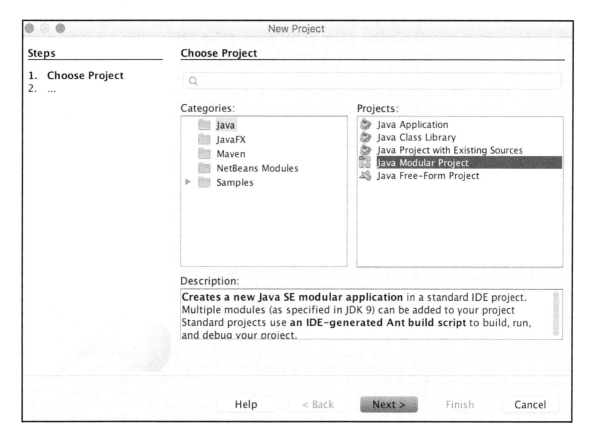

2. Select that and click **Next**. In the next dialog, you can specify the name of your project (I chose addressbookviewer) and the location of your project and click **Finish**:

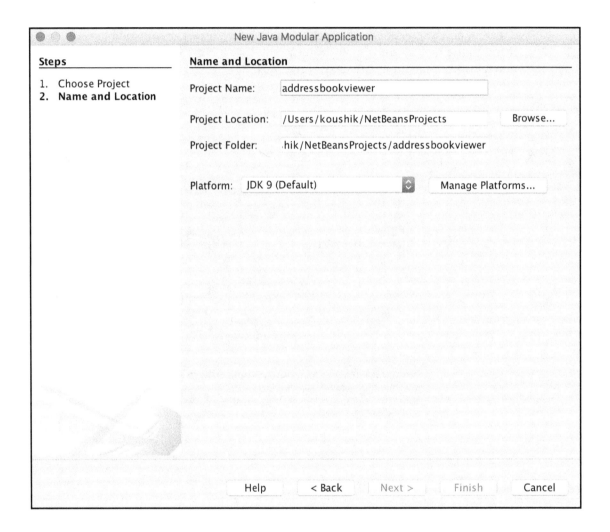

3. Once the new project is loaded onto your IDE, you can right-click on the name of the project in the **Projects** tab and choose the option to create a new module:

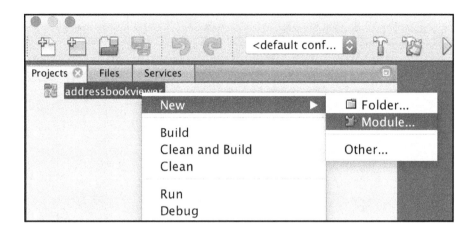

4. In the **New Module** dialog, enter the name of the module `packt.addressbook` and click **Finish**:

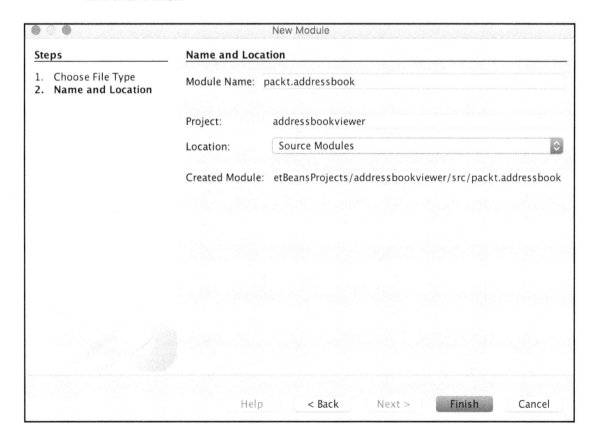

And just like that, you've created a new module! Note how NetBeans has automatically created the module descriptor for your module:

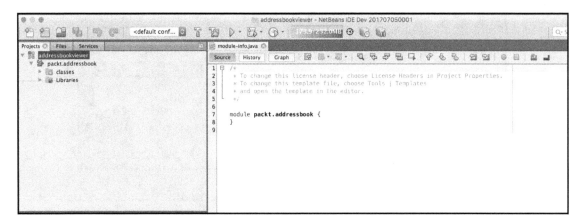

5. Now what's left is to add the `Main.java` class by right-clicking on the module and going through the wizard:

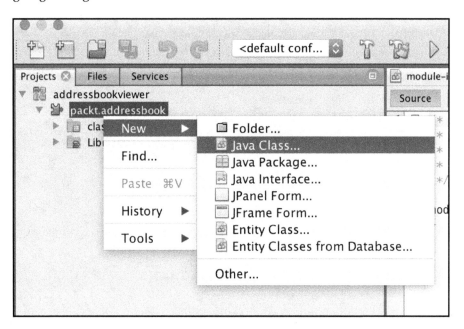

6. After adding the `Main.java` class, you can compile and execute it by right-clicking on the class and clicking **Run File**. You should see the message `Hello World` on the console panel at the bottom:

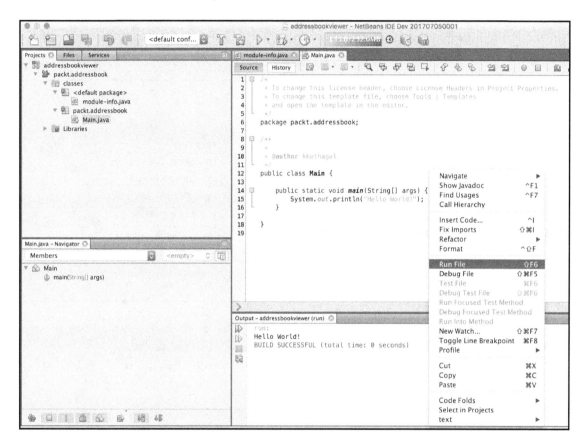

Congratulations! You've created, compiled, and executed your first Java module! This was a module with just one Java type, `Main.java`. Most of the code you'll be writing in this book will have you follow through the same steps that you just did. There will be several variations, of course, but we'll be examining the differences as we learn more about modules.

The address book viewer application

Now that you are comfortable creating, compiling, and executing a simple Java 9 module, let's update it and start adding address book viewer functionality.

The following informal class diagram shows how we'll design the application classes to begin with:

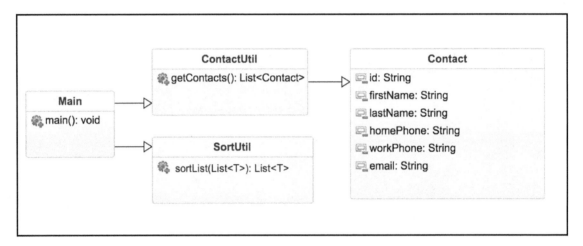

The main class has the `main()` method that displays the list of contacts in ascending order, sorted by the `lastName` property. It gets the list of contacts by calling the `ContactUtil.getContacts()` method and it sorts it using `SortUtil.sortList()`. It then displays the list of contacts to the console.

We'll start with a new model class `Contact`, which represents a single piece of contact information. Apart from the obvious contact-related private member variables and getters and setters, this class also has a couple of additions that'll come in handy later:

- **The constructor with arguments**: This makes it easy for us to create contact objects. This is useful since we'll be hardcoding our contact list to begin with.
- **The toString() method**: This provides readable output when we print `Contact` objects to the console.
- **The compareTo() method**: Since we'll need to sort `Contact` objects, we'll have the `Contact` class, which implements `Comparable`, and the `compareTo()` method, which compares `Contact` instances by their `lastName` property.

Here's what the `Contact` class looks like:

```java
package packt.addressbook.model;
public class Contact implements Comparable {
  private String id;
  private String firstName;
  private String lastName;
  private String phoneNumber;
  public Contact(String id, String firstName,
    String lastName, String phoneNumber) {
      this.id = id;
      this.firstName = firstName;
      this.lastName = lastName;
    this. phoneNumber = phoneNumber;
  }
  // Getters and setters omitted for brevity
  public String toString() {
    return this.firstName + " " + this.lastName;
  }
  public int compareTo(Object other) {
    Contact otherContact = (Contact)other;
    return this.lastName.compareTo(otherContact.lastName);
  }
}
```

Let's move on to the `ContactUtil` class. We need a source of some contact data to start coding with, so for now, we'll hardcode a few `Contact` objects and add them to a list. The `ContactUtil.getContacts()` method just prepares this hard coded list for now:

```java
package packt.addressbook.util;
public class ContactUtil {

  public List<Contact> getContacts() {
    List<Contact> contacts = Arrays.asList(
      new Contact("Edsger", "Dijkstra", "345-678-9012"),
      new Contact("Alan", "Turing", "456-789-0123"),
      new Contact("Ada", "Lovelace", "234-567-8901"),
      new Contact("Charles", "Babbage", "123-456-7890"),
      new Contact("Tim", "Berners-Lee", "456-789-0123")
    );
    return contacts;
  }
}
```

Next is the `SortUtil` class. You don't typically write sort methods, thanks to some good collection libraries that are available out of the box with Java. In this case, however, we will implement our own sorting algorithm for the purposes of learning about modules because it'll help us illustrate some important use cases throughout this book. Instead of creating a method specifically designed to sort `Contact` instances, we'll instead write a generic Bubble Sort method to sort any type that implements `Comparable`. Thanks to `Contact` implementing the `Comparable` interface, we should be able to use the `SortUtil` to sort its instances too:

```
public class SortUtil {
  public <T extends Comparable> List<T> sortList(List<T> list) {
    for (int outer = 0; outer < list.size() - 1; outer++) {
      for (int inner = 0; inner < list.size()-outer-1; inner++) {
        if (list.get(inner).compareTo(list.get(inner + 1)) > 0) {
          swap(list, inner);
        }
      }
    }
    return list;
  }
  private <T> void swap(List<T>list, int inner) {
    T temp = list.get(inner);
    list.set(inner, list.get(inner + 1));
    list.set(inner + 1, temp);
  }
}
```

Now let's bring it all together in `Main.java`. We'll first call the `getContacts()` method on an instance of `ContactUtil` to get the hardcoded `Contact` list. Then we'll pass it to the `sortList()` method on an instance of `SortList`. We will then print the sorted list on the console using `System.out.println()`:

```
package packt.addressbook;

public class Main {
  public static void main(String args) {
    ContactUtil contactUtil = new ContactUtil();
    SortUtil sortUtil = new SortUtil();
    List<Contact> contacts = contactUtil.getContacts();
    sortUtil.sortList(contacts);
    System.out.println(contacts);
  }
}
```

With this, we are done and ready to compile our code. We've seen that the command to compile your code looks like this:

```
$ javac --module-source-path src -d out <all-java-classes-here>
```

The part where we need to specify all Java classes can get tedious. We have a handful of classes at this time, and I already don't want to be bothered with typing all the class names (with paths!) in the command. This can get worse when we have multiple modules in the module source path and we want to compile them. Thankfully, there's a shortcut. The compiler also has the `--module` option that lets you specify the names of the modules that you need to compile. You can specify multiple module names here, separated by commas. The compiler looks for those modules in the module source path and compiles all classes in those modules. And as you can imagine, using this command is much easier!

Since we are compiling just one module here, that's what we'll specify as the value for the `--module` argument:

```
$ javac -d out --module-source-path src --module packt.addressbook
```

The compilation should complete without any errors. Now, let's move on to execute your code. The command remains unchanged:

```
$ java --module-path out --module packt.addressbook/packt.addressbook.Main
```

Here's the sorted output from the hardcoded contacts list:

```
[Babbage 123-456-7890, Lovelace 234-567-8901, Dijkstra 345-678-9012,
 Turing 456-789-0123, Berners-Lee 456-789-0123]
```

If you expand the out directory, you'll again notice the one-to-one mapping between the .java files and the .class files:

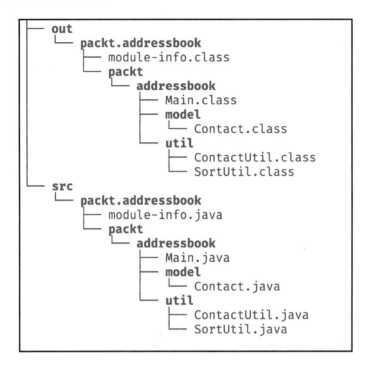

Handling possible errors

Here are some possible errors you could run into when following the steps we previously outlined, along with some solutions:

1. Error during compilation:

   ```
   javac: invalid flag: --module-source-path
   ```

   This is probably because you haven't switched to JDK 9 and are still using the Java 8 compiler. The --module-source-path option has been newly introduced to javac as of version 9.

2. Error during compilation:

```
error: module not found: packt.addressbook
```

This error is because the Java compiler is unable to find the `module-info.java` file. Make sure it is in the right directory path.

3. Error during runtime:

```
Error occurred during initialization of VM
java.lang.module.ResolutionException: Module packt.addressbook
not found
```

This error indicates that the module file is not available in the module path provided. Make sure the path is correctly specified and that the `packt.addressbook` folder contains the compiled `module-info.class` file.

Summary

In this chapter, you have learned what the bare minimum steps to creating a Java 9 module are. You've created a simple module from scratch, as well as compiled and executed code in the module. You've also learned about a few possible error scenarios and how to handle them.

There is something missing though! Since we are dealing with a single module, we are not really leveraging the concepts of modularity here. The concepts of modularity come into play only when we have multiple modules interacting with each other. You'll see just that in action in the next chapter when you create your second Java module and set up inter-module dependency!

3
Handling Inter-Module Dependencies

In the last chapter, we created our first Java 9 module and set up the beginnings of the address book application. However, we built the whole application as a single module, and thus, we didn't really leverage any of the cool new features of modularity. Here's what you'll learn to do in this chapter:

- You'll break the application up into two separate modules, and thereby create your second Java module
- You'll learn how to establish dependencies between those two modules
- You'll learn more about the module descriptor configuration that's required to wire in two separate modules
- You'll revisit the compilation and execution steps with multiple modules

This all starts with breaking our monolithic address book viewer application into two modules. Breaking the single module into two dependent modules has two consequences:

- Breaking the application up into modular parts enables these modular parts to potentially be reused in multiple other applications.
- It's an opportunity to define the interface for the modules. It lets you, as the module author, define what the module exports and how it should be used and consumed.

We'll look at both of these in this chapter.

Creating the second module

Let's start by splitting the address book application into two separate modules. The obvious candidate for moving to its own module is the sorting logic. At this point, there's nothing about the sorting class, SortUtil, that has anything to do with the address book. We've designed the class to be generic and provide functionality to sort any list. That's good practice in general, but it makes additional sense when breaking it out as a separate module. What we will do is move the code related to sorting into a brand new module, called packt.sortutil. Here are the steps at a high level:

1. Create a new module called packt.sortutil.
2. Move the code related to sorting into this newly created module.
3. Configure the packt.sortutil module to define its interface--what it exports and how the module needs to be used.
4. Configure the packt.addressbook module to use the new packt.sortutil module.

Let's start by creating a new module. We've looked at the four steps to create a module in Chapter 2, *Creating Your First Java Module*, already. We know what the module name is. Next, the module structure requires creating a module root directory in the source folder. Just like the packt.addressbook folder resides in the src folder and holds all the contents of the packt.addressbook module, the packt.sortutil module requires the creation of a folder named packt.sortutil in the same src location. What makes this folder a module root folder is the presence of the module descriptor module-info.java:

```
module packt.sortutil {
}
```

Here's the folder structure at this point:

```
src
├── packt.addressbook
│   ├── module-info.java
│   └── packt                          packt.addressbook module
│       └── addressbook
│           └── ...
└── packt.sortutil
    └── module-info.java               packt.sortutil module
```

Now that we have a module, we can move the necessary classes from the packt.addressbook module into the packt.sortutil module. There's just one class related to sorting--SortUtil.java. With the package folders located at the module folder, the folder structure after moving the class over should look as follows:

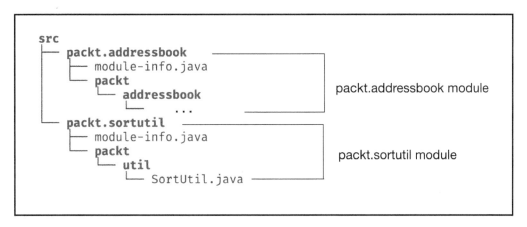

When creating a module, you'd typically also configure the interface, that is, defining the module's inputs and outputs. We didn't do this to the packt.addressbook module in Chapter 2, *Creating Your First Java Module* because it existed as a standalone module. However, that's not the case anymore in this chapter, since we'll now need the two modules packt.addressbook and packt.sortutil to work together. This involves updating the module-info.java file for both the modules to provide this information. But let's skip this step for now and examine the default behavior first. Let's observe what happens if we don't add any module configuration and compile the two modules with empty module definition files.

Compiling two modules

Now the module path (the src directory) has two modules. We can now run the javac command to compile all classes in both modules, since we are supplying src as the module source path.

Here, `packt.sortutil` is the simpler of the two modules. Since it doesn't have any external dependencies, this should just work like the `packt.addressbook` module did in the previous chapter. Let's look at the `packt.addressbook` module. Things are more interesting here. Since we've moved the sort related classes to the `packt.sortutil` module, the `packt.addressbook` module doesn't have the classes in the `packt.util` package anymore. But there is code in the module that still uses it. Notice what happens when we try to compile both the modules with the same command as the previous chapter. This time, since we are compiling two modules, we specify both the module names to the `--module` argument separated by a comma.

```
$ javac -d out --module-source-path src --module
packt.addressbook,packt.sortutil
```

The error you get should look something like this:

```
./src/packt.addressbook/packt/addressbook/Main.java:6: error: SortUtil is
not visible because package packt.util is not visible
import packt.util.SortUtil;
              ^
./src/packt.addressbook/packt/addressbook/Main.java:13: error: cannot find
symbol
SortUtil sortUtil = new SortUtil();
     ^
symbol:    class SortUtil
location: class Main
./src/packt.addressbook/packt/addressbook/Main.java:13: error: cannot find
symbol
SortUtil sortUtil = new SortUtil();
                        ^
symbol:    class SortUtil
location: class Main
```

Firstly, note that the errors are only from compiling the `packt.addressbook` module. This means that the compilation of the `packt.sortutil` module succeeded! The three errors in the preceding output are specifically about the `Main.java` file. The compiler clearly doesn't see the `SortUtil` class and it complains it is missing. But is it really missing? We do have a public `SortUtil` class available in the `src` folder, but since it is in a different module folder, the compiler doesn't seem to see it, even though the class itself is `public`. This brings up an important new change relating to class visibility in Java 9.

Just because a class is marked `public` in Java 9, it doesn't necessarily mean it is visible to all other types.

This is a radical change from the way `public` types work in Java 8 and earlier. Before Java 9, if you had a public class or interface in the classpath, it was available for any other type in the classpath to import and use. This is no longer the case with the module source path in Java 9!

Configuring module dependency

Think of a module being a walled garden by default. By default, any Java type in a module is accessible *only* to the types inside the same module. Previously, the `SortUtil` class was in the `packt.addressbook` module and was thus accessible to other types in that module. Move it to a different module however, and it is not accessible to types in the original module anymore.

Given two modules, **A** and **B**, for any type in module A to access a type in module B, two conditions need to be satisfied:

- Module A needs to declare its dependency on module B
- Module B needs to declare that it's okay with that type being accessed externally by other modules

If either of these conditions isn't met, the type being accessed in module B is said to be *not readable* by module A. We'll cover the topics of readability and accessibility in sufficient detail in Chapter 6, *Module Resolution, Accessibility, and Readability*, but, for now, note that these are two important requirements. Let's apply these to the `packt.addressbook` and `packt.sortutil` modules.

First, we need to have the `packt.addressbook` module declare that it is dependent on the `packt.sortutil` module. It is using a class from that module, and there's no way you can compile or run the module without it. The way to declare a dependency on a module is by using the `requires` keyword:

```
module packt.addressbook {
   requires packt.sortutil;
}
```

Following the `requires` keyword is the name of the module that is required. And yes, you can only require other modules, and not packages or classes. This line is enough for the compiler and runtime to look up types from the module that is being *required* any time those types are being used in the module. A module could depend on multiple other modules. So, it's actually common to have multiple such `requires` lines of code in a module declaration.

When a compiler tries to compile a module, imagine that it looks at this list of modules specified with the `requires` clause and says "Okay, I understand that this module requires all these other modules. While I compile this module, anytime I see a type being used in the code of this module that belongs to another module that is required, I'll go look at the module that contains the type and make sure it exports the type being used." Since every dependent module could potentially require other modules, this is a recursive process.

Now what does a module *exporting* a type mean? This is where we get to the second of the two preceding conditions. Every module needs to specifically declare what types in its module are okay for use outside the module. In our case, the `packt.sortutil` module needs to declare that the `SortUtil` class is allowed to be used outside its own module. This is done in the `sortutil` module's declaration file, using the `exports` keyword followed by the package you want to export. When a module `exports` a package, all the types belonging to that package are allowed access outside the module:

```
module packt.sortutil {
    exports packt.util;
}
```

In our case, we want to export the `packt.util.SortUtil` class. So, we *export* the package `packt.util` thereby exporting the class within it.

Again, note that you *require* modules and *export* packages. There are several reasons why the language designers decided to use the `exports` syntax with packages rather than having developers export individual types. The most obvious reason, of course, is that it is much more convenient than the tedium of having to export each class at an individual type level.

 We've introduced a handful of new keywords so far--`module`, `requires`, and `exports`. You might be wondering if they are reserved words in the Java language as of Java 9. Are you in trouble if you've been using these as variable names all over your code today? The answer is no! These and other module related keywords we'll be learning in this book are what are called *restricted keywords*. You can still continue to use them in your code, but only when they are used in the context of a module descriptor, the compiler knows what they mean and it treats the keywords accordingly.

With both the conditions for cross-module access of types now satisfied, let's compile the code again from one directory above the module path:

```
$ javac -d out --module-source-path src --module
packt.addressbook,packt.sortutil
```

Again, the `--module-source-path` parameter specifies where the compiler can find all the Java modules that are required to do its job compiling your code. And, the `--module` indicates the two modules to be compiled--`packt.addressbook` and `packt.sortutil`. The compiler finds both the module root folders in the module source path and compiles them into their respective classes.

The compilation should quietly succeed. Just like last time, you'll notice that the `out` folder has a `.class` file corresponding to every `.java` file in each of the two modules, including the module descriptors, the two `module-info.java` files.

You can execute the `Main` class in the `packt.addressbook` module like before. For illustration, I'll use the terser `-m` option (instead of `--module`) to specify the module and class to start execution. They both mean the same and can be used interchangeably.

```
$ java --module-path out -m packt.addressbook/packt.addressbook.Main

[Babbage 123-456-7890, Lovelace 234-567-8901, Dijkstra 345-678-9012, Turing
456-789-0123, Berners-Lee 456-789-0123]
```

Here as well, the `--module-path` option specifies where the Java runtime needs to look to find the modules required to execute the code. The runtime detects that the class it needs to start execution with (`Main`) is a part of the module `packt.addressbook` and since that module has a dependency on another module (`packt.sortutil`), it searches the location specified by the `module-path` option (the `out` directory here) to find the depended module. Thanks to our compile step placing the compiled module in the same location, the runtime finds it and the execution proceeds.

You should see the contacts successfully sorted by last name. Note that, to run this code, you just specified the `packt.addressbook` module and the `Main` class, and we didn't have to provide any information to the runtime about the dependent `packt.sortutil` module. This is because the Java runtime is reading off the same module descriptor (the `module-info.class` file this time) to know that the `packt.sortutil` module is required and so leverages the right class files from both modules as and when necessary.

Here is a diagram explaining the behavior of the two modules:

packt.addressbook		packt.sortutil	
Module Definition		Module Definition	
Imports `packt.sortutil`	**Exports** -	**Imports** -	**Exports** `packt.util`
Module Code		Module Code	
Internal packages packt.addressbook.model packt.addressbook.util	**Exported packages** No exported packages	**Internal packages** No internal packages	**Exported packages** packt.util

What we've done is isolated the sorting functionality into its own module so that it can be used by other Java 9 modular applications that need sorting. All that any Java 9 module has to do in order to use `packt.sortutil` is:

1. Add the `requires packt.sortutil` line in the definition of the module that needs the sorting functionality.
2. Import the `packt.util.SortUtil` class and call the `sortList()` method to sort any `List` of objects as long as the objects are `Comparable`.

This is great, but before we share our new `packt.sortutil` library for the world to use, let's think about the library's API for a bit.

 What I mean by a library's API is the code required to be used by the consumers of your library in order to access it. In the case of the simplistic `packt.sortutil` library, for example, the API is a single method `sortList()` on the class `packt.util.SortUtil`. More functional libraries obviously have multiple classes and methods that could potentially be called by their consumers.

When you create a library, before you allow others to use it, you have to very carefully define and finalize the library's API. The reason being that, once others start using your library, it becomes harder to make changes to the library's public API. Any changes to the API in future versions of your library would mean requiring all the consumers of your library update their code to work with the new API.

Right now, the `packt.sortutil` module contains just one class. We will be evolving the module in the next chapters, but for now, one change I'd like to do is to make the `SortUtil` class as lightweight as possible. That class acts as the *programming interface* to the `packt.sortutil` library, so making sure the class is as simple as it can be with fewer lines of code makes it less susceptible to possible changes in the future.

One way to achieve this is by moving the actual sorting functionality to an *implementation* class and have `SortUtil` just delegate the sorting logic to that class.

Let's assume we create a `BubbleSortUtil` class that has the same structure as the `SortUtil` class has so far:

```
public class BubbleSortUtilImpl {
  public <T extends Comparable> List<T> sortList(List<T> list) {
    ...
  }
  private <T> void swap(List<T>list, int inner) {
    ...
  }
}
```

We can then update the `SortUtil` to just call `BubbleSortUtilImpl` class's `sortList` method to delegate:

```
public class SortUtil {
  private BubbleSortUtilImpl sortImpl = new BubbleSortUtilImpl();
  public <T extends Comparable> List<T> sortList(List<T> list) {
    return this.sortImpl.sortList(list);
  }
}
```

This is much better, because if you'd like to change the structure of the library or the sorting logic, as long as you keep the structure of `SortUtil` unchanged, the consumers of your library don't have to change their code. The `SortUtil` class is still tightly coupled to `BubbleSortUtil` in that it is directly instantiating it, but we'll be improving this is in a subsequent chapter, so let's live with it for now.

Running the code at this stage should result in the same output as last time. Now, before we announce to the world that our `packt.sortutil` module is ready for consumption, think back to the problem Jack faced in Chapter 1, *Introducing Java 9 Modularity*. He had created a sorting library JAR file with pretty much the same design as far as classes are concerned--an internal `BubbleSortUtilImpl` and an external `SortUtil`. The problem he ran into was the fact that a certain class is either *internal* or *external* was only a matter of convention and wasn't enforceable without Jack lumping his code into a single package just to leverage the package-private mechanisms. Developers using his library started to use the `BubbleSortUtilImpl` class that they weren't supposed to use. Let's see if we have the same problem with our `sortutil` module, and if so, if there are better tools to protect certain classes using the module system in Java 9.

The answer is simple. Yes, we have the same problem that Jack ran into. Any consumer of the `sortutil` module could easily use `BubbleSortUtilImpl` directly. That's because the class is in a package that's exported from the module. We'd like to avoid that by encapsulating the class and prevent its usage outside the module. How do we do that? Simple! Just move the class to another package! Like we've already seen, the Java Platform Module System expects us to specify what packages are visible outside the module. If any type is accessible outside any module, it's only because it belongs to an exported package in that module. Which is why refactoring the type into a new package is a potential solution. As long as the new package doesn't show up with the `exports` clause in the module definition file of the module, the classes in the package are effectively hidden from outside use, like we've already seen:

```
packt.sortutil/
├── module-info.java
└── packt
    └── util
        ├── SortUtil.java
        └── impl
            └── BubbleSortUtilImpl.java
```

Here's a diagram of the modules, revisited with our newest change:

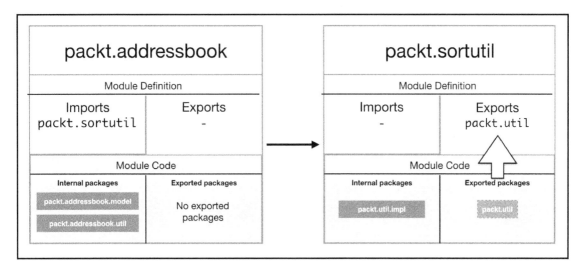

Remember that packages in Java are not hierarchical. In this example, the packages `packt.util` and `packt.util.impl` are two separate packages that are not related in any way. Just because you've exported the package `packt.util`, it doesn't mean that you are automatically exporting `packt.util.impl` also. Nor does it mean that `packt.util.impl` is somehow *within* `packt.util`. That's not how packages work in Java. These are two entirely different packages, and totally unrelated as far as package semantics are concerned.

The state of the code at this time is in the bundled source code. Compiling and executing the code as before should give us the same results. However, we have solved a major problem related to class encapsulation that we discussed in `Chapter 1`, *Introducing Java 9 Modularity*.

Think about the potential impact of this encapsulation on a library developer. Before Java 9, every `public` type that was shipped in a library could have been used and accessed by the consumers of the library. Now, with Java 9 modules, a library developer has full control over what classes can be used and what are just internal. So, the library developer can refactor the *internal* library code without having to worry about them potentially being used. Thanks to the module contract, they are inaccessible and hence guaranteed to be unused in code outside the module.

Module versioning

There's one aspect of module dependency that you might have noticed is missing from what we've covered so far--versioning. When you declare a module definition, can you specify a version number for the module? Also, when you specify that a certain module requires another module, can you also specify which version of module it needs? The answer to both the questions is no. For various reasons, module versioning is not a feature that's available in the Java Module system. It is not a problem the Java platform attempts to solve.

The biggest advantage and utility with module versioning comes with dependency management. Think of tools like Maven or Gradle. These tools allow you to configure specific versions of external dependencies which they can then automatically download for you from some remote repository, and then make them available in the classpath. The Java platform does not attempt to do this, or to solve any dependency management problems. It assumes that all the dependencies are already available, perhaps assembled by a tool like Maven or Gradle. In Chapter 1, *Introducing Java 9 Modularity*, I had mentioned how build tools like Maven or Gradle achieve predictability and consistency in assembling dependencies, but they cannot validate the accuracy or completeness of what's assembled. This is where the Java module system steps in. The platform assumes that all the necessary source files and classes are already there! Whatever your build tools are, and whatever the means you take to assemble your code and libraries, the Java platform works on what you have as a result and *then* makes sure the module contracts are being met.

This is a nuanced topic, and the reasoning can be debated extensively, but it's important to remember that module versioning is not available in Java 9. To manage multiple versions of modules, you are free to use whatever tools or processes you have already been using to pull in jars and libraries. In Chapter 12, *Using Build Tools and Testing Java Modules*, we examine how to integrate a Maven multi-module project with a Java 9 modular application to leverage the best of both worlds.

Rethinking package structure

The fact that you are required to *export* package names from modules has an interesting implication on the way we organize our types into packages in Java 9. Historically, the package construct has been used by Java developers to provide *namespaces* for Java types. While these namespaces created by package names serve the purpose, at least in theory, to prevent type name collisions and to affect visibility of package-private member variables and types, they also serve a slightly more informal purpose of grouping related types for search-ability and maintainability of code.

There's an additional significance to packages in Java 9 that affects how you group your classes and other types into packages--visibility outside modules. For instance, if you need to hide type *A* within a module and export type *B* to outside the module, you are essentially required to place types *A* and *B* in two separate packages. In most cases, typical internal classes of libraries are associated with different namespaces and packages in the pre-Java 9 world anyway, so this shouldn't be a big change in the way we do this. But it's important to note that this new change could factor into our decision to place classes in one package versus another.

Now that we've seen two modules and inter-modular dependency, I'd like you to introduce you to the concept of a module graph. You'll likely see this in a lot of Java documentation over time as a good way to represent relationships between modules. The way to draw a module graph is to plot modules as nodes and the relationships between modules with an arrow. If module *A* depends on module *B*, the arrow is drawn from *A* to *B*.

Here's the module graph for the code we have in the address book application so far:

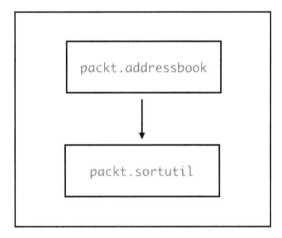

It is very simple at this time, but as we learn more about the module system and evolve our code, we'll be coming back to this module graph and adding detail to it.

Understanding module path arguments

Our example application is comprised of two Java modules. We have the source of both those modules in the module source path. In reality, it's common to be working on module sources that depend on compiled third-party modules pulled in as dependencies. In such cases, you'll need to provide to the compiler the module source path containing the module source files, and the module path for the compiled dependencies. The compiler needs a distinction between the code it needs to compile (in `--module-source-path`) and the location of compiled dependencies and libraries (`--module-path`). When it comes to execution, you just pass in `--module-path` pointing to the compiled modules.

Here are the command line argument values passed to the compiler and runtime:

	`--module-source-path`	`--module-path`
`javac`	Locations of all source modules	Locations of compiled modules that the source modules depend on.
`java`	<Not provided>	Location of all compiled modules - including app modules and compiled module dependencies

Revisiting classpath

We've seen that the new Java 9 platform comes with some new abilities to do module level compilation and execution using the `--module-source-path` and the `--module-path` arguments. It is now module-aware and knows what to do in order to compile and execute Java 9 modules. It's very likely that these flags are going to find increased usage as developers embrace Java modularity.

At the same time, there's a familiar compiler parameter that will, over time, see decreased usage--the `-classpath` parameter. The classpath that has been a concept that's essential to programming in Java for so many years, is for the most part, not required anymore!

For about two decades now, the Java classpath has played the crucial role of being the home for all the classes in any given Java application. Any Java application is obviously made up of multiple classes, often in multiple jar files. As a Java developer, all you had to do to get a class into play was to add it to the classpath. That would guarantee that the runtime would see it. Of course, there are still access modifiers such as `private`, `public`, and `protected` that control who gets to access a given Java type. But still, the presence of a class file in a classpath was all it took to make it *available* to the runtime.

Now, consider the new world where there are no standalone class files and everything is made up of modules. A Java 9 modular application is comprised of a number of different modules that have dependency on one another. Given the module paths, the compiler and runtime can now know where all the classes are. Also, thanks to the module convention, the classes that belong to the module reside in the module folder itself. In this case, why does Java need any other information to access the classes required for an application? The concept of a classpath isn't even needed anymore!

Wait! Before you let go of everything you've learned about classpaths from your memory, I should let you know that what I'm describing is the ideal scenario. Yes, ideally, classpath will likely hold lesser importance in Java in the future. However, we are still not done with it yet. We will be revisiting classpaths a few times in this book, especially in the context of working with older codebases and when migrating code to Java 9. More on that in `Chapter 10`, *Preparing Your Code for Java 9* .

Revisiting the classpath problems

In `Chapter 1`, *Introducing Java 9 Modularity*, we looked at two problems faced by our friends Jack and Amit:

- Jack couldn't easily *encapsulate* internal library types and prevent use of that type outside the library, while retaining the ability to freely use them inside his own library
- Amit couldn't *reliably* assemble a set of compiled Java code and guarantee that all the dependencies and imports of those types are sufficiently met before the program actually hits the dependency at runtime

Have we solved these problems with the module system? Thankfully, yes!

We've already seen how the Java module's encapsulation prevents certain types from being accessed outside the module, even if the type is `public`, unless the package they belong to is explicitly exported. Indeed, we applied the same concept to hide the `BubbleSortUtilImpl` class from external use. When it comes time to upgrade our library, should we feel the need to modify (or even remove) that class, we can rest assured that the only consumer of that code is in the library itself.

How about the second problem--runtime verification? It turns out, the Java runtime refers to the same `module-info` module descriptor (this time in `.class` format) to figure this out. You ran the `Main` class in the `packt.addressbook` module and it worked fine because the runtime found the dependent module `packt.sortutil` in the module path. Let's see what happens if it doesn't find it. If I were to delete the compiled `sortutil` directory in the `out` directory, and run `packt.addressbook/packt.addressbook.Main` again, notice the error you get:

```
$ java --module-path out --module packt.addressbook/packt.addressbook.Main
  Error occurred during initialization of VM
  java.lang.module.ResolutionException: Module sortutil not found,
   required by addressbook
  at java.lang.module.Resolver.fail(java.base@9/Resolver.java:841)
  at java.lang.module.Resolver.resolve(
   java.base@9/Resolver.java:154)
  . . .
```

The error message points out that the `packt.sortutil` module is not found, but the important thing to notice here is *when* the error is thrown. It's not when the class is loaded and the runtime tries to find the dependent types that it encounters this error. The error occurs right at the VM initialization time as the message clearly mentions. This is a huge advantage when it comes to reliability of your Java code. If there are potential errors, the runtime catches that right at initialization and not at some arbitrary point in time during execution.

One of the requirements that the module system was designed to meet is to achieve *fidelity across phases*. What does this mean? You've seen how the module descriptor enabled you to build modules, encapsulate types, and verify availability of the necessary dependencies by allowing you to specify the contract about each module. These benefits affect not only the compilation process of your code, but also the runtime process. The same module definition that lets the compiler know something is wrong when a required module is missing can also provide the runtime with the same information! Thanks to the module descriptor being compiled into the code as a class file, the Java runtime can also read the same descriptor and know well in advance if every module that is depended upon by the code that needs to be run is available. You get the same behavior and error checking across the compilation and execution phases.

Summary

In this chapter, we've created a second Java module and established inter-module dependency. We learned how to set up `requires` and `exports` in module definition files. With two modules, we are finally able to see the modularity features that attempt to solve some of the problems in code organization and management that we've discussed in `Chapter 1`, *Introducing Java 9 Modularity*.

Now that we have a basic understanding of how to create Java 9 modules and use them in other modules, let's focus our attention to the platform itself. Java 9 not only comes with the module system that's meant for developers to use in order to create modules, it also comes with a completely revamped JRE and JDK that are themselves modularized. In the next chapter, you'll learn about the modularization of the platform, how it affects developers, and how it is, in a way, essential for bringing in modularity support into the Java language.

4
Introducing the Modular JDK

In the previous two chapters, you've learnt about the modular API in Java 9 and how to create your own custom modules. There's much more to Java 9 modules than that! The introduction of modularity in Java is not just a new *feature* for developers to use; it has resulted in major changes to the Java platform itself. In fact, Java 9 also has had perhaps the biggest overhaul of the internal Java codebase ever. Java 9 not only comes with the ability for developers to create their own modules, the whole Java platform itself has been modularized. In this chapter, let's examine these important changes, both to learn what the changes are, and to understand *why* they came about. Now that you have warmed up to Java modules by writing modules yourself, it's time to put our thinking caps on and really understand the problems and the requirements that resulted in this major change in the Java language. Not only will it help us appreciate the changes better, learning how and why the JDK was modularized will help us apply these lessons when we learn how to migrate our own Java code to Java 9 in `Chapter 11`, *Migrating Your Code to Java 9*.

Here are the topics that we'll cover in this chapter:

- We'll start by examining two aspects of the JDK as they were before Java 9 and some problems with them. It's important for us to know the way things were, so that we can fully understand the effect of the new changes.
- You'll learn how modularity has transformed the Java platform and be introduced to the built-in modules.
- You'll learn how to browse built-in modules and get information about their module definitions.
- You'll learn how to understand module relationships in a module graph.

Examining the legacy JDK

Java has been around for over two decades now. For the most part of its lifetime, there have been a few things that haven't changed. Let's focus our attention on two aspects of the JDK the way they were in Java 8 or earlier:

- **The JRE structure**: The file and directory structure that **Java Runtime Environment (JRE)** is installed as when it is set up on a computer
- **The state of API encapsulation**: The differences between the *public* Java APIs and the internal platform classes

The JRE structure

When you install the Java 8 Runtime Environment on any machine and examine the installed directory, you'll see, among other files and folders, the following two important directories:

- A `bin` directory with executable files, an important one of which is the Java executable that lets you run Java programs
- The `lib` directory with some key `.jar` files including the all-important `rt.jar`

You may not have had to deal with the `rt.jar` directly when coding in Java, but you should know that it's the single most important `jar` file in the runtime. Can you guess what it's for?

Understanding rt.jar

Let's say you build a Java application that uses some core library classes such as collections and threads. When you compile and distribute your application to be run on another machine with Java installed, you can get away with packaging just the classes you've written in your application, and *not* include the compiled `Collection` and `Thread` classes. That's because every runtime comes with all the compiled platform classes out-of-the-box, so that every developer doesn't have to distribute them with their applications. The way these classes are bundled into the JRE is through a single file--`rt.jar`. You'd place your application classes in the classpath for the runtime to find, but for any of the platform classes, it just finds them in `rt.jar`. The name `rt` stands for **Run Time**, and this single jar file holds the entire Java runtime. Yes, you read that right! `rt.jar` essentially contains all the compiled classes in the Java platform, all bundled into one JAR file. Every. Single. One. Of. Them.

The problem with this model

This has been the state of affairs for multiple Java releases now. The decision to bundle all the platform classes into a single JAR file was made quite early in Java's life and it might have been a good idea at the time. But considering how much the platform has grown and how many new classes have been added to the platform over the years, it's clearly not a good idea anymore. With Java 8, the rt.jar measures close to 60 MB in size. And even if you might find it bearable now, imagine how it would scale, if say, Java continues to grow at a good pace for the next 10 years and ends up having a few thousands more classes added. Would we still be fine with bundling them all into a single jar file then?

In addition to the platform developers having to deal with the monolithic JAR file, here's another logistical challenge that this model brings up. A common practice for application developers to distribute their application is to bundle their app installers with the Java Runtime Environment. Any Java app requires the runtime anyway, but there's no knowing if the users of the Java application have the runtime installed on their machines beforehand. So, bundling the app with the runtime is a great way to make sure anyone who installs the app has the necessary runtime and can execute the app successfully. This is true not just for classic desktop application installers, but also for the newer practice of creating self-contained micro-services. Developers building micro-services create distributables that contain both the compiled micro-services as well as the Java runtime so that a micro-service instance can be kicked off on any virtual machine on the cloud by a single command.

The size of the runtime is clearly a problem here. No matter the complexity of your micro-service or application, irrespective of how many classes in the platform you use, you have to bundle in the complete Java runtime with the rt.jar that contains every Java platform class that's known to exist. So, no matter how small your actual application is, bundled with it is at least 60 MB of rt.jar goodness! Also affected are Java applications that run on smaller devices with resource constraints such as IOT and mobile devices. We briefly discussed in Chapter 1, *Introducing Java 9 Modularity*, the CORBA classes in the Java platform and how it exists in all Java runtimes since a very long time, although hardly anyone seems to use it anymore. As someone creating a self-contained Java executable, it's very fair to ask the question--why do I need to include all these classes in the runtime when I don't need them?

The attempted solution - Compact profiles

With Java 8, there was an introduction of a new concept called **compact profiles** to attempt to solve this very problem. Compact profiles are essentially smaller versions of the Java runtime that does not have to include the entirety of the contents of rt.jar. The runtime was broken down at package level to identify a closed set of core packages and classes that only depend on themselves so that the rest can be broken off and removed. There were three different profiles introduced, varying on how much was stripped off. The smallest and the most minimum profile is called compact1. This version of the runtime contains the very basic language features such as IO, collections, util, security, and concurrency. If your needs aren't met with compact1, you could also choose between compact2 and compact3, and if none of the three work for you, you would go with the full runtime:

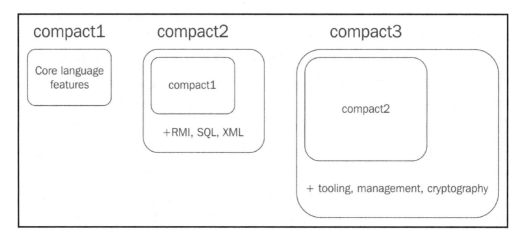

The smallest profile, compact1, measures just about 11 MB in size, and is a significant improvement from the 60 MB of the full rt.jar. But it's obvious that we still haven't eliminated the problem of bundling in runtime classes that aren't needed. We've just minimized them, and there are still going to be classes in whatever profile you choose that your application never uses, but you have to include anyway. Additionally, if you have an application that mostly uses classes from the compact1 profile, but needs just a couple of classes from compact2, well, you have no choice but to bundle the bigger compact2 profile instead.

I would, however, hesitate to call this a failed attempt at solving this problem. In fact, runtime profiles are actually the first steps in the Java platform's journey to modularizing of the runtime. However, it is important to note that this is the best we could do pre-Java 9 to address the issue of a bulky monolithic runtime.

The state of API encapsulation

To best explain the situation (and associated problems) with API encapsulation, all we need to do is recall from Chapter 1, *Introducing Java 9 Modularity*, Jack's trouble with his sorting library. He had an internal public class in his library that wasn't meant for external use, but it did end up getting used. If such a small library with the meagerly count of two classes could run into this problem, imagine the situation with the Java runtime with thousands of classes! The Java language provides documented APIs for developers to use. But it also has many supporting classes to facilitate the inner workings of those APIs that shouldn't be used by developers. However, surely enough, they are all a part of the sole rt.jar, so there's nothing stopping developers from using those classes either.

Understanding internal APIs

There are several internal classes in the Java runtime that developers aren't supposed to use. They aren't documented as part of the language specification, but are necessary for the internal functioning of the runtime, perhaps for other classes that *are* documented. A great example that's much discussed among Java developers in online communities is a class called sun.misc.Unsafe, which we briefly mentioned in Chapter 1, *Introducing Java 9 Modularity*.

The class sun.misc.Unsafe was never meant for public consumption. It was always supposed to be an internal class meant for use by the Java runtime only. It is not documented. It has no public constructors. The source code of the class is filled with warnings about the dangers of using the class. It's funny that even the fact that the class having the ominous sounding name Unsafe hasn't deterred some developers from using it. Of course, sun.misc.Unsafe is one of a handful of internal classes that have been misused by Java developers. But if it's just a handful of classes, you might ask, what's the big deal?

The problem with this model

Java is commonly known to be a very **backwards compatible** language. While the language itself has seen major changes over the years, almost all the changes have been additions to the language, while still retaining the functionality of the older versions. Let's say you picked up a Java codebase written with Java 1.3 and you compiled and ran it with Java 8. Would you be surprised if it ran without issues? Probably not! That's precisely because of the reputation Java has of being backward compatible. And it's a great thing in my opinion, because it gives adopters the confidence that there's not a lot of effort and rewrites required for every major upgrade. This is an aspect where Java has an edge over a few other development platforms.

This backward compatibility comes with a cost, especially when you consider the lack of encapsulation of internal APIs. What if there is an internal API that developers have inadvertently used because of the lack of encapsulation? To maintain backward compatibility, the language team is compelled to not make breaking changes to those internal APIs even though they are, by definition, internal. So, the burden of backward compatibility gets worse for the language--not only do public APIs have to be backward compatible, even the internal runtime classes need to be as well!

The attempted solution - Deprecation, warnings, and documentation

We routinely import classes from packages such as `java.*` and `javax.*` in our code because the classes in those packages house most of the public APIs in the Java language that are meant for public consumption. There are, however, classes in other packages such as `sun.*` that are JDK-internal and you wouldn't find in any API documentation. Many of these classes have been a part of Java since 1.0.

Since the language had no facility to prevent usage of these internal APIs, several other attempts have been made to discourage usage. There was an article on the Sun website titled *Why developers should not write programs that call 'sun' packages*. The Sun website isn't up anymore, but the article's original webpage is still preserved for posterity, thanks to WayBack Machine, and is available here:
`http://web.archive.org/web/19980215011039/http://java.sun.com/products/jdk/faq/faq-sun-packages.html`:

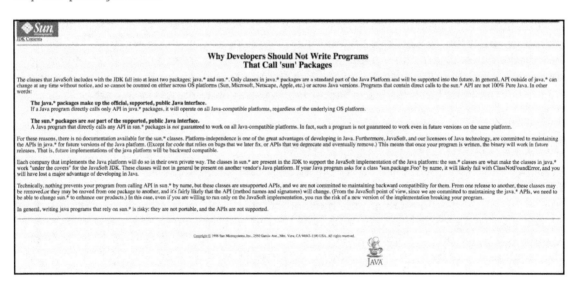

Notice the year mentioned on the article! Yes, it's been around as a part of the official documentation since back in 1996 (then on java.sun.com)! The warning is still around on the Oracle documentation website, by the way. Clearly, 20 years of asking developers not to use certain classes hasn't solved the problem! You might very well ask, what good is such a warning in documentation if nobody pays attention to it? Well, in addition to warnings in documentation, since JDK 6, the compiler has been throwing out warnings if your application uses any APIs from the `sun.*` packages. However, this is also something that developers could easily ignore.

These approaches are clearly not good enough. We need to be able to enforce these rules and provide guardrails to *prevent* developers from using internal APIs. There was no such feature available in the language so far. The language just had to evolve.

Enter Project Jigsaw

Project Jigsaw was the effort to apply the concepts and features of modularity to the Java platform itself. The modularization of the platform essentially solves both the problems described previously. We'll look at how later in this chapter, but let's begin looking at the work that was done for *Project Jigsaw* and how it affects developers interacting with the Java platform.

The project itself was a huge effort that involved the following high-level steps:

1. Re-organizing the platform source code to make it more conducive for modularization.
2. Defining and building modules with predefined input and output interfaces and with a clear dependency map.
3. Encapsulating *internal* classes and allowing usage for only *public* APIs.
4. Providing tools for generating smaller and modular runtime images as an alternative to the monolithic `rt.jar`.

Let's deep-dive into the changes now and see how it affects us.

Platform modularity

With Java 9, the entire Java platform, with every class in it, has been segregated and grouped into modules. Yes, all of the platform Java classes from `Collections` and `Thread` to `Connection` and `Logger`! It doesn't really matter which one; every platform class is now housed in newly created Java modules that come out-of-the-box with the runtime and the JDK. The platform team achieved this by going through both the public APIs and internal classes, grouping them based on the types that usually go well together and are self-contained, and bundling such related classes into modules.

Take Java logging for example. The native logging functionality in Java comprised of a group of classes in the package `java.util.logging`. These classes have now been grouped into a newly created module called `java.logging`. The JDBC and SQL related classes have all gone into a new module called `java.sql`. XML related classes have gone into the module `java.xml`. Here are a few more examples of modules that come out-of-the-box with Java 9:

- `java.scripting`: Provides the scripting APIs for the Java scripting engine
- `java.desktop`: Provides the Java desktop APIs, `awt`, and `swing` packages
- `java.transaction`: Provides transaction related APIs in package `javax.transaction`

There is also a special module named `java.base`. The module `java.base` contains APIs and classes that are fundamental to the Java platform and without which one could not possibly write any Java code. The `java.base` module contains APIs from packages such as `java.lang`, `java.io`, `java.util` and so on. As you can see, it covers a lot of basic Java APIs that most of our Java applications use. Now, why do I call this module special? Hold that thought! We'll get back to it in a bit.

The impact of platform modularity

As you can imagine, the impact of this change is indeed significant, and it pretty much affects the way we write all Java code from now on. In Java 8 and earlier, you didn't have to think twice about using any Java API. All you had to do is import the types you need into your code. Since the JVM knew where to find `rt.jar`, the necessary classes were always found by the runtime. That's no longer the case with Java 9. Remember in Chapter 3, *Handling Inter-Module Dependencies* , when you needed a class in the `packt.addressbook` module from the `packt.sortutil` module? You couldn't just import the class in your code and use it. You had to go to the module definition of `packt.addressbook` and specify the dependency on the module using the `requires` clause. That's exactly what you'll need to do for native Java platform types too!

Need to use Java SQL APIs? They are in the module `java.sql`, so in the module where you need them, you need to specify this in the module descriptor:

```
module mymodule {
   requires java.sql;
}
```

Once you have required the necessary platform module, its APIs are then ready for use in your module. Since the `java.sql` module is built on the same Java module system that you use to write your code, you can bet that there's code in the `module-info` file of the `java.sql` module that exports the `java.sql` and `javax.sql` packages that contain the Java SQL API.

This necessity to *require* modules before using them applies not just to our own modules; it applies to the Java modules too. For example, the `java.sql` module requires logging functionality (for obvious reasons). And the logging APIs are in the `java.logging` module. So, there's a `requires` declaration in `java.sql` module's `module-info.java` file specifying this requirement. That's the only way code in the `java.sql` module can import and use the logging APIs.

This is how the `module-info.java` of `java.sql` module should look to enable the configuration we've discussed so far:

```
module java.sql {
   ...
   requires java.logging;
   exports java.sql;
   exports javax.sql;
   ...
}
```

Module graph

The result of these individual Java modules depending on one another is that we can now draw a complete graph of dependencies with the modules as nodes and the relationships between nodes as module dependencies. This kind of picture is called a **module graph** and is your new best friend to help you track and manage module dependencies in your Java 9 modular applications. We looked at a simple module graph of the address book application in the previous chapter. Here's a simple module graph that specifies the dependencies between a handful of Java platform modules:

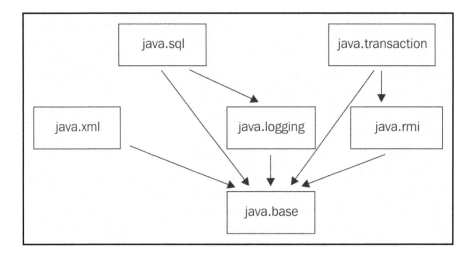

A line drawn from module *A* to module *B* indicates that module *A* `requires` module *B*. So, as this diagram indicates, module `java.transaction` requires `java.rmi`, which in turn requires `java.base`. As mentioned before, since `java.base` contains APIs that are fundamental to the language, it is one module that every other module is sure to need. Which is why, this one module is treated a bit differently.

The java.base module

In `Chapter 2`, *Creating Your First Java Module*, and `Chapter 3`, *Handling Inter-Module Dependencies*, you wrote a few Java 9 modules that used some Java APIs such as `Collection` and `System.out`. These APIs happen to come from the `java.base` module. You might have noticed something wrong with the picture here. Since these core Java APIs are in its own module, shouldn't we have had to add the `requires java.base;` line in all our module descriptors before we used them? How did the compilation succeed without it? Well, let me assure you that there's no trickery involved here. The reason it worked is due to the special nature of the `java.base` module.

When was the last time you had to write the line `import java.lang.*` in your Java class? Never, I hope! You don't need to import classes from the package `java.lang` because it is imported and available to your Java code by default. That's because the classes in that package are so commonly used that it's a sensible default to always have the types in the package imported.

Java 9 has a similar shortcut for requiring the `java.base` module. This module contains the `java.lang` package among other fundamental Java APIs that almost no Java module can be written without. So, rather than every Java module in existence having to *require* the `java.base` module, it is just required by default, so you don't have to explicitly specify it. Now, since the `java.lang` packages are in the `java.base` module, the default behavior is seamless in both cases! See how that works?

Remember, though, that this is the only module that has this behavior. Every other Java module in existence, platform or otherwise, will have to be explicitly *required*, if the module is needed as a dependency.

Since there is always an implicit dependency on `java.base`, a common practice when writing module graphs is to skip the dependency on this base module in order to make things more legible. The idea is to show a module depending on `java.base` only if the given module's *only* dependency is `java.base`. If a module depends on other modules, we show only that and skip the `java.base` dependency. Here's how the module graph from earlier looks with this approach:

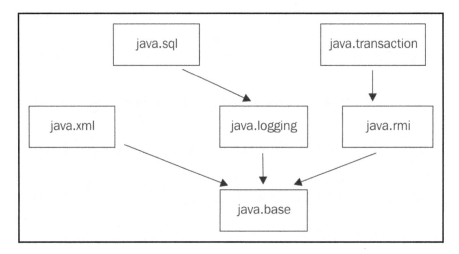

I hope you'll agree this graph looks a bit cleaner. This is a practice that people seem to be increasingly following, so when you come across such module graphs, don't forget the implicit `java.base` dependency. It's always there!

Browsing modules

Now that you've looked at some of the modules that come with Java, you might be wondering how you can get more information about them. How can you find out what the list of modules are that come with the platform? Given an API, how can you know which platform module contains it? And given a module, how can you know what are the packages it exports?

The answer is a couple of new arguments to the `java` command. First is an option called `--list-modules`. This command lets you examine the modules that are available for you from the platform.

When you run the following command from the **Command Prompt**, this is what you'll see:

```
$ java --list-modules
  java.activation@9
  java.annotations.common@9
  java.base@9
  java.compiler@9
  java.corba@9
  java.datatransfer@9
  java.desktop@9
  . . .
```

The list you see there is the list of all the Java platform modules! As you scroll the list, notice that the modules we discussed previously are all there! This is a great way to browse through and get a good idea of what's available.

There's another new option `-d`, which helps in examining the details of a single module. The syntax is:

```
$ java -d <module-name>
```

You can also use the longer form `--describe-module` to do the same:

```
$ java --describe-module <module-name>
```

For example, if you want to look at more details about the `java.base` module, run the following command:

```
$ java -d java.base
  module java.base@9
  exports java.io
  exports java.lang
  exports java.lang.annotation
  . . .
```

The output has been truncated for brevity, but as you scroll down the result of the command, you'll notice various details about the module listed.

Here's the output of the command run on the module `java.sql`:

```
$ java -d java.sql
  java.sql@9
  exports java.sql
```

```
exports javax.sql
exports javax.transaction.xa
requires java.base mandated
requires java.logging transitive
requires java.xml transitive
uses java.sql.Driver
```

In these module-level outputs, you'll notice the following categories of information displayed:

- **Exports**: This is the list of all the packages exported by the module. In the `java.base` module, you'll see familiar packages such as `java.io` and `java.lang` here. The `java.sql` module exports packages `java.sql` and `javax.sql`. These packages marked with `exports` are all the packages that the module exports. Thereby, when you `require` the module, (which you do by default with `java.base`), your module gets access to the types in the *required* module that also belong to those *exported* packages. In the output, you'll notice some statements in the form `exports <package-name> to <module-name>`. These are called qualified exports. We'll be covering qualified exports in Chapter 6, *Module Resolution, Readability, and Accessibility*.

- **Contains**: This is the list of internal packages that the module *contains* but does not export. These packages are, by definition, not visible outside the module. It is still handy for us developers to know what the packages are that belong to the *internal* module API because a lot of these had been APIs that existed in Java 8 and thus, used to be available publicly earlier. For example, look at the packages `jdk.internal.*` and `sun.util.*` in the `java.base` module. They are not in the `exports` list so they are now effectively encapsulated in the module.

- **Requires**: This is the list of modules that a given module requires. The `java.sql` module requires three other modules--`java.base`, `java.logging`, and `java.xml`. The requirement of `java.base` is by default, and so it is qualified with a `requires mandated` clause. Note that you *do not* have to do this in your own modules, since that's default behavior. Ignore the `requires transitive` clause for now. That's related to making modules available to dependent modules, a concept we'll explore in detail in Chapter 6, *Module Resolution, Accessibility, and Readability*. Also, as is obvious, `java.base` does not `require` any other module.

- **Uses and provides**: These are related to the concept of Services, which we'll be exploring in Chapter 7, *Introducing Services*.

I recommend using the `java --list-modules` and `java -d <module-name>` commands to explore other modules in the platform. As you start writing modular code in Java 9, you'll often need to import platform classes, and that requires the identification of modules that export them. Initially, you'll need to use these commands to get to the right module, but when you do this a few times, you'll be committing to your memory the common packages and the modules that have them available, and so you don't need to do this anymore. What also helps is the intuitive names for the modules. Need to use SQL classes? You just *know* they are in `java.sql`! Granted, some packages may not be all that intuitive, but still, the naming convention followed goes a long way in helping developers get to the right modules quickly.

Module types

Speaking of naming conventions, you might have noticed the different prefixes to the module names when you ran the `java --list-modules` command. The three prefixes to the platform modules are--`java.`, `javafx.`, and `jdk.`. The prefix indicates the nature of the module:

- `java`: Indicates the core Java platform module. These are what's referred to in the official documentation as *standard modules.*
- `javafx`: Indicates modules of Java FX, the platform for building desktop applications in Java.
- `jdk`: Indicates core JDK modules. These are not part of the language specification, but contain valuable APIs and tools for the Java developer, including the `jdk.compiler` and `jdk.javadoc`, as well as debugging and serviceability tools and APIs such as `jdk.jdi` and `jdk.jconsole`.
- `oracle`: If you've downloaded the Oracle Open JDK, you might see a couple of modules beginning with this prefix. Remember that these are non-standard modules that are specific to this flavor of the JDK implementation and they will not be available in other implementations. For this reason, it's a good idea to completely ignore these modules.

The `java.` prefixed modules themselves can be classified into three categories:

- **Core Java modules**: These are necessary for the Core Java functionality. Modules such as `java.base`, `java.xml`, and so on, which are APIs usually referred to as Core Java SE APIs. This is in contrast to Enterprise APIs, the next category.

- **Enterprise modules**: This category contains modules such as `java.corba` that contains APIs leveraging CORBA technology and `java.transaction`, which provide database transaction APIs usually required in an Enterprise application context. Note that this is different from Java EE, which is the completely different spec. However, there has always been a small overlap between what got bundled with the Java SE and Java EE SDKs. To avoid this overlap, as of Java 9, these Enterprise modules have been marked as deprecated and might be removed in a future Java version.

- **Aggregator modules**: These are modules that do not contain any APIs by themselves, but instead act as a convenient way to bundle multiple modules together. Specifying a `requires` dependency on the aggregator module is equivalent to individually specifying the `requires` dependency on all the individual modules that the aggregator module aggregates. You'll learn how to build your own custom aggregator modules in Chapter 6, *Module Resolution, Accessibility, and Readability*. For now, note that there are a couple of aggregator modules that come bundled with the platform. They are:

  - `java.se`: This is a convenient aggregator module that gathers all the *standard* Java SE modules together.
  - `java.se.ee`: This aggregator module gathers all the `java.se` modules and adds in the APIs that overlap with the Java EE specification.

While aggregator modules provide a level of convenience, I'd recommend using them with care. When writing a Java application, it can be tempting to just `require` the `java.se` module, for instance, to pull down the entire Java SE platform. That way, you don't have to bother with identifying which platform modules contain the APIs you want and thus need to import. With just one line--`requires java.se`, you have the whole platform at your disposal. But then, you are losing several advantages of the modularization of the platform. You then end up with a bulky Java platform with unnecessary classes, no different from Java 8 and earlier. The aggregator modules are provided for convenience to be used only when necessary. So, make sure you use them right.

Examining platform file structure

Let's now examine how these changes to the platform manifest in the file structure of the installation. Historically, the Java platform has come in two flavors--The **Java Runtime environment** (**JRE**) and the **Java Development Kit** (**JDK**). The JDK is the superset, in that it contains the JRE. Here's a high-level structure of the classic JDK with only a few important files shown for the sake of simplicity:

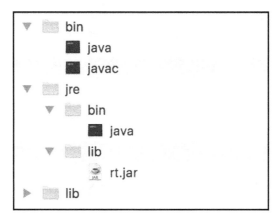

The Java 9 JDK looks very different. You can navigate to the directory using the `cd $JAVA_HOME` command. Here's what the new JDK looks like, again with only a few important files displayed:

There are a couple of important differences that should be noted:

- There is no JRE folder within the main folder anymore. The structure is now collapsed into one common folder. JDK 9 moves away from the distinction between JRE and JDK to create a common runtime binary file structure. This structure contains the `bin`, `lib`, and `conf` folders at the top level, with no nested folders for the runtime. This change was implemented to provide the ability to create custom runtime images that are now supported in Java 9. You'll learn more about generating such images in `Chapter 8`, *Understanding Linking and Using jlink*.

- There's a new folder called `jmods` that contains all the packaged platform modules that we've learnt about so far. With Java 9, it's time to say goodbye to `rt.jar`. There is no single monolithic jar file that houses the entire platform. Each platform module has a corresponding file in the `jmods` folder. So, what would have formerly been a single `rt.jar` file is now split into separate module files, one for each platform module.

- Notice the `.jmod` file extension of the module files. Shouldn't those be `.jar` files? With Java 9, a new format called JMOD has been introduced as a new way of bundling libraries specifically for development time, and not for runtime. The traditional jar format is great for bundling classes for runtime use, but since they are just a ZIP file of compiled classes, they aren't very useful when using them during development time. The new JMOD format goes beyond the JAR format by including the ability to bundle in things such as native code and configuration files, which makes it useful for distributing libraries for development use. This is the format used by the JDK to bundle all built-in platform modules. The details of the format are beyond the scope of what we are covering here. Just think of it as the new dev-time-only alternative to the JAR format.

Observable modules

There are two module path values we pass to the `javac` and `java` commands--the module source path (passed to `javac`) containing the uncompiled Java source modules and the module path (passed to `javac` and `java`) containing the compiled Java modules. These options point to the locations of all the modules that are available for the compiler and the runtime to look up and use when necessary. Notice that we didn't have to add the path to the Java platform modules. That's because the Java runtime modules are included by default in the module path for compiling with `javac` and executing with `java`. You have to add the path only to the modules that are not a part of the platform, but you intend to include for compilation or execution.

This complete set of modules including modules in the module path that you supply to the platform *and* the out-of-the-box platform modules that are automatically available are together referred to as *observable modules*. As the name indicates, these are the modules that the platform *observes* in order to satisfy module dependencies. If a required module is not among the set of observable modules, the platform complains that the module is missing.

How do you know what the observable modules are? When we've used the `java --list-modules` command to list the platform modules, what we are actually doing is listing all observable modules. And, by default, only the platform modules are observable. You can also find out what are the observable modules for a given module path. You do that by specifying the `--module-path` option to the same command. You can specify as value a set of directory locations that form the module path. In that case, the command would display the list of observable modules *for that module path*, which would include all the platform modules along with any compiled modules in that module path.

For example, if you were to run the command with the module path being the compiled modules in the `out` folder from the previous chapter (`03-two-modules`), here's what you'll see:

```
$ java --module-path out --list-modules
java.activation@9
java.base@9
java.compiler@9
...
addressbook file:///Users/koushik/code/java9/03-two-
 modules/out/addressbook/
sortutil file:///Users/koushik/code/java9/03-two-modules/out/sortutil/
```

Notice that in addition to the platform modules, there are two of our own modules showing up in the list. This is because they are in the module path we've passed as a parameter to the command, thus adding them to the list of observable modules for that module path. For non-platform modules, the output also includes the path of the module. This makes it handy to locate modules when there are multiple directories passed to the `--module-path` option.

Revisiting the two problems

We started this chapter looking at two issues with the Java platform:

- The monolithic runtime
- The lack of API encapsulation features

Interestingly, the modularization of the Java platform provides solutions to both these problems.

Solving the monolithic runtime

There is a distinct advantage of knowing which platform modules your application belongs to. It is a clear indication of which platform modules it doesn't need--which is anything the modules in the application doesn't use! So, for example, if your application contains modules that only `require` the platform modules `java.base` and `java.logging`, you can essentially create a small subset of the Java platform consisting of just those two modules. That slice of the platform is all that your application needs to function. If you are bundling the runtime with your application, you now know the exact portion of the runtime you need to bundle, no more no less!

Java 9 comes with a brand-new *static linking* step that lets you create custom runtime images with only the modules that your applications need. This results in smaller and leaner application distributable, micro-service executables, and so on. You'll learn more about the linking phase and how to create your own runtimes in `Chapter 8`, *Understanding Linking and Using jlink*.

Solving the API encapsulation problem

Thanks to Java platform modules leveraging the encapsulation concepts of modularity, the platform now has the means to effectively protect internal classes from external usage. The platform can evolve to modify or even completely remove and replace the internal APIs, and still ensure backward compatibility as long as the *public* exported APIs remain the same. I believe this enables better and faster evolution of the Java platform, and we all get to benefit from it.

On the other hand, remember that there are some classes that were publicly accessible in earlier Java versions that are now encapsulated in Java platform modules. This implies that there are possibly some backward incompatibilities with applications that were formerly depending on those internal APIs (even though they really shouldn't)! This is a problem many of us will have to tackle when we migrate code written in Java 8 or earlier into Java 9. We'll learn more about that, as well as strategies to handle such situations in `Chapter 10`, *Preparing Your Code for Java 9*.

Summary

We've covered a lot of ground in this chapter. We started looking at a couple of problems with the earlier versions of the Java platform and how the language didn't really provide sufficient features to solve them. We then learned how the Java platform has been modularized, what the modules are, and how to browse and get information about them. We then wrapped up with how the new modular Java platform has effectively solved the two major problems we began the chapter with.

In the next chapter, you'll put these concepts into practice by wiring in the Java platform modules into the address book application and getting familiar with the process of using platform modules and APIs in your custom Java code.

5
Using Platform APIs

In the previous chapter, we looked at how the Java platform has been modularized, what the modules look like and how to navigate and find more information about them. In this chapter, we'll get hands-on and implement and extend functionality in the address book viewer application by using some of the platform APIs. In the process, I'll walk you through the typical process of finding and using platform APIs, as well as how to organize application modules to have better reusability and modularity.

Here are the enhancements we'll make to the address book viewer application in this chapter:

- We'll add logging logic to the application using the Java Logging APIs. This is not really a user-facing feature, but it's handy as a developer to be able to log informational and error messages from your application.
- We'll use XML APIs to read contact information from an XML file. The application currently has a bunch of hardcoded users. We'd like to update that to read from an XML file on a path that's provided by the user.
- We'll add a graphical user interface to the application by displaying a list of names. Clicking on a name in the list then displays detailed contact information of that contact. We'll be building this using the Java FX APIs.

All of the preceding features requires the usage of Java platform APIs. By achieving the preceding three objectives, you will have had good practice in establishing dependencies on and using the Java platform modules. Note that the focus in this chapter is on using the platform APIs and not on learning about the specific APIs themselves. So, even though you don't plan to use or learn about the Java XML APIs or the Java FX APIs, I still recommend you open your editor and follow through the steps covered in this chapter hands-on. Using these specific APIs in this chapter is just a means to learning about using platform APIs in general. Once you are done working on this chapter, you'll be in a much better position to browse and use other Java Platform APIs too.

We have a lot to cover, so let's get started!

Adding logging ability

Let's start with using the logging API in Java to log messages to the console. As an example, we want to be able to log some sample messages during the application start and completion.

What we'd typically do in Java 8 or earlier is just import the necessary logging classes and start using the logging APIs. That is, the `Logger` class from the `java.util.logging` package. However, as we've learned in the previous chapter, there's an additional step in Java 9. Using the logging APIs directly will result in a compilation error. That's because the logging APIs aren't available in the `java.base` module. We've seen that the best way to search for a module is using the `--list-modules` parameter to the `java` command. Let's run that and see if we find a module related to logging:

```
$ java --list-modules
. . .
java.jnlp@9
java.logging@9
java.management@9
java.naming@9
java.prefs@9
```

As you can see, there's a module called `java.logging`. That looks promising! The next step is to see if that module exports the APIs we need:

```
$ java -d java.logging
module java.logging@9
  exports java.util.logging
  requires mandated java.base
  provides jdk.internal.logger.DefaultLoggerFinder with
  sun.util.logging.internal.LoggingProviderImpl
  contains sun.net.www.protocol.http.logging
  contains sun.util.logging.internal
  contains sun.util.logging.resources
```

Good news! It does. The `java.logging` module exports the package `java.util.logging`, which is just what we need. Let's add this module as a dependency in the `packt.addressbook` module first:

```
module packt.addressbook {
  requires java.logging;
  requires packt.sortutil;
}
```

Now, we are free to use the logging APIs in our code. In the `Main.java` class, first import the `Logger` class and create a static `logger` variable by initializing `Logger` with the class name:

```
package packt.addressbook;
...
import java.util.logging.Logger;
...
public class Main {
  private static final Logger logger =
    Logger.getLogger(Main.class.getName());
  ...
}
```

Next, we can use the logger to log a message both at the start and the end of the application:

```
public static void main(String[] args) {
  logger.info("Address book viewer application: Started");
  ...
  System.out.println(contacts);
  logger.info("Address book viewer application: Completed");
}
```

Compile the modules by running this command in the project root directory:

```
$ javac --module-source-path src -d out --module
  packt.addressbook,packt.sortui
```

Execute with the `java` command and you should get output that looks like this:

```
$ java --module-path out -m packt.addressbook/packt.addressbook.Main
Mar 27, 2017 7:41:51 PM packt.addressbook.Main main
INFO: Address book viewer application: Started
[Charles Babbage, Tim Berners-Lee, Edsger Dijkstra, Ada Lovelace, Alan
Turing]
Mar 27, 2017 7:41:51 PM packt.addressbook.Main main
INFO: Address book viewer application: Completed
```

With this, we've successfully integrated logging APIs into our application. This is the simplest of the three use cases we'll be looking at in this chapter. The usage of the logging platform API involved:

- Declaring the need for a platform module--with the `requires` statement
- Usage of the platform module APIs in the Java source

Using an alternative compiler command

As we begin creating more modules, the compiler command will continue to grow. This is because we need to specify every module in the module path that needs compilation directly in the command.

If you are using a macOS/Unix/Linux operating systems, there's an alternative way you can get all the modules compiled, and I find this method shorter and easier. Remember in Chapter 2, *Creating Your First Java Module*, we listed all the Java classes directly in the command for the compiler to compile. Now rather than entering all the classes in all the modules manually in the command, the idea is to use the Unix `find` command with a command line wildcard to get all the file names with the `.java` extension and plug them in directly. The below command illustrates how this works:

```
$ javac --module-source-path src -d out $(find . -name '*.java')
```

The part of the command `$(find . -name '*.java')` expands all the file names of the Java files (as specified by `-name '*.java'`) in the current folder (as specified by the `.`), including nested subfolders, in one go. Since this command is shorter and much easier on the eyes, I'll be using this version from now on. This format also has the additional advantage of being consistent. You can pretty much copy-paste this command to compile all modules in the module current directory, irrespective of how many modules you have. If you are on Windows, or if you prefer to use the `--module` format, make sure you specify all the individual module names following the `--module` option.

Reading contacts from an XML file

The next improvement we'll make is to have the address book viewer application read an XML file to get contact information instead of a hard-coded list. There are a couple of nuances with this integration, so let's try that out now!

The list of contacts being displayed by the address book viewer is from hard-coded data in the `ContactUtil` class. Here's the sample structure of the XML file we'd like to read it from:

```xml
<?xml version="1.0"?>
<addressbook>
  <contact>
    <firstname>Edsger</firstname>
    <lastname>Dijkstra</lastname>
    <address>
      <street>5612</street>
      <city>AZ</city>
      <state>Eindhoven</state>
      <country>Netherlands</country>
    </address>
    <phone>345-678-9012</phone>
  </contact>
  <contact>
    . . .
  </contact>
  . . .
</addressbook>
```

The root node is `addressbook` and within it are several `contact` child nodes. Each `contact` node has `firstname`, `lastname`, and a nested `address` node, as shown.

In order to have the application read from an XML file, what we'd like to do is the following:

1. Remove the existing hardcoded logic from the module `packt.addressbook`.
2. Implement functionality of opening and reading the XML file in a separate module. This module will contain code to read from the source XML file and return a list of contacts.
3. Update the *main* address book module to depend on this new module to get the list of contacts.

The fact that we need to do #1 is obvious. But why #2 and #3? Why move that portion of the code to its own module? Well, as you can imagine, there's no *right* answer for this one.

The goal of modularization is to achieve the separation of monolithic code into modular building blocks that can be freely reused and replaced. Consider the scenario where, in the future, you decide to *not* use an XML file to store the data, but instead, read from a JSON file. Or a database. Or even a REST API! No matter what the new source is, the fact that there is this one separate module that acts as a *provider* of the list of contacts makes the change relatively easy. All you have to do then is to remove the XML-based module we'll create now and plug in a new module that reads from the new source of data. Granted, you'll still need to change the consumers to depend on the new module. But the change will be minimized, and so will the scope of any side effects.

Removing the hard-coded contact list

Let's begin by removing the hard-coded source of contacts. This is fairly simple. You'll need to delete the `ContactUtil.java` class in the package `packt.addressbook.util`. We are now left with a couple of lines of code in `Main.java` that are not valid anymore. Let's remove those two lines too:

```
ContactUtil contactUtil = new ContactUtil();
List<Contact> contacts = contactUtil.getContacts();
```

Creating the module

Now let's create a new module that holds code that acts as a source of contact information. I'll call the module `packt.contact`. You should know the drill by now. Create a new module root folder with the name `packt.contact` in the `src` folder, just where the other module root folders reside. Next, create a `module-info.java` module descriptor in the module root folder.

What modules do we need here? Since this module needs the XML APIs, we'll have to declare it with the `requires` statement. We saw in the previous chapter that there's a module called `java.xml` that contains the XML APIs. Of course, a way of searching for the right module is using the `java --list-modules` command as before. here's the module descriptor with this dependency added.

```
module packt.contact {
  requires java.xml;
}
```

The source code in this module belongs to two classes. First is the class `ContactLoader` in the package `packt.contact.util`. This class contains the method `loadContacts` that takes in the filename of the XML file to read and it returns the list of `Contact` objects. This is the method that consumers of this module will call:

```
package packt.contact.util;
public class ContactLoader {
  public List<Contact> loadContacts(String fileName) {
    ...
  }
}
```

Note that the name of the method is the generic `loadContacts`, and contains no particular indication that what it's loading from is an XML file. This is again useful to achieve the abstraction, and the module could very well change its functionality in the future to read contacts from another source or file format.

The second class `XMLUtil` consists of some generic but handy XML utility methods. These are methods that the `ContactLoader` class will use to read and parse XML. Since this aspect of dealing with XML is not the *purpose* of this module, this class will be in a separate `packt.contact.internal` package so that it can be protected against use outside the module:

```
package packt.contact.internal;
public class XmlUtil {
    ...
}
```

Here's the file and folder structure of the module at this time:

```
packt.contact/
├── module-info.java
└── packt
    └── contact
        ├── internal
        │   └── XmlUtil.java
        └── util
            └── ContactLoader.java
```

Coding the XmlUtil class

Let's now add the first of two methods to the XmlUtil--a loadXmlFile() method that takes in an XML filename as a String, parses it, and returns an XML document object.

The code involves opening the file to get a File object. Then, using the DOM XML API, we create a DocumentBuilderFactory. With that, we create a new DocumentBuilder. And with that, we parse the input file.

The following is the method in its entirety:

```
public Document loadXmlFile(String fileName) throws
 ParserConfigurationException, SAXException, IOException {
    File inputFile = new File(fileName);
    DocumentBuilderFactory dbFactory =
      DocumentBuilderFactory.newInstance();
    DocumentBuilder dBuilder = dbFactory.newDocumentBuilder();
    Document doc = dBuilder.parse(inputFile);
    doc.getDocumentElement().normalize();
    return doc;
}
```

Note the exceptions that the method throws. The three exceptions are a result of using the File API to open the file and the XML API to parse it. Rather than have the method catch the exception, which it wouldn't really know what to do with, it throws them. These exceptions have an interesting implication to modularity that we'll look at shortly.

The second method is getElement(), which takes in an XML node and the element name to return the value of that element in the node. If no value is found, an empty string is returned. This is all XML API specific and not too interesting for us in the context of this chapter, so here's the method in its entirety:

```
public String getElement(Node nNode, String tagName) {
  if (nNode.getNodeType() == Node.ELEMENT_NODE) {
    Element eElement = (Element) nNode;
    return eElement.getElementsByTagName(tagName)
      .item(0).getTextContent();
  }
  return "";
}
```

With this, we are done with XmlUtil. We'll now move on to the more interesting ContactLoader class.

Coding the ContactLoader class

We've already seen that `ContactLoader` should have a single method `loadContacts()`, which takes as argument the file name and returns a list of `Contact`s:

```
public List<Contact> loadContacts(String fileName) {
}
```

In the method, we initialize a new instance of `XmlUtil` and use the `loadXmlFile` method to get the XML Document object:

```
XmlUtil xmlUtil = new XmlUtil();
Document doc = xmlUtil.loadXmlFile(fileName);
```

Now what's left is processing the resulting DOM object structure and constructing the list of contacts in the model type we need. Again, to avoid getting into too much detail about XML, I'll just point you to the bundled source code at `05-jdk-modules/src/packt.contact`.

There are a couple of problems with the `packt.contact` module right now--shared classes and dependency leakage. One of which you might have already noticed.

Shared classes

This is the more obvious of the two problems. We've created a new module and designed a method in a class to return a list of `Contact` instances. The problem is that the `Contact` and `Address` model classes are not in the module! They are in the `packt.addressbook` module. Compiling this module now will result in a compilation error about the two classes not found. How do we solve this?

Here's a thought. How about depending on the module that contains the classes? The `packt.contact` module needs the `Contact` and `Address` classes that are available in the `packt.addressbook` module. Could we have the `packt.contact` module require the `packt.addressbook` module? We'll of course also need the dependency the other way round. `packt.addressbook` needs to `requires packt.contact` to get the list of contacts. Can this be done? Turns out it cannot, because it introduces circular dependencies, which are not allowed by the Java module system.

 A **circular dependency** is when two or more modules depend on each other in such a way that the dependency graph forms a loop. Both of the examples in the following diagram represent circular dependencies.

The following diagram shows two circular dependency scenarios. Modules **A** and **B** depend on each other, forming a circular dependency. In the second example, to the right, module **Z** reads **X**, **X** reads **Y**, and **Y**, in turn, reads **Z**. This is also a circular dependency, now between three modules. If the Java platform encounters circular dependencies like these, it'll throw an error and fail to work:

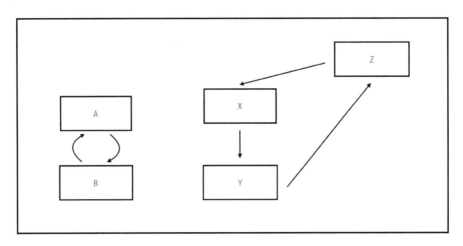

Circular dependencies are disallowed by the Java module system because it invalidates the concept of modules having **directed** dependencies. Think back to the module graph we've been drawing. There is a sense in which dependencies have **direction** and when one module depends on another, there's a directed arrow drawn from the former to the latter. Having circular dependencies, or as they are often called, **cyclic** dependencies implies that the two modules are so closely tied to each other, that the idea of splitting them into two separate modules becomes moot. If one module cannot exist without the other, what's the point in having them as separate modules anyway?

It is important to have the module graph as a **directed acyclic graph**. This is a type of graph, which as the name says, is **directed**, as in you can arrange all the nodes in such a way that there is a top-down direction of all dependencies, and it is **acyclic,** as in there are no loops.

Since we cannot implement circular dependencies, we are left with two options to solve this problem. First option--move the model classes from `packt.addressbook` to `packt.contact` and have `packt.contact` export them. This way, since `packt.addressbook` requires `packt.contact` anyway, it gets to use the model classes too.

The second option is to create a separate module for the model classes and have both
`packt.addressbook` and `packt.contact` require them. This also allows for other
modules to possibly use the model classes. For the sake of simplicity, I'll go with the first
approach and move the model classes into `packt.contact` for now. In a similar real-world
use case, you may want to consider the anticipated usage of such shared classes to decide
whether they warrant a separate module.

With the model classes in the `packt.contact` module, here's how the module looks:

```
packt.contact/
├── module-info.java
└── packt
    └── contact
        ├── internal
        │   └── XmlUtil.java
        ├── model
        │   ├── Address.java
        │   └── Contact.java
        └── util
            └── ContactLoader.java
```

The `module-info.java` needs to be updated to `export` the util and model packages:

```
module packt.contact {
    requires java.xml;
    exports packt.contact.model;
    exports packt.contact.util;
}
```

Dependency leakage

Here's the second problem with the way we've built the `packt.contact` module, and this
one may not be all that obvious. Here's the method signature of the method in
`ContactLoader` that we want consumers of this module to call:

```
public List<Contact> loadContacts(String fileName)
  throws ParserConfigurationException, SAXException, IOException
```

What does a consumer of this module need to do to access this method? First, the consuming module needs to `require packt.contact`. With that, they have access to `ContactLoader` in their module. They can then call the `loadContacts` method in one of their classes. But wait! Since the `loadContacts()` throws three exceptions, the consuming method will need to catch them too!

```
try {
   contacts = contactLoader.loadContacts("input.xml");
} catch (ParserConfigurationException | SAXException |
   IOException e) {
      // Handle error here
}
```

And herein lies the problem. The code from the consuming module is forced to use XML exception classes in order to catch them. `IOException` is from `java.lang`, so all modules get it because of the implicit `java.base` dependency. But the consuming modules don't automatically have access to `ParserConfigurationException` or `SAXException`, since they are classes from the `java.xml` module. The only way `loadContacts()` can be used by other modules is if they also `require java.xml` overtime they use `packt.contact`. Even if they are not using any XML APIs themselves. So much for encapsulating XML functionality!

While this is a workable solution, we don't want to build modules that enforce dependencies like this. Ideally, a module should be self-sufficient, and shouldn't necessitate other peer dependencies just to make it usable. There are a couple of ways to solve this problem. One way is to establish what's called a *transitive* dependency in the `packt.contact` module. Transitive dependency is a way in which the module system allows you to configure modules to declare automatic peer dependencies. For example, you can have a dependency on `packt.contact` also establish a dependency on `java.xml` automatically, so that any module that has a dependency on the former also gets the latter. We'll learn more about transitive dependencies in Chapter 6, *Module Resolution, Accessibility, and Readability*.

However, in this case, that's not ideal either. We want to tuck away anything XML-related into `packt.contact` and not have any XML classes leak into the consuming module. So, in this case, we'll create a custom exception and throw that when anything goes wrong. We'll make sure the exception is in an exported package, so that the consuming module gets the exception automatically.

We'll call the class `ContactLoadException` and place it in the `packt.contact.util` package:

```
package packt.contact.util;
public class ContactLoadException extends Exception {
  ...
  public ContactLoadException() {
    super();
  }
  public ContactLoadException(String message) {
    super(message);
    // TODO Auto-generated constructor stub
  }
}
```

Now `ContactLoader` needs to catch the XML exceptions and throw the custom exception instead:

```
public List<Contact> loadContacts(String fileName) throws
 ContactLoadException {
  ...
  Document doc;
  try {
    doc = xmlUtil.loadXmlFile(fileName);
  } catch (ParserConfigurationException | SAXException |
    IOException e) {
      throw new ContactLoadException("Unable to load
      Contact file");
  }
```

Great! Now we've completely isolated the XML-related functionality into `packt.contact` and none of the modules that uses it needs to deal with the XML APIs.

With this, we are done with the `packt.contact` module. We can now move on to `packt.addressbook` and use this module.

Consuming the new module

First, we establish a dependency in `packt.addressbook`. Here's the `module-info.java` file:

```
module packt.addressbook {
    requires java.logging;
    requires packt.sortutil;
    requires packt.contact;
}
```

Then, in `Main.java`, we create a new instance of `ContactLoader` and call the `loadContacts` method by passing in the path to the XML file. Using the `input.xml` file that is bundled with the source code, here's what it takes to read the file and return `Contact` instances:

```
try {
      contacts = contactLoader.loadContacts(
        "/Users/koushik/code/java9/input.xml");
    } catch (ContactLoadException e) {
        logger.severe(e.getMessage());
        System.exit(0);
    }
```

The `catch` block uses the `logger` instance previously created to log the exception message and exit the application.

Here's the complete `Main` method with these changes:

```
public class Main {

  private static final Logger logger =
    Logger.getLogger(Main.class.getName());

  public static void main(String[] args) {

    logger.info("Address book viewer application: Started");
    List<Contact> contacts = new ArrayList<>();
    ContactLoader contactLoader = new ContactLoader();
    SortUtil sortUtil = new SortUtil();
    try {
      contacts = contactLoader.loadContacts(
        "/Users/koushik/code/java9/input.xml");
    } catch (ContactLoadException e) {
        logger.severe(e.getMessage());
        System.exit(0);
    }
```

```
        sortUtil.sortList(contacts);
        System.out.println(contacts);
        logger.info("Address book viewer application: Completed");
    }
}
```

Compiling and executing the application now will result in an output as follows:

```
$ java --module-path out -m packt.addressbook/packt.addressbook.Main
Mar 28, 2017 3:25:41 PM packt.addressbook.Main main
INFO: Address book viewer application: Started
[Charles Babbage, Tim Berners-Lee, Edsger Dijkstra, Ada Lovelace, Alan
Turing]
Mar 28, 2017 3:25:41 PM packt.addressbook.Main main
INFO: Address book viewer application: Completed
```

Nice work! In the process of adding XML functionality into the address book viewer application, you've handled a couple of issues and design considerations when dealing with modules. Let's move on to the third objective in this chapter--integrating with the Java FX APIs to create a UI for our address book viewer application.

Adding UI with Java FX

Let's now create a UI application that allows us to click and browse contact information. We will be using the Java FX APIs to create and display the UI. As in the last section, I should highlight that the focus here is not for us to learn the JavaFX API itself. In fact, I'll be glossing over most of the Java FX API details in this section because that's beyond the scope of this book, although the full working code is available for you to peruse if you are interested. The intention of this exercise is for us to learn how to use Java APIs and how to handle the different usage scenarios and nuances that come with it.

Here's what we'll do to add UI to the address book application:

1. Create a new module called packt.addressbook.ui which contains code to display the address book in a Java FX powered user interface.
2. Have the packt.addressbook.ui module depend on packt.contacts to get the list of Contact instances. Also have the module depend on packt.sortutil to sort the Contact instances by last name.

Creating the module

Let's start by creating the new module `packt.addressbook.ui`. As before, create the module root folder with the same name in the project folder, and then create the module descriptor `module-info.java`. We already know that we need to depend on `packt.contacts` and `packt.sortutil`, so let's add those two dependencies first:

```
module packt.addressbook.ui {
   requires packt.sortutil;
   requires packt.contact;
}
```

We need to use the JavaFX libraries in this module, so we need to use the `requires` clause in the module descriptor to specify this dependency. How do we know what the libraries are? The answer is the same as earlier--using `java --list-modules` and `java -d <module-name>`. But before we browse for what modules to depend on, we should know what APIs we need! Let's look at the code we'll need to write to build the UI.

We'll create a Main.java class in the package `packt.addressbook.ui`. This class will launch the UI. As with any Java FX app, the class that *launches* the application is required to extend `javafx.application.Application`. We then override the `start` method and add the functionality of building the UI in it. This method is called by the JavaFX framework to launch our application. Remember this method! We will revisit this shortly when we execute the code:

```
public class Main extends Application {

  public static void main(String[] args) {
    launch(args);
  }

  @Override
  public void start(Stage primaryStage) throws Exception {
    // Build JavaFX UI and application functionality
  }
}
```

In the `start` method, the logic to get the `Contact` instances and to sort them is exactly the same as the command-line application in the `packt.addressbook` module:

```
ContactLoader contactLoader = new ContactLoader();
SortUtil sortUtil = new SortUtil();
try {
    contacts = contactLoader.loadContacts(
      "/Users/koushik/code/java9/input.xml");
```

```
    } catch (ContactLoadException e) {
        logger.severe(e.getMessage());
        System.exit(0);
    }

    sortUtil.sortList(contacts);
```

What's different in this case is what we do with the sorted list of Contacts. We don't just print it to the console. Instead, we will build a JavaFX ListView that displays the list. We'll also add a click handler to each element in the list, so that when a name is clicked, we can display the details of that contact to the right of the list. Here's what we'd like the UI to look like:

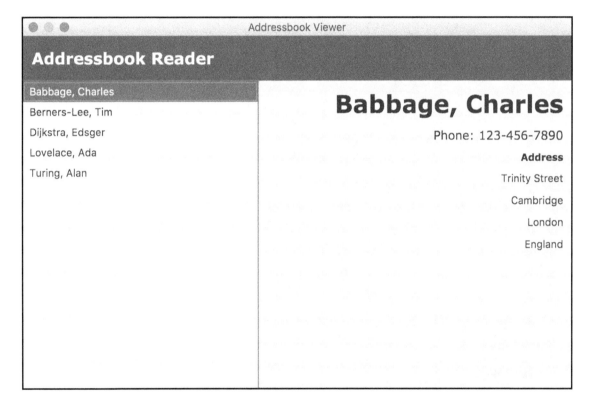

Without going into too much detail of how the JavaFX controls are built and displayed, here's the core functionality that builds the list of Contacts from the list that sortutil has sorted, and handles click events on the list item:

```
// Create a new JavaFX ListView
ListView<String> list = new ListView<String>();
// Collect a String list of Contact names in lastName,
```

```
                    firstName format
                    List<String> listContactNames = contacts.stream()
                          .map(c -> c.getLastName() + ", " + c.getFirstName())
                          .collect(Collectors.toList());
                    // Build an ObservableList from the list of names
                    ObservableList<String> obsContactNames =
                          FXCollections.observableList(listContactNames);
                    // Pass that to ListView to have them displayed in a list
                    list.setItems(obsContactNames);
                    // Add listener to handle click events
                    list.getSelectionModel()
                          .selectedItemProperty()
                          .addListener((obs, oldVal, newVal) -> {
                             // Get the selected index in the ListView
                             int selectedIndex =
                               list.getSelectionModel().getSelectedIndex();
                             name.setText(newVal);
                             // Get the Contact instance which was clicked
                             Contact contact = finalContactList.get(selectedIndex);
                             // Set the values to each of the labels on the right
                             street.setText(contact.getAddress().getStreet());
                             . . .
```

The preceding code wires in the logic we are already familiar with (the `ContactLoader` and `SortUtil`) into the JavaFX code that displays that data in a UI for browsing. We have used quite a lot of JavaFX APIs here, as we normally would when building a JavaFX application like this. Now that we know what the APIs we need to use are, we next need to find the modules that `exports` these APIs and set up dependencies in the `packt.addressbook.ui` module.

Using the `java --list-modules` command, we see there are multiple modules associated with JavaFX. Those are the ones that start with the `javafx.` prefix:

```
$ java --list-modules
. . .
javafx.base@9
javafx.controls@9
javafx.deploy@9
javafx.fxml@9
javafx.graphics@9
javafx.media@9
javafx.swing@9
javafx.web@9
. . .
```

To know the packages we use, all we need to do is look at the list of imports in the
`Main.java` class. We can examine the package level information for each of the JavaFX
modules to get the set of modules that together have all the packages we need.

For example, `javafx.base` exports `javafx.collections` that we use in `Main.java`. So,
that's a module we'll be adding. Here are more modules we are interested in. The left
column shows the package we need, and used in our Java code. The right column is the
Java platform module that exports that package (which we find by running `java -d`
`<module-name>`):

```
Package                       Module
-------------------------------------------
javafx.collections            javafx.base
javafx.scene.control          javafx.controls
javafx.application            javafx.graphics
javafx.scene.layout           javafx.graphics
javafx.geometry               javafx.graphics
```

Based on this, the three modules we'll need to require are `javafx.base`,
`javafx.controls`, and `javafx.graphics`. Let's add these three into the
`packt.addressbook.ui` module definition using the `requires` clause. Here's `module-`
`info.java` when we are done:

```
module packt.addressbook.ui {
    requires java.logging;
    requires javafx.base;
    requires javafx.controls;
    requires javafx.graphics;
    requires packt.sortutil;
    requires packt.contact;
}
```

While we've found the packages exported by the modules and we are technically not wrong
in what we've required, this step could be done in a much better way. We actually needed
to require just one JavaFX module here! This is thanks to a certain qualifier called
`transitive`. We will be covering more about what that is and how it affects our
dependencies in Chapter 6, *Module Resolution, Accessibility, and Readability*. But, since we
haven't covered it yet, let's go with adding all three JavaFX modules for now.

If you feel like the process of finding these dependencies by running the `--list-modules` command is tedious, well, you are not alone! This is something that I hope will quickly be unnecessary once IDEs get support for Java 9. Ideally, an IDE should be able to help us identify the modules based on the packages we import into our Java applications, and preferably add the modules to the module descriptor automatically. This feature might already be available in most of the standard IDEs by the time you are reading this!

OK, so with this, we have all the dependencies established. Let's give this a go! Compile all modules using the `javac` command:

```
$ javac --module-source-path src -d out $(find . -name '*.java')
```

The code should compile without any errors. Let's try to execute it. Since we are running the Main.java file in the new module `packt.addressbook.ui`, make sure you specify that in the command this time. Notice that we get an error when we run the code:

```
$ java --module-path out -m packt.addressbook.ui/packt.addressbook.ui.Main

Exception in Application constructor
Exception in thread "main" java.lang.reflect.InvocationTargetException
...
Caused by: java.lang.IllegalAccessException: class
com.sun.javafx.application.LauncherImpl (in module javafx.graphics) cannot
access class packt.addressbook.ui.Main (in module packt.addressbook.ui)
because module packt.addressbook.ui does not export packt.addressbook.ui to
module javafx.graphics
...
```

The error indicates that the module `javafx.graphics` is trying to access our Main class and is unable to access it because our module `packt.addressbook.ui` doesn't export it! You might be wondering what business the module `javafx.graphics` has with a class we wrote! Why would it need to access our class?

Turns out the answer is because of the way JavaFX works. Remember that I mentioned about the `start()` method in `Main.java` and how the JavaFX framework calls that method to launch the application. The framework uses reflection to identify classes that extend the `Application` class. The framework then uses that information to launch the JavaFX application by calling the `start()` method.

And there is our problem. In the module descriptor of `packt.addressbook.ui`, we don't export the package that `Main` is in, that is `packt.addressbook.ui`. So, `Main` is not accessible to any code outside the module, and so JavaFX cannot launch the application! The encapsulation that applied to static access of types outside the module is in effect even for runtime reflective access!

One way to solve this problem is by making `Main` public. We just need to export the package that the type is in. That's enough for JavaFX to access it. That also actually enables *any* module to access it! This may or may not be what you want. But for now, let's export the package and make `Main.java` available externally. We'll revisit this too in `Chapter 6`, *Module Resolution, Accessibility, and Readability,* and find a better way to do this.

Here's the final `module-info.java`:

```
module packt.addressbook.ui {
  exports packt.addressbook.ui;
  requires java.logging;
  requires javafx.base;
  requires javafx.controls;
  requires javafx.graphics;
  requires packt.sortutil;
  requires packt.contact;
}
```

Compile and run the application again, and everything should work this time around. A GUI window should load with the list of contacts sorted by last name. Clicking on a name should display the details on the right-hand side. You can close the application by clicking the close button on the title bar.

Summary

We've made several enhancements to the address book application to make use of some platform APIs and learnt some lessons on how to find and use platform modules, as well as how to handle some tricky scenarios that showed up along the way. Here's what we have done so far:

- We used the `java.logging` module to add logging functionality to the `packt.addressbook` module.
- We used the `java.xml` module and created a new custom module that reads and parses an XML file to return a list of model objects.

- We encountered two problems--shared code and dependency leakage and we implemented a strategy to get around those problems.
- We used the JavaFX modules to build a UI for the address book. We created a new module that leveraged our existing contact and sort modules to build this UI. We learnt about the impact of modularity on reflection. We got around the problem by just exporting the class that needed access by the framework, although we'll be learning a better way to do this in the next chapter.

One additional point that I want to highlight is how, in this chapter, we were able to leverage the modules that we'd already built to create a new custom GUI module. Notice that we didn't have to mess around with existing code and pile up logic and functionality on them with if clauses. We were easily able to create a new module for GUI, and thanks to the other core functionality being separate modules, we were just able to use them as building blocks to create a brand new module with all the functionality we needed. The `packt.contact` and `packt.sortutil` aren't aware of where they are being used, so they technically don't care!

In the next chapter, we'll look at a few more tricks that the Java module system has up its sleeve! We'll also deep-dive into concepts related to readability and gain an understanding of more powerful ways to make different modules accessible to one another.

6
Module Resolution, Readability, and Accessibility

In the previous chapter, we significantly enhanced the address book viewer application by leveraging multiple platform APIs to add extra functionality. We implemented logging, XML parsing, and a UI module using JavaFX. The address book viewer application has come a long way from its simple *Hello world* origins. And in the process, you have acquired a good amount of knowledge about the Java module system and you should have the required know-how and tools to build any Java application of similar complexity.

Here's what you will be learning in this chapter:

- You'll be introduced to two important concepts and related terminologies--readability and accessibility
- You'll learn some of the nuances about what makes modules readable and packages accessible
- You'll learn some powerful new ways to tweak the default methods of specifying dependencies--implicit dependencies and qualified exports
- You'll then apply these two new ways in the address book viewer application to tweak and optimize the dependencies using aggregator modules and qualified exports

In this chapter, we'll do a significant deep-dive on some of the concepts we've learned only at a high level along the way. While you can use everything we've covered so far to build various different applications, there are certain nuances to several of the topics covered that will be helpful to learn and understand. Knowing about these concepts will help you use the module system in powerful new ways. In addition, some of the terminologies we'll learn in this chapter will help you understand and describe concepts and processes that run under the hood every time you use the module system.

Readability

Readability is an important concept in modularity and it describes how modules work with each other. We've been using module dependencies to have one module require another module and use its APIs. Whenever a module depends on another module, the first module is said to read the second module. Also, the second module is said to be readable by the first. When a module reads another module, it has access to the types exported by the second module. In other words, the readability relationship between two modules is the arrow in the module graph that we've seen so far.

For example, in the address book viewer application, the module `packt.addressbook` *reads* `packt.sortutil`, `packt.contact`, and `java.logging`. That's because it `requires` those modules in the module descriptor.

Consider an example. The following diagram shows the relationships between three modules **A**, **B**, and **C**:

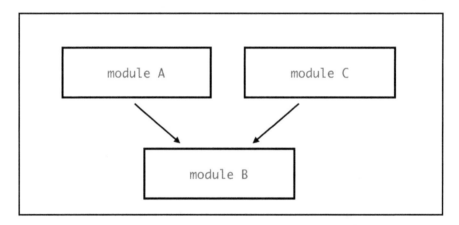

Module A requires **module B**. So, **module A** *reads* **module B**. **Module B** is *readable* by **module A**. **Module C** also *reads* **module B**. However, **module C** does not read **module A** and vice versa.

As you can tell, the *reads* relationship is not symmetric. If **module A** *reads* **module B**, it does not mean that **module B** reads **module A**. In fact, in the Java module system, we can guarantee that the *reads* relationship between modules is asymmetric. Why? Because if two modules *read* each other, what we'll end up with is a cyclic dependency, which is not allowed (see `Chapter 5`, *Using Platform APIs*). So to summarize, firstly, the *readability* relationship is established through the usage of the `requires` clause. Secondly, if a module *reads* another module, we can guarantee that the second module does not *read* the first module.

There are, however, two exceptions to this, and you can probably guess what they are, since we've already covered them. First, every module *reads* the `java.base` module. And this dependency is *automatic* and there's no explicit usage of the `requires` qualifier. Secondly, every module *reads* itself by definition, because a module automatically has access to all the public types in the module by default.

The readability relationship is fundamental to achieving one of the two primary goals of the Java module system--reliable configuration. We want to be able to reliably guarantee that the dependencies of all the modules in an application are satisfied. An additional advantage that we'll see more over time is the performance optimization of these formal modular relationships. No longer does the runtime need to scan the entire class path to find a given type. There are ways in which the runtime can optimally find the right module and thus the location to find types. This is a huge win!

Accessibility

Accessibility is the other side of the Java modularity coin. If the *readability* relationship specifies what modules can read a given module, *accessibility* indicates what they actually do get when they read it. Not everything in a module is accessible to the other modules that read it. Only the public types in packages that are marked with an `exports` declaration are.

Thus, for a type in module B to be *accessible* in module A, the following needs to happen:

- Module A needs to *read* module B
- Module B needs to export the package that contains the type
- The type itself should be `public`

Let's look at an example and examine the readability and accessibility relationships. Consider two modules, `app` and `lib`. Module `app` has a `requires` qualifier for module `lib`. Module `lib` exports its package `lib.external`:

```
module app {
  requires lib;
}
module lib {
  exports lib.external;
}
```

Let's say the `lib` module has the following structure:

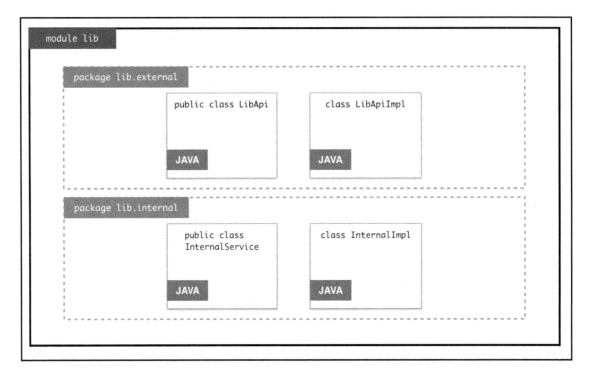

It has two packages--`lib.external` and `lib.internal`. Both packages contain one public interface and one package-private implementation.

 Note: The implementation classes in this example don't have the `public` keyword in the class declaration, which makes them visible only in the same package. They have the *default* package-private access level.

Let's try to answer the following questions:

1. Does module `app` read module `lib`?

   This one should be simple. The answer is yes, because of the `requires` qualifier.

2. Does module `lib` read module `app`?

   The answer is no. Hopefully equally simple!

3. Is the type `LibApi` in module `lib` *accessible* to module `app`?

   Let's verify the two requirements for accessibility. Is the type `public`? Yes. Is the type in a package that's exported by the module? Yes. So, the answer is `LibApi` *is* accessible to module `app`.

4. Is the type `InternalService` in module `lib` *accessible* to module `app`?

   No. Because even though the type is `public`, it belongs to a package that is not exported in the module definition of the `lib` module. The type `InternalImpl` is also not accessible to the `app` module.

5. Is the type `LibApiImpl` in module `lib` *accessible* to module `app`?

   The answer is no, because it fails the requirement--is the type public? Since `LibApiImpl` is package-private, it is not accessible outside the module, since it's not `public`. This is true even though the type belongs to an exported package. This scenario is, however, more interesting with a couple of important lessons we can learn from it. Let's look at them in detail.

Interface and implementation accessibility

What does it mean for an interface to be accessible to a module in Java 9? Quite obviously, it means that you can use the interface type in the code in that module. However, an interface is quite meaningless without an implementation. Does this mean that when you export a public interface (as in `LibApi`), but not the implementation (`LibApiImpl`), the implementation is essentially useless outside the module? Not quite!

Consider we add a static method in the `LibApi` interface to create an instance of `LibApiImpl`. We'll also add a handy `testMethod()` to the interface for us to call from another module to verify if it works. Notice that while the `createInstance` method is creating a new instance of `LibApiImpl`, its return type is the interface, and not the implementation. This is important, as we'll see in a bit:

```
package packt.lib.external;
public interface LibApi {
  static LibApi createInstance() {
    return new LibApiImpl();
  }
  public void testMethod();
}
```

Let's build a simple implementation class that prints a message to the console. Note the missing `public` keyword in front of the class declaration. This means that this class is package-private, not `public`. So, even though it's in the package that's exported by the module, it's not *accessible* outside the module:

```
package packt.lib.external;
class LibApiImpl implements LibApi {
  public void testMethod() {
    System.out.println("Test method executed");
  }
}
```

What happens if we access these types outside the `lib` module? Let's find out! Let's create a class `App.java` in the module app. Let's first try creating an instance of `LibApiImpl`:

```
package packt.app;
import packt.lib.external.LibApiImpl;
public class App {
  public static void main(String[] args) {
    LibApiImpl api = new LibApiImpl();
    api.testMethod();
  }
}
```

What happens if we compile this?

```
$ javac --module-source-path src -d out $(find . -name '*.java')
./src/app/packt/lib/external/App.java:3: error: LibApiImpl is not public in
packt.lib.external; cannot be accessed from outside package
import packt.lib.external.LibApiImpl;
                         ^
...
```

Just as we thought. The package-private class isn't accessible, even though it's in the exported package. How about we use the interface to get its instance?

```
package packt.app;
import packt.lib.external.LibApi;
public class App {
  public static void main(String[] args) {
    LibApi api = LibApi.createInstance();
    api.testMethod();
  }
}
```

We are now using the `createInstance()` method of the interface `LibApi` to create an instance of `LibApi`. It then calls `testMethod` on that instance. We know that `LibApi` is creating a new instance of `LibApiImpl`, and we know that that class is not accessible. Will this work now?

```
$ javac --module-source-path src -d out $(find . -name '*.java')

$ java --module-path out -m app/packt.app.App
  Test method executed
```

It does! Since we are not referring to the type `LibApiImpl` directly in the code, the compiler and runtime are perfectly happy to allow access to the instance through the interface. This is a valuable pattern in modules, as this lets you provide APIs that are public while still managing to change and rewrite the implementation underneath. This applies not just for non-public implementation classes in an exported package (as in this case); it also applies to public types sitting in packages that are *not* exported, thereby being equally inaccessible. So, let's revisit the question. Is the `LibApiImpl` accessible outside the module now? The answer is still no. However, the important lesson here is that the accessibility rules apply to usage of types and do not apply to dynamic instances of types at runtime. This is by design and is a great pattern to use to achieve implementation-level encapsulation.

Split packages

Here's a question that some of you might be asking already. The `LibApiImpl` class is package-private. So, there's no way it is accessible to a type outside the `packt.lib.external` package it is in. So, our attempt to access the type in `packt.app.App`, a completely different package, was bound to fail anyway! In fact, it would have failed even in Java 8 or earlier! How about if we try to access it from the same package in another module? If we were to create the same package `packt.lib.external` in the `app` module and create a new class there, would *that* class be able to access `LibApiImpl`? In this scenario, the consuming class is in the same package. Let's give it a try! You don't have to go too far. Just creating the same package from one module into another module doesn't work. Let's say you recreate the package in the `app` module and add any arbitrary Java type in it:

```
package packt.lib.external;
public class App {
  public static void main(String[] args) {
    System.out.println("Test");
  }
}
```

We are not even using `LibApiImpl` here! We've just used the same package in another module. The compilation step will fail with the error:

```
$ javac --module-source-path src -d out $(find . -name '*.java')
./src/app/packt/lib/external/App.java:1: error: package exists in another
module: lib
package packt.lib.external;
^
1 error
```

Yes! A package cannot exist in two modules at the same time. Well, not in two observable modules, at least! In other words, given a package in an application, it should be a part of one and only one module on the module path!

This is a significant deviation from how we've traditionally thought of libraries in Java. Having come this far, I don't have to highlight that modules are different from traditional JAR libraries. But here is yet another aspect that breaks the traditional *library* paradigm. Traditionally, multiple jars in the class path can contain the same package. We've seen this figure already in `Chapter 1`, *Introducing Java 9 Modularity*:

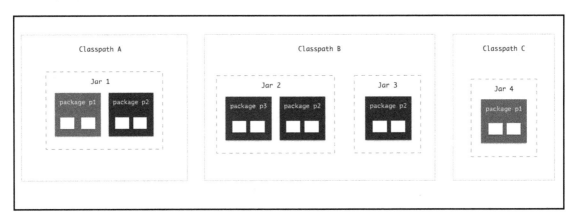

With modules not allowing *sharing* of packages, or *split packages* as they're often called, we now end up with a new hierarchy. Modules at the top, packages under them, and then types under packages, as shown in the following diagram with a couple of example modules:

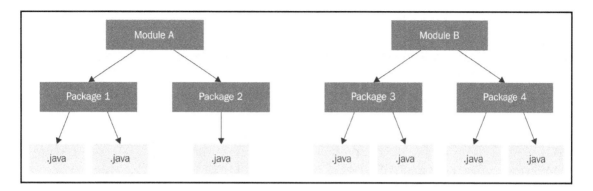

This now results in another change to the way we think about packages. Packages are not grouping of types in the entire application anymore. Packages are grouping of types only inside a single module. When you create a package, you are *forced* to choose which module the types should all be in. One advantage of this approach, if we design our packages well, is clearer organization. There are also performance optimizations. The Java class loader internally maps each package to a single module, so when it's looking up types to load, it immediately knows where (and in which module) to find a given type.

This restriction of avoiding split packages will come back to be a bitter pain in the neck when migrating legacy Java codebases to Java 9 modules which we'll cover in Chapter 11, *Migrating Your Code to Java 9*. Also note that there are ways to bypass this restriction by using multiple class loaders, but that's beyond the scope of what we are covering here.

Tweaking modularity

We've looked at two language constructs you can use in the module descriptor--*requiring* modules and *exporting* packages. Together, they give you sufficient control over the interface of your modules and they address the two main goals of modularity--reliable configuration and strong encapsulation. However, in many real-world situations, you might sometimes find that these two alone are not enough to achieve certain things you want to do. For example, you may want to export a package from a module, only for it to be consumed by a certain other module, and not for public consumption. To handle many such special cases, the module system has some powerful features that we'll take a look at in this part of the chapter.

Implied readability

We looked at the problem of dependency leakage in Chapter 5, *Using Platform APIs*. The module that you depend on might have APIs that might also require you to use another module. Here's an example:

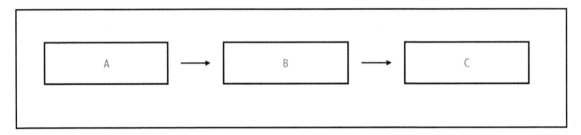

```
module A {
    requires B;
}

module B {
    requires C;
}
```

The module A requires module B, which in turn requires C. We know that with this, A does not read C, since module dependencies are not *transitive* in nature. But what if it needs to? For instance, if B has an API whose return type is in module C.

A good example can be found in the platform module itself. Let's say you write your custom module that reads java.sql. And you'd like to use the Driver interface from the module. The Driver interface has a method called getParentLogger() that returns the type Logger. Here's what the method in the Driver interface looks like:

```
Logger getParentLogger() throws SQLFeatureNotSupportedException
```

Here's your code in your custom module that calls the API from java.sql:

```
Logger myLogger = driver.getParentLogger();
```

To get this to work, you just need to add requires java.sql in your module definition, and you should be good to go, right? Not so fast! Think about the return type Logger. That type is actually coming from java.logging, like we've already seen. The java.sql module depends on java.logging for logging capabilities, so it isn't a problem for *that* module. But how about yours?

Since `yourmodule` does not directly require `java.logging`, in order to use the `java.sql` API, you'd have to `require` the `java.logging` module too!

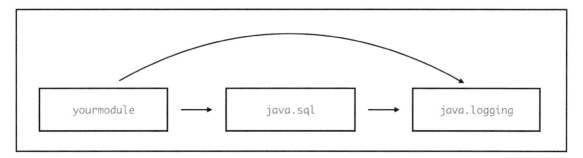

As you can tell, this is not very convenient. If the usage of a certain module requires the use of other modules too, it just adds to the complexity of the API. Here, you'd need to have some documentation for the developers that says, *If you happen to use java.sql, don't forget to also require java.logging.*

Is there a better way? Although dependencies aren't transitive by default, what we'd like is the ability to selectively make only certain dependencies transitively available, for situations like this. Thankfully, this is possible in Java 9 by using the `transitive` keyword. When you declare `requires` on a module, you can also have that module be available and readable to any modules that depend on your module. The way to use this feature is like this--`requires transitive <module-name>;`

In the following example, module A requires B. But module B *requires transitive C*:

```
module A {
   requires B;
}

module B {
   requires transitive C;
}
```

Now, module C is readable by not only module B, but by all other modules that read module B. So here, A gets to read C too!

Notice that the `transitive` keyword is adding an additional semantic to the `requires` keyword. The line `requires transitive C` now makes C readable by all modules that read B, while at the same time retaining the meaning of `requires` that we've known all along--that B needs to read C too!

How does this affect the *readability* relationship we have just discussed? We know that A *reads* B because of the explicit `requires` relationship? But does A *read* C as well? The answer is yes, and this kind of readability relationship is referred to as *implied readability*. The relationship is not *explicit*, since there's no direct dependency declared by A on C. The readability is implied due to its transitive nature.

This feature is leveraged in the `java.sql` module to solve the problem with the `Logger` return type. If you run `java -d` on `java.sql`, you'll see this:

```
$ java -d java.sql
  module java.sql@9
  exports java.sql
  exports javax.sql
  exports javax.transaction.xa
  requires transitive java.logging
  requires transitive java.xml
  requires mandated java.base
  uses java.sql.Driver
```

Notice that the two modules `java.xml` and `java.logging` that `java.sql` requires are both marked `transitive`. Like we've just seen, this means that any module that requires `java.sql` *will* get access to the APIs in `java.xml` and `java.logging` automatically! This is a decision taken by the platform team because using many of the APIs in `java.sql` requires the use of the other two modules as well. So rather than having all the developers remember to `require` those too, the platform has made it *automatic*. This is why any module that depends on `java.sql` and calls the `Driver.getParentLogger()` will have no problems using the `Logger` type, since that module will have an implied readability on `java.logging`:

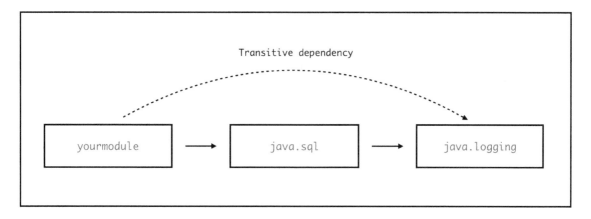

Note that you need to be cautious about adding a lot of transitive dependencies in your modules. I mentioned dependency leakage in Chapter 5, *Using Platform APIs,* and how it's better to have all of your module's dependencies restricted in usage in your module. Any usage of APIs that the module exposes should only need to deal with types that are all exposed and available in the same module as well. The concept of transitive dependencies in a way seems to run counter to that philosophy. Thanks to transitive, any dependency leakages can be handled easily by making the modules containing the leaked types as requires transitive. But that's a slippery slope. Imagine having to depend on a module and inadvertently getting a dozen other module dependencies because they are all marked requires transitive in the module you need! Such module designs clearly violate the principles of modularity, and I highly recommend avoiding them unless absolutely required.

There is, however, a really interesting and handy usage of transitive dependencies that will help library developers. That is *aggregator modules.*

Aggregator modules

An aggregator module is a module that does not provide any functionality on its own, but instead, its sole purpose is to gather and bundle together a bunch of other modules. As the name implies, these modules *aggregate* several other modules.

Let's assume you have a group of your favorite library modules that you often use together in your applications. Let's say this is a list of some core libraries, and whenever you write a module, it's very likely that you'll use pretty much every library in that list. Now, using every module in that list in any of your own modules involves specifying each of those modules using the `requires` clause. Depending on how big that list is, it can be tedious to specify the same set of core dependencies in every one of your module descriptors. Even if you were to do that once, it's hard to change the list of core libraries, perhaps to add a new one. Your only option would be to go through all your module descriptors again and make that change. Wouldn't it be nice if you could create a new module that bundles all your core libraries? That way you have the list in one place and you don't have to specify the complete list anywhere else. Any module that needs all those libraries can now express a dependency to this new *module bundle*! You can do just that by creating an essentially *empty* module with all the dependencies transitive.

Consider this example:

```
module librarybundle {
    requires transitive core.foo;
    requires transitive core.foo;
    requires transitive core.baz;
}
```

Here's a module called `librarybundle` that does not really export *anything*, since there are no `exports` packages specified in the module descriptor. This module doesn't really need to contain a single Java class! What it does do, however, is `requires transitive` three other libraries. So, any module that depends on the `librarybundle` module automatically reads those three libraries too.

Java platform aggregator modules

The Java platform has a couple of aggregator modules to represent the *complete* JRE, at least as we knew it in Java 8 and earlier. The `java.se` module essentially re-exports the entire Java SE platform. The `java.se.ee` module contains the subset of the platform that overlaps with Java EE and contains APIs such as web services, transactions, and the legacy CORBA APIs.

Running `java -d` on the `java.se` module shows us how it's implemented:

```
$ java -d java.se
  java.se@9
  requires java.scripting transitive
  requires java.xml transitive
  requires java.management.rmi transitive
```

```
requires java.logging transitive
requires java.sql transitive
requires java.base mandated
...
```

Again, I hope you resist the temptation to use these aggregator modules in any new modules you create in your Java 9 code. You could practically throw in `requires java.se` in all your module definitions and not have to worry about doing any other `requires` ever again! But that again defeats the purpose of modularity and you are back to using the Java platform the way we did in Java 8 and earlier--by depending on the entirety of the platform APIs irrespective of what part of them you really need. These aggregator modules are mainly to be used for legacy code migration purposes, and that too as a temporary measure, in an attempt to get to more fine-grained dependencies eventually.

Although the `java.se.ee` module is deprecated and is not encouraged for use, there's an interesting observation to be made by examining it. While `java.se.ee` is a super set that includes all modules in `java.se` and then some more, its module definition doesn't re-declare a entire list of all the modules in the platform. What it does is simply require transitive the `java.se` module:

```
$ java -d java.se.ee
  java.se.ee@9
  requires java.corba transitive
  requires java.base mandated
  ...
  requires java.se transitive
```

You can use this approach in your own modules to create aggregator modules of other aggregator modules! Pretty powerful stuff!

Qualified exports

In the previous section, we looked at transitive dependencies that let us tweak the *readability* relationship between modules to handle some special use cases. In this section, you'll be introduced to a way you can tweak the *accessibility* relationships in some special cases. This can be done using a feature called **qualified exports**. Let's learn what they are.

You've already learned that the `exports` keyword lets you specify which packages in a module are allowed to be used outside the module. The exported packages form the *public contract* of the module, and any module that reads such a module automatically gets *accessibility* to those exported packages.

But there is a catch here! Ideally, you'd like to design your modules and APIs as standalone entities and you always have a clear idea about what the modules should export. But you might encounter real-world scenarios where that isn't the case. Sometimes you'll have to design modules to make them work well with others, and that incurs an interesting cost.

Consider that you have built a library module called **B** that is being used by a consumer module **A**:

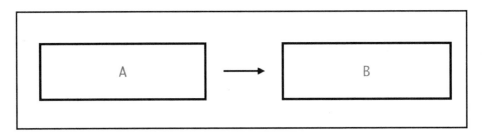

The developer of module A can obviously call the exported APIs of B now. But then, it so happens that they also need this one other API in module B that isn't exported yet. You didn't initially want to export that private package from module B because it's not something that's commonly needed outside B, but it turns out there's just one other module, module A, that really needs it! So, to make the developer of module A happy, you add that private package to the `exports` list from module B:

```
module B {
   exports moduleb.public;
   exports moduleb.privateA; // required only for module A
}
```

After a while, a new module, module C, depends on module B. It too has an interesting use case where it needs another private API from module B. It's very likely that it's only C that'll ever need that API outside of B, but in order to make module C work, you have no option but to add that package to the exported packages of module B:

```
module B {
   exports moduleb.public;
   exports moduleb.privateA; // required only for module A
   exports moduleb.privateC; // required only for module C
}
```

I hope you notice the problem already. Now two originally private packages in module B are now public for use by every module that reads B, although the intent for exporting those packages was to satisfy two very small and specific use cases. If this goes on, the exported APIs in your module end up being the greatest common set of APIs that are sure to keep every consumer module happy. In the process, you've lost the advantages of encapsulation. Now that an internal package is exported, albeit with the intention to satisfy one module, it is available for *any* module to use. Wouldn't it be great if when exporting packages to a module, you could selectively specify *which modules* the packages need to be exported to? If so, then only those selected modules could access those specially exported packages. All other modules would only get the *publicly exported* packages.

This is possible using qualified exports. The `exports` clause in the module definition optionally lets you specify which module you need to export the package to. If you do that, the `export` is not public anymore. Only the module you specify has access to it. The syntax is:

```
exports <package-name> to <module1>, <module2>,... ;
```

Applying this concept to our example module B, we can still have better encapsulation of our private packages by selectively giving modules A and C access to what they alone need:

```
module B {
  exports moduleb.public;          // Public access to every module
                                    //    that reads me
   exports moduleb.privateA to A; // Exported only to module A
   exports moduleb.privateC to C; // Exported only to module C
}
```

With this change, package `moduleb.privateA` is *accessible* to A, but not to B or any other module that reads B. Similarly, `moduleb.privateC` is *accessible* only by C. Now, while the private APIs are still not fully encapsulated, you at least know for sure what modules they are accessed by, and so any changes are easier to manage.

An example usage of this feature in the Java platform is in the `java.base` module. This module contains a lot of core internal packages that have been deemed *internal* and that we Java developers are ideally not supposed to use. Unfortunately, other platform modules still need to use them, and encapsulating these internal packages prevents access to those platform modules too! Thus, you'll see a lot of these qualified exports where the internal APIs are exported just to the platform modules that need them. You can run the `java -d` command on `java.base` to see many instances of these:

```
$ java -d java.base
  module java.base@9
  . . .
```

```
exports jdk.internal.ref to java.desktop, javafx.media
exports jdk.internal.math to java.desktop
exports sun.net.ext to jdk.net
exports jdk.internal.loader to java.desktop, java.logging,
  java.instrument, jdk.jlink
```

Remember that using qualified exports is generally not recommended. The principles of modularity recommend that a module should not be aware of who the consumers are. Qualified exports, by definition, add a certain level of coupling between two modules. The coupling is not forced--if you have a qualified export to a certain module, and that module isn't even in the module path to take advantage of it, there are no errors. But the coupling is there nevertheless, and so it's not a good idea to use qualified exports unless it's absolutely required.

Applying the concepts to address book viewer

We've learned about a couple of powerful ways in which we can tweak the *default* behavior of module dependencies in Java 9. Let's get hands-on now and apply some of these to our address book viewer application.

Creating a custom aggregator module

Notice that we have two modules in the address book viewer application that provides a view of the address book. The `packt.addressbook` module shows a simple list of contacts in command line. The `packt.addressbook.ui` module shows the address book contacts and details in UI form. Both these modules happen to use the two utility modules to get the list of contacts (`packt.contact`) and to sort them (`sort.util`). Here, we have just two modules, so it's not that big of a deal to add the requires descriptor for both of these modules in two places. But imagine if there were many more libraries and many more consumers! You'd be duplicating the list multiple times.

To avoid that, let's create an aggregator module that bundles and re-exports the `packt.contact` and `sort.util` modules. We can then have the `packt.addressbook` and `packt.addressbook.ui` modules depend on the aggregator module directly.

Let's call the aggregator module `packt.addressbook.lib`. This module acts as the *library* for all `addressbook` modules. Create a directory with the name of the module in the `src` folder and add the following code in its module descriptor:

```
module packt.addressbook.lib {
  requires transitive packt.contact;
  requires transitive packt.sortutil;
}
```

This is actually the only file that this module would need. It doesn't provide any APIs of its own. It just has the module descriptor that `requires transitive` all the modules that it wants to re-export. Here, we choose for it to re-export the two custom utility modules we've created. We have the option here to add `requires transitive` on some of the platform modules as well, like `java.logging`. But we'll just stick with our custom modules for now.

The next step is to go to the consumer modules and change the direct dependencies to the aggregator module instead.

Here's the module descriptors for the two address book modules:

```
module packt.addressbook {
  requires java.logging;
  requires packt.addressbook.lib;
}
module packt.addressbook.ui {
  exports packt.addressbook.ui;
  requires java.logging;
  requires javafx.base;
  requires javafx.controls;
  requires javafx.graphics;
  requires packt.addressbook.lib;
}
```

Compile and execute the two modules, and you should still see the output as before. Here's the updated dependency graph of our address book application now, excluding the platform modules. Notice that the transitive dependencies are illustrated with a dotted arrow to convey that while the dependency is not direct, it's still there!

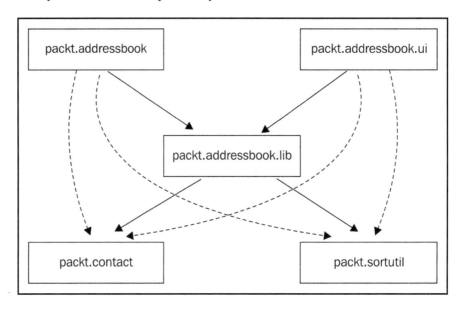

Optimizing module imports

In the previous chapter, we created the GUI address viewer module that required the Java FX modules necessary for building the UI. Here's what the module descriptor looked like:

```
module packt.addressbook.ui {
    exports packt.addressbook.ui;
    requires java.logging;
    requires javafx.base;
    requires javafx.controls;
    requires javafx.graphics;
    requires packt.addressbook.lib;
}
```

We'll now see that not all the modules imported are actually required, and we can optimize this list a bit, thanks to our new knowledge of transitive dependencies. Running `java -d` on `javafx.controls` gives us:

```
$ java -d javafx.controls
  module javafx.controls@9
  ...
  requires transitive javafx.base
  requires transitive javafx.graphics
```

Turns out the `javafx.base` and `javafx.graphics` modules are transitive dependencies of `javafx.controls` already. So, any module that *reads* `javafx.controls` also *reads* `javafx.base` and `javafx.graphics`! So, we can remove those two modules and just declare our dependency on `javafx.controls`, since that module alone pulls in all the dependencies we need. Here's the updated module descriptor for `packt.addressbook.ui`:

```
module packt.addressbook.ui {
  exports packt.addressbook.ui;
  requires java.logging;
  requires javafx.controls;
  requires packt.addressbook.lib;
}
```

You should be able to recompile and execute the UI module to make sure things still work just the same.

Optimizing module exports

At the end of the previous chapter, we begrudgingly added the `exports` qualifier for the package containing the main JavaFX class in the module descriptor for the `packt.addressbook.ui` module. We did this because the way the JavaFX framework works, it needs to be able to access the class that extends `javafx.application.Application` that launches the UI application. We said how that isn't an ideal solution because not only are we exporting the package to the JavaFX framework, we are essentially exporting it to the whole world, that is, any module that reads `packt.addressbook.ui`.

With our new knowledge of qualified exports, we have just the solution for this problem! Instead of exporting `packt.addressbook.ui` globally, we can use a qualified export in order to export it just to the JavaFX module. Here, the module that needs access to the class is the module `java.graphics`. We've removed the explicit dependency, although the dependency is still implicitly there! With the qualified export to `java.graphics`, here's what the module descriptor looks like:

```
module packt.addressbook.ui {
    exports packt.addressbook.ui to javafx.graphics;
    requires java.logging;
    requires javafx.controls;
    requires packt.addressbook.lib;
}
```

Again, you should be able to compile and run the code to make sure everything works well. With this change, you've retained encapsulation of the `Main` class while still making it available to the right JavaFX framework module that needs access to it.

There is a slightly better way to achieve this by using the `opens` keyword if the problem is with reflective access only. We can use the concept of open modules. We'll be covering open modules in detail in `Chapter 9`, *Module Design Patterns and Strategies*.

Summary

In this chapter, you've learned some important concepts and terminologies related to modularity, including *readability* and *accessibility*. You've also learned how the default behavior of the module system can be tweaked for certain specialized needs--using implied dependencies and qualified exports. And more importantly, you've understood some scenarios where such needs might be required, like aggregator modules and certain encapsulation challenges, and how these tweaks might be useful in such cases. We then looked at a few places in the address book viewer application where these tweaks helped us optimize and simplify dependencies while improving encapsulation.

In the next chapter, you'll learn about a whole new way of handling depended abstractions using a powerful concept in Java modularity--using services.

7
Introducing Services

In this chapter, we'll learn about yet another exciting new feature in Java modularity called **services**. Services offer an additional layer of indirection between modules when compared to direct dependencies, and we will see that they add extra flexibility to how we can get modules to work with each other. In this chapter, you will:

- Understand one of the limitations of module dependencies the way we have been doing things so far
- Understand what services are and how they solve this problem
- Learn how to create and expose services
- Learn how to consume services using the `ServiceLoader` API

Before we learn what services are, let's examine and understand the actual problem that they were created to solve. It's the problem of tight coupling between modules with direct dependencies, at least the way we've been hooking them up so far.

The problem of coupling

The phrase **tight coupling** in programming is referred to situations where two entities are so highly dependent on each other that in order to change either of their behavior or relationship, it is required to make actual code changes to one (or often both) of those entities. The term **loose coupling**, on the other hand, refers to the opposite scenario--entities that are not highly dependent. In such cases, entities ideally don't even know about each other's existence, but can still be made to interact with each other.

With that in mind, what would you say the coupling of two modules in the Java module system could be called? When one module depends on another, are the two modules tightly coupled or loosely coupled? The answer is obviously that they are tightly coupled. Think of the following facts that apply to module relationships:

- Modules need to explicitly state which other modules they depend on. In that sense, each module is *aware of* the existence of other modules it needs.
- Modules are also coupled to and *aware of* the APIs exposed by the dependent modules. If module A reads module B and calls an API, it is by using the actual Java type that is available in and exported from module B. Thus, module A knows the internals of module B, at least as much as the types exported by module B and used by module A.

Because of these two factors, it is obvious that this kind of tight coupling results in a very *strict* and *rigid* behavior of the modules at runtime. Consider the address book viewer application. The set of modules compiled is the exact set of modules that is involved in execution at runtime. Once modules are compiled, there's no way you can remove one of those modules, replace it with something else, and execute them. The modules involved have to be *exactly* the same. Although we get an impression of Java 9 modules being building blocks that can be assembled into multiple combinations, that advantage only applies to development time. What we've seen so far is that once the modules are coded and the dependencies established, the result is pretty much a cohesive, unalterable monolith.

Now you might wonder, *Well, isn't that what we want?* The benefits of *reliable configuration* require a strict check to make sure the exact modules we intend to have are present, don't they? Well, yes, but we could still have runtime flexibility without giving up reliable configuration. An analogous example for that is in the Java language itself. Even though Java is strictly typed, you can achieve powerful runtime flexibility and loose coupling between types by using the concepts of polymorphism. The idea is that classes don't directly depend on each other. Instead, they depend on abstract classes or interfaces. At runtime, instances of those interfaces can be dynamically initialized and used anywhere the interface is used. Could we have something similar to this with modules? If so, how would it work?

Let me give you an example. We have a sorting utility module called `packt.sortutil` that has an API to sort lists. We have configured the module to export an interface and encapsulate an implementation, but in reality, that distinction is currently useless. It has only one implementation, and all that the module can do now is bubble sort. What if we wanted to have multiple sorting modules and we let the consuming module choose which sorting algorithm to use?

Current:

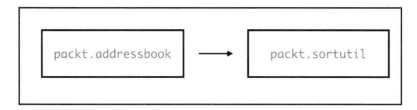

What we'd like:

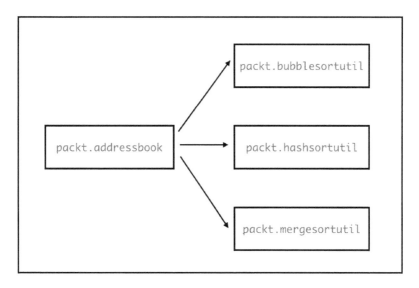

We'd like to be able to use multiple modules providing different implementations of sorting in our application. However, thanks to tight coupling, in order for a module to use another module, it has to *require* it. This means that the consumer `packt.addressbook` module has to declare `requires` on each and every one of those different implementation modules it might need, even though, at any time, it might possibly be using just one. Wouldn't it be nice if there was a way you could define an interface type somewhere and have the *consumer* module depend only on that? Then the different *provider* modules with different sorting algorithms just provide implementations of the interface that you can plug in at runtime without needing explicit dependencies, and with no coupling between the actual consumer and the various implementation modules?

The following diagram shows what we'd like. Rather than `packt.addressbook` requiring all of the modules that provide the implementation logic, it instead requires a single module that somehow acts as an interface, and has some mechanism to get the implementations dynamically:

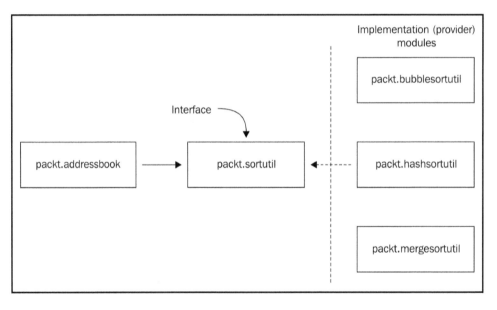

By now you must have guessed that anytime I ask the *Wouldn't it be nice ...* question, it probably means that such a feature already exists! At least in this case, it's true. This is where services come in. The concept of services and the Service API together add a whole new layer of indirection on top of the existing modularity concepts you've learn so far. Let's dive into the details.

Understanding services

Let's begin our journey of understanding services with a concept that you should be very familiar with as a Java developer--polymorphism. It starts with one interface and (possibly multiple) implementations of that interface. Although interfaces are not strictly *necessary* for services, they are still a good place to start. Let's say you define a service interface called MyServiceInterface that looks like this:

```
package service.api;
public interface MyServiceInterface {
  public void runService();
}
```

Now you can have multiple modules containing classes that implement this interface. Since all those modules need access to this interface, let's throw this interface into a module of its own, called service.api, and expose the package that the interface MyServiceInterface is in. Then each implementation module can require the service.api module and implement MyServiceInterface.

Consider there are three implementations of MyServiceInterface in three corresponding modules. Since they need the interface to implement it in the first place, all three implementation modules *read* the service.api module to get access to MyServiceInterface. Imagine each module does just that, and that each contains a class that implements MyServiceInterface:

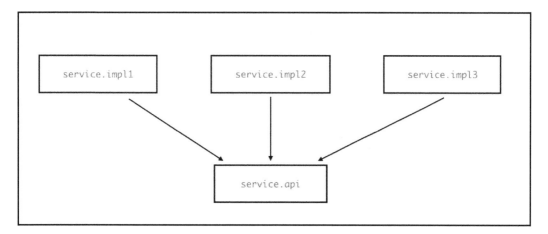

Now, the consumer module needs to call one of these implementations to actually run the service. The goal here is not to have the consumer module directly *read* the various implementation modules, since that's tight coupling. What we want is for the consumer module to read just the *interface* module `service.api` and deal with the interface type only, but still somehow manage to get access to instances of that interface's implementations. Remember, we *do not* want the consumer to require the individual implementation modules (the *Xs* in the following diagram):

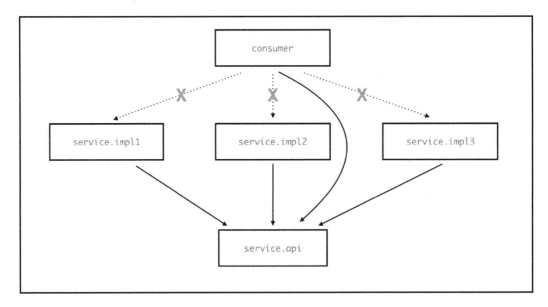

The service registry

In order to cross this bridge between the consumer and the implementation without direct tight coupling, imagine a layer between them called *the service registry*. The service registry is a layer provided by the module system to record and register implementations of a given interface as *services*. Think of it as a kind of phone book or yellow pages, but for services. Any module that implements a service needs to register itself in the service registry. Once that's done, the service registry has all the information about the different service implementations of the interface that are available. The following diagram illustrates this interaction:

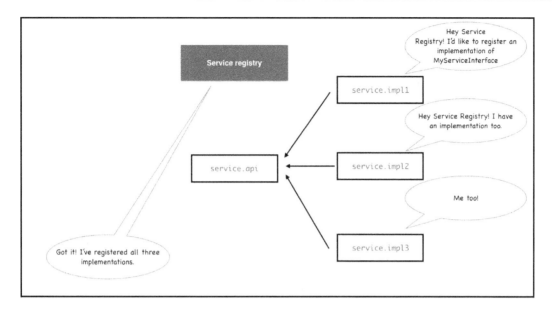

Now when the consumer needs an implementation, it uses the services API to talk to the service registry and get instances of the available implementations. The following diagram illustrates this interaction:

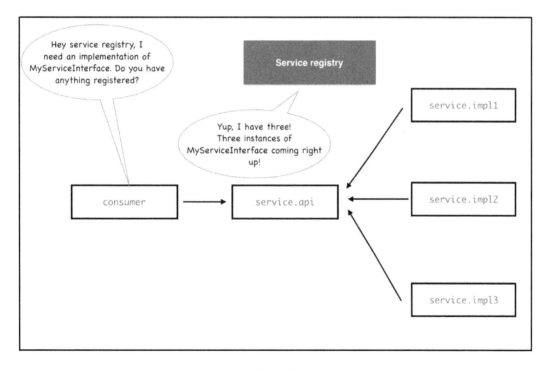

What the consumer module gets is an `Iterable` of instances of all available implementations. There doesn't have to be multiple instances, of course. There could be just one implementation! Either way, the Service API hands over the available instances to the consumer when accessed.

As you can see, we have broken the coupling between the *provider* and the *consumer*. Every module in this figure reads just one module in common--the module containing the interface. The interface is the only **common** entity that all these different modules share, since that's the means of the interaction between them. Since the other modules are completely unaware of each other, you could pretty much remove one implementation module and drop in another. As long as it does the right things--that is, implements the right interface and registers with the service registry--it is available for the consumer to use.

Now that you've understood the concept of services at a high level, let's get into the specifics. How do the modules *register* their implementations? How does the consumer module access the instances from the registry? Let's look at the implementation details.

Creating and using services

Here are the end-to-end steps to create, register, and implement a service:

1. **Create the Java type that defines the service**: Every service is based off of a single Java type that defines the service API. The type could be an interface, an abstract class, or even a regular Java class. Most of the time, the service type will be an interface. Having an interface is ideal because that way, you can have multiple implementation types for it.

   The service type is the means through which both the providers and consumers talk to each other. This begs the question of which module the service type should be in? Since it is shared by multiple modules, and we don't want the providers and consumers to be tightly coupled, the ideal solution is to create the service types in a separate module. This module exports the service type and is read by both the provider and consumer modules.

   In our example, that would be the module `service.api`. It exports the package `service.api`, thereby exporting the interface:

   ```
   module service.api {
     exports service.api;
   }
   ```

This module contains the interface `service.api.MyServiceInterface`, as previously shown. This fully qualified interface type name itself is the service type. Services in the Java module system don't have special names. They are simply referred to by the name of the Java type that acts as the service.

2. **Create one or more implementation modules that read the interface module and implement the interface**: For example, if you need to have two modules `service.implA` and `service.implB` that provide two implementations of `MyServiceInterface`, both the modules will *require* the `service.api` module to access the interface. They each have an implementation of the `MyServiceInterface` interface. Each implementation of the service interface is referred to as a *service provider*.

3. **Have the implementation modules register themselves as service providers**: This is the part where the implementation modules tell the service registry that they would like to register their implementation of the interface. This is done in the module descriptor by using a new keyword called `provides` and specifying both the interface and the implementation type information. The syntax is as follows:

```
provides <interface-type> with <implementation-type>;
```

For example, if the module `service.implA` has the implementation class `packt.service.impla.MyServiceImplA` that implements `MyServiceInterface`, the module definition should read:

```
module service.implA {
  requires service.api;
  provides service.api.MyServiceInterface with
   packt.service.impla.MyServiceImplA;
}
```

This is sufficient for the module system to know that this module would like to register the `MyServiceImplA` class as a service that provides for the interface `MyServiceInterface`.

A few observations here:

- Note the fully qualified name for both the interface and implementation types. This is important in order to avoid name conflicts and make sure the Java platform knows exactly which types you are referring to.

- Note that the interface type referred to in the `provides` clause does not belong to the module itself. It's in a completely different module that this module reads from (using the `requires` clause)! But that's okay; it works. However, it's important for the implementation class to be in the module that the module descriptor belongs to. This makes sense when you consider the fact that with the `provides` line of code, the module is essentially claiming to provide the implementation mentioned. So, it had better have it!

- This is an observation about what's *not* in the preceding module descriptor. Notice that we haven't added an `exports` clause here in order to make the `MyServiceImplA` class accessible to other modules. When providing services, you don't have to expose the implementation classes and make them accessible. This is because this class is not accessed with the usual module *readability* and *accessibility* relationships that we've been working with so far. The consumer module will get the instance of the implementation through the service APIs and does not read the module directly. That's the point of services after all, to avoid this tight coupling.

With this step, we have now successfully registered the service providers with the module system. Every implementation that does this is now mapped to the service *name* which is, for all practical purposes, the fully qualified interface name-
-`service.api.MyServiceInterface`.

Now let's turn our attention to the consumer module. Getting the consumer module to have access to the service implementation instances is a two-part process:

1. **Have the consumer module register itself as a consumer of the service**: Just like the service providers *register* their intent to provide implementations, the service consumers need to *register* the fact that they'll need to *use* the service. The module that needs the instances will have to formally declare this need in the module descriptor. This is done using the `uses` keyword. The syntax is:

   ```
   uses <interface-type>;
   ```

   In our example, if we have a module named consumer that needs instances of `MyServiceInterface`, the module definition will read:

   ```
   module consumer {
     requires service.api;
     uses service.api.MyServiceInterface;
   }
   ```

This is sufficient for the module system to know that this is a module that will use a service implementation instance of the mentioned interface.

A few observations:

- The consumer module too `requires` the module that exposes the interface. It has to, because when the module requests service instances from the service API, what it'll get back are instances that are of the same type as the interface.
- Here, the `uses` clause is referring to a type that's not available in the module.
- As you must have guessed, there's no direct dependency on any of the implementation modules. Loose coupling for the win!

After this step, on the one hand, we have the provider modules register their implementations with the service registry. And on the other hand, we have the consumer module register that it is a consumer of the service. Now, how does the code in the consumer module get access to the instances of the provider implementations? This is the final step, and this involves calling the `ServiceLoader` API.

2. **Call the ServiceLoader API to access the provider instances in the consumer module's code**: With no direct dependencies, the service implementation types are completely unknown to the consumer. All it has is the interface type. So, there's no way it can instantiate types using `new`.

   In order to access all registered implementations of the service, you'll need to call the Java platform API `ServiceLoader.load()` method in the consumer module's code. Here's the code to get all registered service provider instances of the interface `MyServiceInterface`:

   ```
   Iterable<MyServiceInterface> sortUtils =
       ServiceLoader.load(MyServiceInterface.class);
   ```

What the API returns is an `Iterable` of all available implementations of the service that have been registered in the Service Registry. Thanks to the return type being `Iterable`, you can loop through the instances and maybe pick one of them. Or you could even use all! It really depends on the application need and what it's trying to do. What's important to note is that each one of the objects in this `Iterable` is an instance of the provider implementation types that were registered in step 3 of creating services mentioned earlier. There could be several other classes that implement the interface, but if they aren't registered using the `provides` syntax, they will not be considered in this process.

There's a common pattern in many Enterprise Java frameworks that's used to handle various implementations of services and is accessed through the interface. It's called *Dependency Injection*. This pattern is available in frameworks such as Spring, as well as Java EE technologies like EJB. This pattern requires the consumer classes to simply *declare* dependency on services. The framework then performs the job of creating instances and automatically *injecting* them to the consuming classes.

What we are doing here is *not* that. There's no automatic injection of instances to the consuming code. As you've noticed, you have to write code that uses ServiceLoader to *look up* provider instances. This is by design, and is an important distinction to make when compared to those other patterns. This is a *dependency lookup*, not *dependency injection*.

Implementing sorting services

Now that we have an understanding of how to create and consume services, let's put this to practice in the address book viewer application. We'll create multiple sorting implementation modules and register these implementations as services. We'll then update the packt.addressbook module to use the ServiceLoader API to get the sorting instances, and then use one of these instances to sort the contacts list. Let's run through the five steps we've just learned in order to achieve this:

1. **Create the Java type that defines the service**: We'll retain the interface SortUtil to be the common interface that various implementation types will use. The packt.sortutil module contains both the interface and implementation types now. We'll remove the implementation and leave just the interface in there. We'll also remove the default static dependency on BubbleSortUtilImpl and make this a pure and abstract interface:

```
package packt.util;
import java.util.List;
public interface SortUtil {
  public <T extends Comparable> List<T> sortList(List<T> list);
}
```

This will be the only type in the `packt.sortutil` module. The module exports the `packt.util` package to make the interface available to both the providers and consumers. Here's `module-info.java`:

```
module packt.sortutil {
    exports packt.util;
}
```

2. **Create one or more implementation modules that read the interface module and implement the interface**: Let's create a couple of implementation modules-- `packt.sort.bubblesort`, which provides the BubbleSort implementation, and `packt.sort.javasort`, which provides an implementation using the default sorting API of Java collections:

```
├── packt.sort.bubblesort
│   ├── module-info.java
│   └── packt
│       └── util
│           └── impl
│               └── bubblesort
│                   └── BubbleSortUtilImpl.java
├── packt.sort.javasort
│   ├── module-info.java
│   └── packt
│       └── util
│           └── impl
│               └── javasort
│                   └── JavaSortUtilImpl.java
└── packt.sortutil
    ├── module-info.java
    └── packt
        └── util
            └── SortUtil.java
```

 Make sure you don't put both the implementation classes in the two modules in the same package. For example, both the implementation classes cannot be in the same `packt.util.impl` package, because then you'll run into the problem of split packages, with both modules containing the same package, and the runtime will throw an error. We've covered the split packages problem in Chapter 6, *Module Resolution, Accessibility, and Readability*.

Both the modules `requires` the module `packt.sortutil` in order to access the `packt.util.SortUtil` interface. Each has an implementation of the interface.

Here's `BubbleSortUtilImpl`, which is a class we've already seen, so here's the truncated version:

```
public class BubbleSortUtilImpl implements SortUtil {

  public <T extends Comparable> List<T> sortList(
   List<T> list) {
    ...
     return list;
  }''
}
```

Here's `JavaSortUtilImpl`, which simply uses the `Collections.sort` API:

```
public class JavaSortUtilImpl implements SortUtil {
  public <T extends Comparable> List<T> sortList(
   List<T> list) {
     Collections.sort(list);
     return list;
  }
}
```

3. **Have the implementation modules register themselves as service providers**:
   Let's register both the implementation modules as providers using the `provides` keyword. The service type is the interface `packt.util.SortUtil` and the implementation types are the two implementation classes in the two modules, respectively.

   Here's the `module-info.java` file for the `packt.sort.bubblesort` module:

   ```
   module packt.sort.bubblesort {
     requires packt.sortutil;
     provides packt.util.SortUtil
      with packt.util.impl.bubblesort.BubbleSortUtilImpl;
   }
   ```

   And here's the `module-info.java` file for the `packt.sort.javasort` module:

   ```
   module packt.sort.javasort {
     requires packt.sortutil;
     provides packt.util.SortUtil
      with packt.util.impl.javasort.JavaSortUtilImpl;
   }
   ```

4. **Have the consumer module register itself as a consumer of the service**: We'll be needing instances of `SortUtil` in the `packt.addressbook` and `packt.addressbook.ui`. I'll showcase the steps in the `packt.addressbook` module alone here, because it has relatively fewer things going on. But the steps are the same and need to be applied to both modules.

   Here's the module descriptor of `packt.addressbook` with the `uses` clause:

   ```
   module packt.addressbook {
     requires java.logging;
     requires packt.addressbook.lib;
     uses packt.util.SortUtil;
   }
   ```

5. **Call the ServiceLoader API to access the provider instances in the consumer module's code**: In `Main.java`, use the `ServiceLoader` API to get all provider instances of `SortUtil`:

   ```
   Iterable<SortUtil> sortUtils =
     ServiceLoader.load(SortUtil.class);
   ```

Now, iterating through, you can access each instance. I'll loop through and sort the list using *both* of the sorting implementations. This is clearly unnecessary, but it's just for illustration:

```
for (SortUtil sortUtil : sortUtils) {
  System.out.println("Found an instance of SortUtil");
  sortUtil.sortList(contacts);
}
```

And we are done! You've used the service mechanism to create, register, and use sorting service implementations.

 Make sure you apply the same changes to the `packt.addressbook.ui` module as well! If not, the compilation step will fail for that module, for obvious reasons.

Compiling and running the code now should work without any errors:

```
$ javac --module-source-path src -d out $(find . -name '*.java')
$ java --module-path out -m packt.addressbook/packt.addressbook.Main
Apr 09, 2017 12:03:18 AM packt.addressbook.Main main
INFO: Address book viewer application: Started
Found an instance of SortUtil
Found an instance of SortUtil
```

```
[Charles Babbage, Tim Berners-Lee, Edsger Dijkstra, Ada Lovelace, Alan
Turing]
Apr 09, 2017 12:03:19 AM packt.addressbook.Main main
INFO: Address book viewer application: Completed
```

As you can see from the output, there have been two instances of SortUtil returned by ServiceLoader, corresponding to the two implementations we have registered.

Drawing the module graph

Let's draw the module graph that represents the interaction between the service provider and consumer modules. We know how to represent *readability* relationships. How about service consumer and provider dependencies? The following diagram uses arrows to depict both the **uses** and **provides** dependencies, with labels to identify them:

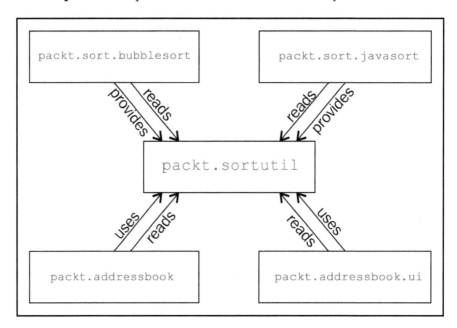

The lack of dependencies between the consumer and provider modules is the key to loose coupling that is enabled using services.

Advanced services

The services concepts covered so far should address a lot of typical use cases, but there are a few additional features and concepts that might come in handy in certain special scenarios. We'll look at a few such concepts in this section.

Supporting singleton and factory providers

Suppose your service instances cannot be created simply by a constructor. What if you need to reuse instances, maybe to have a singleton provider instance? Or maybe execute some logic whenever a new service instance is created? There is a handy feature of services that lets you create factory methods to get service instances. All you need to do is add a method with the name `provide()` in your provider classes. The method needs to be a public static method and it shouldn't take any arguments. Also, the return type should be the same as the type of the service being provided. If the `ServiceLoader` sees this method, it calls it, and uses the return of the method as the service instance. If it doesn't find such a method, it calls the public no-args constructor like we've already seen. This allows you to hook into the provider instance creation step, and here you can execute any necessary code, as well as get an opportunity to create the object that the `ServiceLoader` will use as the provider instance.

Implementing service priorities

In the last example, we got two instances of `SortUtil`, and we did something ridiculous with them--we sorted the list twice, once per implementation! You wouldn't typically do that. What you'll most likely need to do in applications when you receive more than one service implementation is something a bit trickier. You'll need to choose one!

Unfortunately there is no way you can give service implementations distinct priorities. So, there's no way you can say something like `BubbleSortUtilImpl` is your favorite sort implementation, and that's the implementation to be used if it's available, irrespective of whatever other implementations are found. As per design, it's not the responsibility of the service implementations to specify priority. It's the job of the consumer to decide what to do with the multiple implementations it receives from `ServiceLoader`, since the *best* service implementation for the job is usually dependent on the consuming application itself. What is the best service implementation for one consumer might not be ideal for another.

Now, how does the consumer choose one provider among all available ones? All it sees is a bunch of instances of the same interface! So, what we do is enhance the interface to contain methods that the consumer can use to query provider instances. The consumer calls these methods to find out more about the provider classes and thus make an informed decision about which provider instances it would like to go with.

Take the case of the SortUtil implementations. Let's assume we want to use the sorting algorithm depending on the size of the list. For instance, let's say we wish to choose bubble sort only if the list is very small, but use the Collections API sorting for larger lists.

What we could do is add a method to the SortUtil interface called getIdealInputLength(). Each implementation then provides an integer length that it can deal with ideally.

Bubble sort is far from the best sorting algorithm you can use. It's an algorithm many programming courses use to teach sorting, but in reality it's horribly inefficient. For the sake of our simple example, let's say we use bubble sort on lists that are four elements or smaller, and use Collections sort for the rest. I'll admit this is a contrived example, but it'll let us implement a basic strategy for choosing providers. In reality, you'd almost always want to use the Collections API for sorting lists.

Here's SortUtil with the new method declaration:

```
public interface SortUtil {
  public <T extends Comparable> List<T> sortList(List<T> list);
  public int getIdealMaxInputLength();
}
```

Here's the BubbleSortUtilImpl implementation of this method that returns 4 as the ideal maximum size of the input list:

```
public class BubbleSortUtilImpl implements SortUtil {
  ...
  public int getIdealMaxInputLength() {
    return 4;
  }
}
```

The `JavaSortUtilImpl` is OK with any list size, so for the ideal maximum, we'll just return the maximum integer value:

```
public class JavaSortUtilImpl implements SortUtil {
  ...
  public int getIdealMaxInputLength() {
    return Integer.MAX_VALUE;
  }
```

Now that each provider has a method that can be used to choose one implementation over the other, the consumer can use this to identify which of the implementations it would like to use.

Here's the section in `Main.java` (in both the `pack.addressbook` and `packt.addressbook.ui` modules) that loops through the providers to pick one:

```
Iterable<SortUtil> sortUtils =
  ServiceLoader.load(SortUtil.class);
for (SortUtil sortUtil : sortUtils) {
  logger.info("Found an instance of SortUtil with ideal
   max input: " + sortUtil.getIdealMaxInputLength());
  if (contacts.size() < sortUtil.getIdealMaxInputLength()) {
    sortUtil.sortList(contacts);
    break;
  }
}
```

Given the size of the `contacts` list we'd like to sort, we'll check each provider to see if the list size is greater than the maximum size the provider would ideally like to handle. We then pick the first provider that passes this check, use that instance to sort the list, and `break` off the loop.

Run the code and observe the output. If the `BubbleSortUtilImpl` is the first instance in the iterator, the logic skips it and moves to the `JavaSortUtilImpl` and uses it to sort:

```
$ java --module-path out -m packt.addressbook/packt.addressbook.Main
Apr 09, 2017 8:01:20 PM packt.addressbook.Main main
INFO: Address book viewer application: Started
Apr 09, 2017 8:01:20 PM packt.addressbook.Main main
INFO: Found an instance of SortUtil with ideal max input: 4
Apr 09, 2017 8:01:20 PM packt.addressbook.Main main
INFO: Found an instance of SortUtil with ideal max input: 2147483647
[Charles Babbage, Tim Berners-Lee, Edsger Dijkstra, Ada Lovelace, Alan
Turing]
Apr 09, 2017 8:01:20 PM packt.addressbook.Main main
INFO: Address book viewer application: Completed
```

This is a simple example of how provider implementations give *clues* about the implementation to any consumers. Different consumers could then choose different implementations, depending on their unique needs and business problems.

Service interface provider lookup

The lookup logic to get service instances is now in the Main classes in both the `packt.addressbook` and `packt.addressbook.ui` modules. This is less than ideal. We don't want to repeat the lookup logic in multiple places. One way to solve this is to move the logic to a common place that's accessible by all the consumers of the service. Now, what's the module that's shared by every consumer of the service? It's the module that exports the interface. Wouldn't it be a great idea to move the dependency lookup logic and tuck it away as a default method in the interface? Then none of the consumer modules would need to mess with the `ServiceLoader` APIs directly. They would just have to call the right interface method to look up the instances.

Let's create two new methods on the `SortUtil` interface. One to get all service provider instances, and the second to get single instances based on the size of the list (which is a criterion that affects which instance is picked, like we've already seen).

Here are the two new static methods on `SortUtil`:

```java
public static Iterable<SortUtil> getAllProviders() {
  return ServiceLoader.load(SortUtil.class);
}

public static SortUtil getProviderInstance(int listSize) {
  Iterable<SortUtil> sortUtils =
    ServiceLoader.load(SortUtil.class);
  for (SortUtil sortUtil : sortUtils) {
    if (listSize < sortUtil.getIdealMaxInputLength()) {
      return sortUtil;
    }
  }
  return null;
}
```

Here we are returning `null` if no service instances that matched our requirement were found. This could easily be enhanced to provide a default service in case a suitable instance wasn't found.

Now, `Main` doesn't have to talk to `ServiceLoader` and loop through instances anymore:

```
SortUtil sortUtil = SortUtil.getProviderInstance(contacts.size());
sortUtil.sortList(contacts);
```

I hope you'll agree that the consumption of the service has become much simpler now.

One other change you'll have to do is to move the `uses` clause from the `packt.addressbook` and `packt.addressbook.ui` modules to the `packt.sortutil` module. That's because the service is consumed and the `ServiceLoader` APIs are invoked from the `packt.sortutil` module now:

```
module packt.sortutil {
   exports packt.util;
   uses packt.util.SortUtil;
}
```

Compiling and running the code should give you the same output as before. But this time, the service lookup logic is now refactored into a common module usable by all consumers.

Selective service instantiation

In the preceding examples, we have queried the `ServiceLoader` APIs to get *all* provider instances in an `Iterable`. We then looped through them and picked one. This is not a problem here because our services are simple and lightweight Java classes. That may not always be ideal. Imagine if services are more complex and need time and resources to instantiate. In such cases, you wouldn't want to instantiate every service provider when you know you won't use all of them.

The Java module system is quite smart about how it manages service instances in an application. First of all, all service instances are *lazily loaded*. In other words, service provider instances are not automatically instantiated when the application starts up. The runtime creates a service instance only when the type is needed, like when some consumer asks for instances of the service using `ServiceProvider.load()`.

Secondly, any service instances that are created during the lifetime of the application are always cached. The service loader maintains this cache and keeps track of all the service instances that have been created. When the second consumer requests the service, the instance is fetched off of the cache directly. It also intelligently makes sure that the order of the service instances returned always includes the cached instances first.

Caching is automatic with service instances. If you want to clear the entire service provider cache during application execution, you can do so using the `ServiceProvider.reload()` API.

The `ServiceLoader` API has an option of streaming instances of an intermediate type called `Provider`, which can then be used to create service provider instances. Rather than getting all the service instances directly, what you get instead is `Provider` instances--one instance per service implementation found. You can then instantiate only the service providers you want by using the `Provider.get()` method on those instances.

As an example, consider the `getProviderInstanceLazy()` method on `SortUtil`. Rather than directly use `ServiceLoader.load(SortUtil.class)`, we can instead use `ServiceLoader.load(SortUtil.class).stream()`, which returns a `Stream` of `Provider` instances:

```
Stream<Provider<SortUtil>> providers =
    ServiceLoader.load(SortUtil.class).stream();
```

The `Provider` instances can then be inspected for things such as annotations and other type information. Here, we are just sorting them by type name, which is silly, but it works as a minimal example:

```
Stream<Provider<SortUtil>> providers =
    ServiceLoader.load(SortUtil.class).stream()
     .sorted(Comparator.comparing(p -> p.type().getName()));
```

At this time, no service instances are created. The actual instantiation of the service provider types happens when the `Provider.get` is called:

```
SortUtil util = providers.map(Provider::get)
                         .findAny()
                         .orElse(null);
```

In the preceding code, we call `Provider.get()` on each provider instance through the map function and pick one. This way, we can defer the creation of instances as well as selectively instantiate provider types by calling `Provider.get` only on the ones we need.

Services and the module system goals

Since services are a part of the Java module system, how do they align with the two goals of the module system--strong encapsulation and reliable configuration?

Let's begin with strong encapsulation. Services provide an alternative way of having types in modules interact with one another, which does not involve having to expose types to all consuming modules. The service provider packages do not have to be `exported` and thus they are encapsulated even from modules that *read* the module containing the service! At the same time, they are published as implementations of a service type, and thus can be used by modules that do not even *read* the service implementation module. So, in a way, the types are still encapsulated, although not in the same way as what we've seen so far.

How about reliable configuration? Since the service providers and the service consumers *declare* the fact that they are providing and consuming services respectively, it's easy for the runtime and the `ServiceProvider` API to make sure that the right consumers get the right services. However, you can easily compile a bunch of modules without any service implementations available in the module path.

For example, you can delete the `packt.sort.bubblesort` and `packt.sort.javasort` modules from your source code and compile the rest of the modules. It works! You can execute the `Main` module. It still works, although the `ServiceProvider` API does not find any service instances. We are returning `null` in our example, but we could easily handle this scenario by providing a default service implementation (assuming there's a default implementation called `DefaultSortImpl`) in case nothing is found:

```
SortUtil util = providers.map(Provider::get)
                         .findAny()
                         .orElse(new DefaultSortImpl());
```

Why is this? When there's a module that clearly declares itself as a service consumer, why do the compiler and runtime not check if at least one service implementation is available? The reason is, it is by design. Service dependencies are *meant* to be optional. Remember the concept of loose coupling we started the chapter with. We want to be able to plug-and-play service consumers and providers at runtime. This works perfectly well with services.

The reliable configuration checking of the platform, however, does come into play when there's a service module that does not have some of its dependencies met. For example, let's say we have a service consumer module **C**. You can compile and execute this module without the presence of a service provider. In the following picture, the Java platform won't complain:

However, if you do add a provider module, you'll need to make sure it has all the dependencies met. For instance, let's say you drop in a provider module **P** that provides an implementation for the service that **C** needs. Now this provider module needs to follow all the rules for reliable configuration. If this module reads module **D** and module **D** doesn't exist as an observable module, the platform complains:

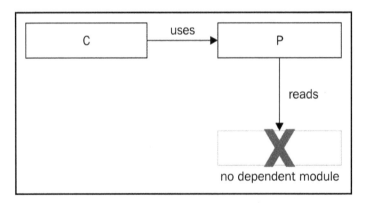

It seems strange that while the platform was perfectly fine when there was no provider module available, it complains when a provider module exists, but it doesn't have a dependency met. Why could it not ignore module **P** then? The answer is, again, reliable configuration. The absence of a provider module could be intentional. But if the platform finds a module that it could technically use, but cannot, because of an unmet dependency, that indicates a *broken* state, and thus, it errors out accordingly. Even allowing loose coupling through services, the platform is essentially trying the best it can to provide reliable configuration for us.

Summary

In this chapter, we've taken a detailed look at the services feature in the Java module system. We've learned the disadvantages of tight coupling of modules, and how loose coupling provides more flexibility. We then dove right into the syntax of creating and using services and then implemented a sorting service with two provider implementations. We then looked at some advanced concepts related to services, such as mechanisms for prioritizing service instances, using the service interface itself to handle service lookup, and deferring service instance creation using the `Provider` type in the case of heavy-weight services.

We then revisited the two goals of modularity--strong encapsulation and dependency injection--and evaluated how the services feature impacts those goals.

In the next chapter, we'll learn about the new *linking* phase that now applies to Java development thanks to modularity features. We'll also revisit the problem of the monolithic JDK that we discussed in `Chapter 1`, *Introducing Java 9 Modularity*, How can we make that better? How can we leverage the concepts of modularity to create leaner and meaner runtimes that are smaller and perform better? The answers to these questions and much more can be found in the next chapter!

8
Understanding Linking and Using jlink

In the previous chapters, we've learned about some advanced concepts relating to Java modularity, including handling readability and accessibility of module relationships, and the powerful concept of services. In this chapter, we'll move on to the final step in any application development--building and packaging your application.

Here's what you'll learn in this chapter:

- You'll learn about the module resolution process, an important process that happens every time you compile or execute a modular Java application.
- You'll be introduced to a new phase in the development process--linking. Linking, or static linking, is a new step in Java 9 modular development. It sits between the familiar compilation and execution phases that you should already be familiar with. In this chapter, you'll understand what linking is and the benefits of this step.
- You'll learn how to use `jlink`, the new tool built into the platform to facilitate the linking phase and help build runtime images.
- You'll learn about some `jlink` plugins that optimize runtime images that are created by `jlink`.
- You'll learn how to build a modular JAR file, which is an alternative way to distribute your compiled library modules for use in other applications.

Module resolution process

Before we get into the details of the linking process and what it can do for us, let's understand an important step that happens every time you compile and execute a modular Java application. This is a step called **module resolution**.

Traditionally (pre-Java 9), the Java compiler and Java runtime would to look at a set of folders and JAR files that form the **classpath**. The classpath is a configurable option that you pass to the compiler during compilation and to the runtimes during execution. In order to have any class file be under the purview of the compiler or runtime, you'd need to first place it in the classpath. Once it's there, every Java type is *available* for the compiler or the runtime.

Things are different with modules. We don't have to use the generic classpath anymore. Since every module defines its *inputs* and *outputs*, there's now an option to know exactly what portion of the code is needed at any time.

Consider the following module dependency graph:

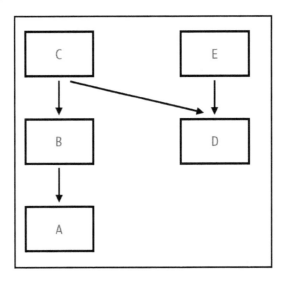

Let's assume that you have the modules **A**, **B**, **C**, **D**, and **E** in the module path. Let's imagine that you are playing the role of the Java runtime, and you want to execute the main method in module **C**. What is the minimal set of modules that are *required* for this to happen? You'll obviously need module **C**, since that has the main method. Next you'll need its dependencies, modules **B** and **D**. Next you'll need those modules' dependencies as well, which in this case is module **A**, which **B** depends on:

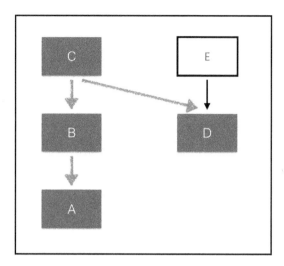

Using this process, it's safe to say that the minimum set of modules required to execute a `main` type in module **C** is **A**, **B**, **C**, and **D**--module **E** is unnecessary.

Let's repeat the exercise, but this time to execute a type in module **E**. This time, we'll just need modules **E** and **D**; all other modules can be skipped:

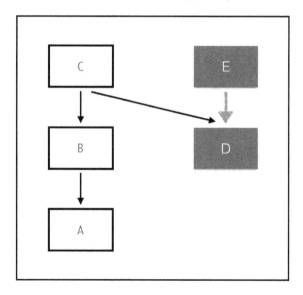

Now why are we doing this? What's the advantage of finding this *minimal set of modules?* Contrast this with the older classpath model where every type in the classpath is a part of the application, and any type could be *in use*. There's no way for the compiler and runtime to figure out where a given type exists unless it scans the entire classpath. That's not the case anymore! Since both the compiler and runtime now have a precise idea about what part of the code base is *needed* to execute anything and what part is not, it puts this advantage to good use, as we'll soon see. But in order to get this information, the platform runs a process of resolving modules, which is, in principle, similar to what we did in the preceding example. This process is called the module resolution process.

In graph theory, this process is referred to as finding *transitive closure.* Given a graph, the idea is to find a set of nodes that are *reachable* from a given node. The graph on which we perform transitive closure should be what's called a **directed acyclic graph** (**DAG**). The graph should be **directed**, in that the relationships between nodes are directional (with arrows), and **acyclic**, in that there shouldn't be cyclical relationships. Does the DAG remind you of any graphs you've seen recently? Yes! The Java module graph is a great example of a directed acyclic graph!

Module resolution steps

Here are the high-level steps that the platform runs through when it resolves modules:

1. Add the root module to the resolved set of modules. Remember that when you execute your code, you specify the type containing the main method and the module it belongs to. This module is the root module and forms the starting point for the module resolution process. Note that this starting point doesn't have to be just one module--there could be several modules, as we'll see shortly.

2. Identify all the `requires` dependencies of the module(s) added. Here, each module's descriptor file is looked up to identify all the modules that it *reads*. This includes both `requires` and `requires transitive`.

3. From the list from step 2, remove all modules that are already in the resolved set of modules.

4. Add the remaining modules to the resolved set of modules. Repeat step 2 for this list.

As you can imagine, this is a recursive graph operation that starts with one or more modules and ends up with the minimal set of modules that are needed as dependencies. Since the platform does this during every compilation and runtime phase, it uses this opportunity to check for several different kinds of errors. In fact, many of the module errors we've encountered so far happen because of checks during and around the module resolution process. Here are a few of them:

- **Unavailable dependent modules**: This one is obvious. While looking up dependencies, if a module isn't found among the observable modules, the process errors out. This, as we've seen, is the key to reliable configuration.
- **Multiple modules**: Not only do all dependent modules have to be available, there needs to be only one of each. If there happen to be two modules in the module path that have the same name (even if they have entirely different contents), the platform catches this right away and throws an error.
- **Cyclic dependencies**: If two or more modules depend on each other and form a closed loop cycle in the module graph, the platform throws an error, as we've already seen.
- **Split packages**: The platform assumes that each package is available in just one module. The class loaders maintain a map of each package to the module it is found in. Thus, if there are multiple modules that contain the same package, the process terminates with an error.

Examining module resolution in action

There's a new command option added to Java that prints out debug information that describes the module resolution process. You can activate it by passing the option `--show-module-resolution`. When passed this option, the `java` command prints out console messages for each step of the module resolution. You can use this to see the process that the runtime goes through to resolve all the modules, much like we did in the preceding exercise.

This is how you ran the command-line address book module in the previous chapter, without the flag:

```
$ java --module-path out -m packt.addressbook/packt.addressbook.Main
```

Here's how you run it with the module resolution diagnostics enabled:

```
$ java --show-module-resolution --module-path out -m
  packt.addressbook/packt.addressbook.Main
```

The verbose output gives a clear indication of what's happening here. Things start off with the root module `packt.addressbook`, as expected:

```
root packt.addressbook file:///Users/koushik/code/java9/07-
services/out/packt.addressbook/
```

Next, it finds the dependent modules from the module descriptor. For every module it finds, the output lists the name of the module, where it found it (the path), and why (which module required it):

```
packt.addressbook requires packt.addressbook.lib
file:///Users/koushik/code/java9/07-services/out/packt.addressbook.lib/
packt.addressbook requires java.logging jrt:/java.logging
```

It also figures out the service providers based on the modules that declared themselves as consumers:

```
packt.sortutil binds packt.sort.bubblesort
file:///Users/koushik/code/java9/07-services/out/packt.sort.bubblesort/
packt.sortutil binds packt.sort.javasort
file:///Users/koushik/code/java9/07-services/out/packt.sort.javasort/
packt.addressbook binds packt.sort.bubblesort
file:///Users/koushik/code/java9/07-services/out/packt.sort.bubblesort/
packt.addressbook binds packt.sort.javasort
file:///Users/koushik/code/java9/07-services/out/packt.sort.javasort/
```

The runtime continues to look for subsequent dependencies as it traverses the nodes of the module graph. After it's done adding all the necessary modules to the resolved set, it then executes the main method and the expected program output is printed on the console:

```
Aug 16, 2017 11:07:02 PM packt.addressbook.Main main
INFO: Address book viewer application: Started
[Charles Babbage, Tim Berners-Lee, Edsger Dijkstra, Ada Lovelace, Alan
Turing]
Aug 16, 2017 11:07:03 PM packt.addressbook.Main main
INFO: Address book viewer application: Completed
```

Now that you've understood the process of module resolution and how it benefits the process of compile-time and runtime enforcement of reliable configuration, let's now look at another problem that it can solve. We briefly introduced the problem of the monolithic JDK in Chapter 1, *Introducing Java 9 Modularity*. We'll quickly recap the problem and then learn how that it is no longer a problem with Java 9.

Revisiting the state of the JDK

In `Chapter 1`, *Introducing Java 9 Modularity*, we examined the large size of the JDK, both in terms of the file size of `rt.jar` as well as the number of classes that are bundled in it. Typically, you wouldn't think about the JDK when developing Java applications. Once you've installed the JDK on your development machine, it sits in a remote corner of your hard disk at `$JAVA_HOME` and it doesn't bother you. There are, however, a few instances where you would need to worry about the size of the JDK, especially when bundling an application executable. Here are a couple of such occasions:

- **Runtime bundles for embedded devices**: Java has been known to run on portable and embedded devices, such as compact music players, microwaves, and washing machines. Many of these are devices with scarce hardware capacities for memory and processing power, and for Java to run on those devices, the runtime should obviously be a part of the installed application. The size of the Java SE runtime is so prohibitive that there is a separate platform (Java ME) for such scenarios.

- **Runtime images for microservices**: A common trend in recent years is to deploy lightweight microservices in the cloud. Instead of having one centralized web application that does everything, the application is split into separate smaller services that run on different machine instances and communicate with each other over the network. The runtime image for each instance is a self-sufficient set of binaries that include the application classes and the Java runtime. These microservices are ideally stateless, scalable, and disposable, so they'd ideally need to be lightweight and performant. Bundling a 75 MB runtime that needs to be a part of every instance doesn't really help.

Think for a minute about why this problem even exists. Well, it's because of the classpath model of previous versions of Java. Any piece of code can potentially refer to any other Java type in the classpath, and there's no saying what's required and what's not, so we had no choice but to add the whole platform.

This is no longer the case with modular programming! We've seen that with module resolution, given a starting point, we can precisely identify which modules are required for its execution. This applies equally to both application and platform modules, since they both follow the same contract. Thanks to this, we can now apply the module resolution process and come up with a unique bare minimum set of platform *and* application modules that you'd need to run any application. Thus, when distributing an application with runtime, for example, you don't have to include the entire platform. Instead, you just include the platform modules that are necessary, and we do just that by introducing a whole new step in Java application development that we didn't have before--linking.

Linking using jlink

JDK 9 comes bundled with a new tool called `jlink` that lets you build your own complete runtime image that contains everything necessary to execute a given application. Remember the new structure of the JDK that we looked at in `Chapter 4`, *Introducing the Modular JDK*:

With `jlink`, you can create a similar custom image of your own to distribute your application. The generated image contains:

- The minimal set of your application and library modules that you've authored or added
- The minimal set of platform modules needed for your application to work

This effectively solves the problem of the huge overhead incurred to ship the platform along with your application. What you ship is just what the application needs--no more, no less. There are further benefits to this process, but before we get into that, let's learn how to use `jlink` to create this image.

The jlink command

The `jlink` command needs the following inputs:

- **The module path**: This is where it needs to look for modules. This is the directory (or directories) where the compiled modules are available.
- **The starting module**: This is the module from which to begin the module resolution process. This could be one or many, separated by delimiters.
- **The output directory**: This is the location where it stores the generated image.

The usage looks something like this, with the command broken into separate lines for readability:

```
jlink --module-path <module-path-locations>
      --add-modules <starting-module-name>
      --output <output_location>
```

To run this command on our sample codebase and generate an image for the address book UI module, we first need to compile the modules in the same way that we usually do:

```
$ javac --module-source-path src -d out $(find . -name '*.java')
```

Here, `out` is the location of the compiled modules, and thus, that is the module path for `jlink`. The module that serves as the starting point is `packt.addressbook.ui`.

In the same directory that we ran the `javac` command, we can now run `jlink`. To run the command, either make sure the `$JAVA_HOME/bin` directory is in your operating system's path, or use the path to access `jlink` directly:

```
$ $JAVA_HOME/bin/jlink --module-path out
    --add-modules packt.addressbook.ui --output image
```

Note that we get an error:

```
Error: Module java.base not found, required by packt.addressbook.ui
```

We are missing the platform modules! Note that `java.base` is a core platform module and is not available in the module path we've specified in the preceding command. Platform modules don't get special treatment; their module location needs to be explicitly specified to the `jlink` command!

We've already seen that the core Java modules are available in $JAVA_HOME/jmods. Let's add that to the --module-path parameter. As before, in order to specify multiple paths there, we need to separate the paths with the : symbol (; on Windows operating systems):

```
$ $JAVA_HOME/bin/jlink --module-path $JAVA_HOME/jmods:out
    --add-modules packt.addressbook.ui --output image
```

jlink will now get to work and quietly generate the runtime image for us. Let's look at the structure of the image generated:

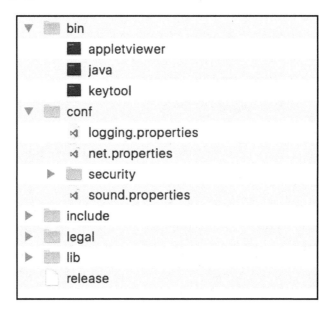

This should look familiar now. The structure is very similar to the JDK file structure we've already seen. One notable exception is that the jmods folder isn't here. This makes sense because this is a *runtime* image, and the jmods format is not designed to be used for runtime. Since this image contains only the modules necessary, they are all bundled into a common modules file in the lib folder.

Now that the image contains the runtime and the compiled application modules, it is a self-sufficient bundle. You can deploy this image on a computer that does not have the Java runtime installed and execute it without any problems.

Now, to execute our module from the runtime image, we need to execute the `java` executable that's available in the `bin` directory of the image, not the one in `$PATH`. You also don't have to specify the `--module-path` this time because the module resolution is already done! The generated image is already bundled with every module it needs, and thus already knows where to find them:

```
$ cd image/
$ bin/java -m packt.addressbook.ui/packt.addressbook.ui.Main
```

You should see the address book UI application pop up. That's great, but you can probably tell something isn't right:

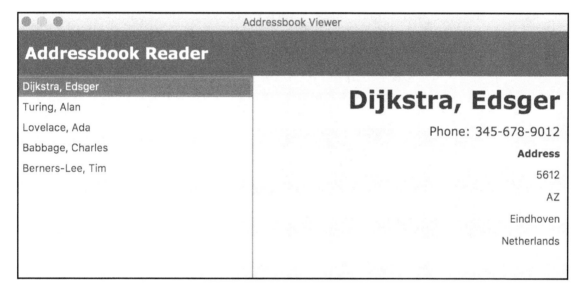

The names aren't sorted. Can you guess why? It's because the sorting modules haven't been bundled in! If you run the `java --list-modules` on the `java` executable in the image, you can see all the modules that have been bundled in. Note that the sorting service modules aren't included:

```
$ bin/java --list-modules
java.base@9
  . . .
packt.addressbook.lib
packt.addressbook.ui
packt.contact
packt.sortutil
```

Remember that the module resolution process traverses the module graph and adds modules that have a **direct dependency** using the `requires` clause. Services, by definition, are loosely coupled and so are not required by any module. Because of this reason, both the service modules--`packt.sort.bubblesort` and `packt.sort.javasort`--haven't been included. This behavior of `jlink` is intentional. The bundling of service modules needs to be explicitly stated to the command.

Note that the `java --list-modules` command displays the observable modules that are available in the runtime image on which the command is run. All along, we've run the command on the installed JDK, so it listed all (and only) the platform modules. This time, we have run the command on the generated runtime image, which is a combination of our application modules and a select few platform modules. Thus, the output of the command reflects that accordingly.

There are a couple of ways we can fix our problem. The first way is to add the service modules to the list of **starting-point modules** for module resolution using the `--add-modules` option. Multiple module names can be specified for this option, with the names separated by commas. These modules and their dependencies will then also get bundled into the image, since the module resolution process will run starting from each of those modules, too, and add them to the resolved set:

```
$ $JAVA_HOME/bin/jlink --module-path $JAVA_HOME/jmods:out
    --add-modules
packt.addressbook.ui,packt.sort.bubblesort,packt.sort.javasort
    --output image
```

Now, running `java --list-modules` in the generated image should show the sorting modules. Also, when executing the application, the UI should now show the list of contacts sorted by last name:

```
$ bin/java --list-modules
  java.base@9-ea
  . . .
  packt.addressbook.lib
  packt.addressbook.ui
  packt.contact
  packt.sort.bubblesort
  packt.sort.javasort
  packt.sortutil
```

Another alternative to bundling in services is to use the `--bind-services` option of `jlink`:

```
$ $JAVA_HOME/bin/jlink --module-path $JAVA_HOME/jmods:out
    --add-modules packt.addressbook.ui --bind-services --output image
```

This parameter automatically identifies any services consumed by modules when it checks each module through the module resolution process. Then, all observable modules that declare that they are providers for those services will be automatically bundled in. This is an easier option because you don't have to explicitly mention service modules yourself, but there's a chance that you might pull in more modules than you really require. Let's say there's some random module in the module path that your application doesn't use, but it just happens to implement one of the service types you've used. Well, that module gets pulled in with this option!

Link phase optimizations and jlink plugins

There have always been two steps to get Java code to execute--the compile step (using `javac`) and the execution step (using `java`). During the compilation step, `javac` doesn't just try to convert Java code into byte code, it also tries to perform any optimizations it can and generate the most optimal and efficient byte code possible. Over the years, the Java compiler has learned several new tricks and strategies to better optimize the resulting byte code. But there has always been a challenge--the compiler works on a handful of classes at a time and it doesn't have the opportunity to see the big picture by looking at the entire application, which could have helped it implement better optimizations. That option is available for runtime, but some of the optimizations end up being too expensive when done at runtime. With the introduction of the new linking step in between the compile and execution phases, an opportunity opens up to do application-level optimization for our Java byte code. In fact, one of the goals of the platform team for the linking phase is to do **whole-world** optimizations--optimizations that span multiple classes and modules across the application, having been given the **bigger picture**.

Remember that the linking step is optional, of course. We've executed our application in the previous chapters without having to use `jlink`, and thereby without doing any such optimizations. However, if you were to use `jlink`, there's an opportunity to do optimizations--things such as compressing the image, identifying and removing unreachable code and types, pre-optimizing code, and methods where the possible inputs are constant and known ahead of time. These optimizations can happen when running `jlink` and are done using a series of `transformers`, which are built as plugins.

Here's an approximation of how `jlink` works to create the runtime image:

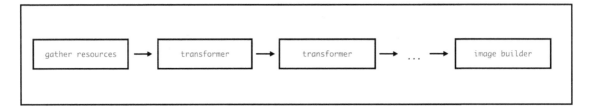

The process starts with gathering all the necessary resources and running them through a series of transformers that can do various tasks and optimizations. The `jlink` tool has a plugin API so that anyone can create custom plugins that hook into this process and have the opportunity to transform the resulting image. After the transformers are done, the image is written to the output directory, where, again, plugins can be written to control what happens.

The Java 9 platform comes with built-in plugins that do several of these optimizations. In fact, some of these optimizations are so important and have such a significant impact that they have been turned on by default! It's important to know some of these options that are available to you while you generate your runtime image:

- **Module descriptor optimizations with the system-modules plugin**: During the initial development of modules in Java, it was noticed that the Java runtime ended up spending a significant amount of time and resources examining, parsing, and validating the module descriptors (`module-info.class`) of each module in the system image. Since the set of modules that are going to be bundled in an image is known at link time, the process of scanning and validating all the module descriptors can be done at link time too. There is a `jlink` plugin that does this bundled with the platform, and is called `system-modules`. This plugin generates a pre-processed and pre-validated system module graph so that the runtime doesn't have to. The process results in such significant gains in performance that it's enabled by default whenever you run `jlink`.

- **Compressing the image with the compress plugin**: This plugin allows you to apply compression to the generated image to reduce the size of the output runtime image. There are two types of compression that this plugin can perform on the generated image. The first identifies all usages of UTF-8 strings and generates a global string table so that any common `String` values have to be stored only once and can be reused across the application. The second type of compression is the ZIP compression of files in the resulting image to shrink its overall size.

Unlike system-modules, this plugin is not enabled by default. To use it, you'll need to pass the `--compress` option to `jlink`. You can pass three values--`0`, which means no compression, `1`, which enables string sharing, and `2`, which does ZIP compression.

Running the two levels of compression while generating the address book image on our sample code shows the gains in size of the generated images:

```
$ $JAVA_HOME/bin/jlink --module-path $JAVA_HOME/jmods:out
    --add-modules packt.addressbook.ui --bind-services
    --compress=1 --output image1

$ $JAVA_HOME/bin/jlink --module-path $JAVA_HOME/jmods:out
    --add-modules packt.addressbook.ui --bind-services
    --compress=2 --output image2
```

Examining the sizes of the resulting images shows us how much space the compression has saved us. The following table summarizes the folder sizes on my machine after running these commands:

Compression	Address book image size
None	167.5 MB
Level 1	129.4 MB
Level 2	95.9 MB

- **Locale information with the include-locales plugin**: By default, the runtime image bundles in all installed locale information. If you are targeting your application runtime only for certain locales, you can use the `--include-locales` option and pass the comma-separated list of locales you need. Only those locales will be included in the resulting image, thus freeing up more space:

```
$ $JAVA_HOME/bin/jlink --module-path $JAVA_HOME/jmods:out
    --add-modules packt.addressbook.ui --bind-services
    --compress=2 --include-locales=en --output image3
```

The preceding command regenerates the image with full compression, and with the English locale included (`--include-locales=en`). On my machine, this resulted in further space savings, with the image size at 88.2 MB.

There are several other handy plugins that come bundled in the JDK. To get to know what plugins are available, and to learn how to use them, you can run `jlink` with the `--list-plugins` option. The complete list of installed plugins will be displayed, including the plugins we've just learned about and much more:

```
$ $JAVA_HOME/bin/jlink --list-plugins
```

Building a modular JAR file

We've looked at creating complete modular runtime images and learned about the advantages of the linking process, but sometimes that may not be what you want. Suppose you are a library developer and you just want to bundle a single utility module as a jar file. When building a jar file from a module, you have an option of creating a **modular JAR file**. A modular jar file is just like any other jar file, but with the `module-info.class` file in the root directory. You can use this to distribute compiled modules as a single file instead of the whole module folder. You can drop a modular JAR file in a module path when running the `java` command, and it behaves just like the compiled module folders that we've been dealing with.

To illustrate this, let's replace a couple of modules in the `out` folder of the address book application with modular JAR files.

The way to create a modular JAR file is by using the `jar` utility. In order to convert the `packt.contact` module into a modular JAR file, we run the following command:

```
$ jar --create --file out/contact.jar --module-version=1.0
    -C out/packt.contact .
```

The `--create` option tells the `jar` utility that it needs to create a JAR file. The `-C` option specifies where it can find the classes. The value is of the format `<folder> <file>`. In our case, the folder is `out/packt.contact`. This is followed by `"."` which indicates that all files in this location need to be included. The `--module-version` option specifies a module version for the `jar`. Finally, the `--file` option provides the JAR output file name.

Running this command will create a modular JAR file, with the `module-info.class` file at the root. There's also a `META-INF` folder with a manifest file that records the version number specified: `Manifest-Version: 1.0`.

Even modules with an executable `main` method can be converted to modular jars. Here's how we'd convert the `packt.addressbook.ui` module into a modular JAR:

```
$ jar --create --file out/addressbook-ui.jar --module-version=1.0
      --main-class=packt.addressbook.ui.Main -C out/packt.addressbook.ui  .
```

Most of the parameters should be familiar here, except for the `--main-class`. This option, as the name says, specifies the type with the `main` method.

With these two modules converted to modular JAR files and placed in the module path, you can now delete the corresponding compiled module folders and still execute the application. The runtime treats the modular JAR file the same way as the expanded module folder:

```
$ rm -rf out/packt.contact/
$ rm -rf out/packt.addressbook.ui/
$ java --module-path out
      -m packt.addressbook.ui/packt.addressbook.ui.Main
```

The application should still work the same way, although this time, it's executing two of the modules from the JAR file.

Summary

This chapter examined the part of the application development process after you are done writing code--building and packaging your application for distribution. We started the chapter by examining the module resolution process. We then looked at the process of linking, which uses module resolution to build a runtime image containing just the modules needed for a given application. We then looked at some of the built-in plugins that allow us to optimize and preprocess the generated image. Finally, we learned how to generate a modular JAR file to bundle reusable library modules for use in other applications.

We've looked at a lot of features so far and how they work. In the next chapter, we'll start looking at how to work with Java 9 modules in the context of an existing legacy Java codebase. You'll learn ways to write code that is interoperable between different Java versions. You'll also learn techniques and strategies to migrate existing code written using Java 8 or earlier to the new modular application development of Java 9. See you in the next unit!

9
Module Design Patterns and Strategies

In the previous few chapters, we did a deep dive into several modularity features in Java 9 that enable you to build Java applications with modules. You've learned how to use the dependency declarations and services to establish module dependencies. You've also learned how to use jlink to build modular runtimes that can be distributed. In this chapter, we'll look at a slightly less objective concern--how to build good applications with modules in Java. Now that you've acquired the knowledge to create and use modules, what are the recommended ways to do that? What are the best practices and patterns that you should use? Here's what we'll cover in this chapter:

- Understanding how to design modules--what a module should ideally be and where module boundaries should be drawn
- Understanding how to design good APIs for those modules
- Learning about several best practices to create modules, as well as patterns, to use the module system effectively

Many of the patterns discussed in this chapter come with usable code examples, available in the folder `09-module-patterns`. Each example has been carefully crafted to help explain the pattern being discussed with minimal information overhead. Feel free to use and experiment with these code examples as you explore these patterns. Also, remember to revisit this chapter during your Java 9 modularity journey to brush up your knowledge of these patterns. It's often the case that rereading and thinking about design patterns at any time offers new perspectives to the challenges you have going on at that time.

Let's get started!

Designing modules

Over the years, the first step in designing a Java application has usually involved the design of the packages and classes, as well as the interactions between them. It also perhaps involved designing some shared libraries. For instance, you'd move reusable code into a separate project and bundle it into your application as a JAR file. With Java 9 modules, you now have a new aspect to consider that significantly impacts the design process. Irrespective of whether you are creating a new application from scratch or you are migrating an existing classpath application into a modular application, there are some common questions you'll need to answer--How do you come up with a modular design? How do you choose what a module should be? How much code and functionality should be in a module? Where do you draw module boundaries in specific scenarios? For example, a question you might often run into is--Given a functionality or a set of classes and packages, should they belong to *Module A* or *Module B*? And how do you achieve good design principles for modules such as reusability, extensibility and maintainability?

As with most software design challenges, there are no right answers that apply for all scenarios. In fact, some of the -ility factors pull against each other, and most designs involve making a calculated trade-off. However, having some guidelines and best practices should get us started with tackling these challenges that can then be refined and tweaked as per specific use cases.

Among the first steps in designing and building a modular application, it helps to have a high level idea of what the modules and APIs will be. For simple projects, it can be tempting to just fire off the IDE and start coding. But for anything serious, it helps to spend some time and design a rough picture of the modules involved, their public APIs and their dependencies on each other before you start coding. Let's start looking at some principles and factors to keep in mind when designing modules and deciding what it should do.

Scoping

Perhaps the most obvious way of deciding what makes a module is based on what it is about. In other words, its *scope*. If you were to break down any reasonably complex application, you'd immediately come up with high level functional areas that begin to separate out from each other. For instance, a banking application might have account related functionality that's separate from credit functionality and so on. In the case of existing Java applications, these different concerns might already be under different top-level packages. In the case of new applications, the various aspects of the business problem can give us clues. Distinct business areas stand out to form an initial high level classification, which can then perhaps be broken down into further chunks. So, in our banking example, account functionality might be split into savings and checking account functionality, account transfer related code, bill pay, and so on. This way of using the business concern to break down the application problem domain is a good strategy to get to smaller units that can then be good candidates for modules. You'll likely have to go through several levels of breaking down the scope until you arrive at a level where each unit feels like they could be separate modules.

Note that, while this is a good strategy to start breaking the problem in a top-down manner, it doesn't help you decide when to stop breaking things down! How do you know if your modules are too big? Or too fragmented? You'll have to look at other factors in this section to help make that decision.

Team structure

There's a popular adage in software design called **Conway's Law**, which suggests that the design of software in any organization is influenced by the structure of teams in the organization and the way they communicate with each other. It makes perfect sense if you think about it. Software development teams often tend to work on isolated libraries and code bases (or at least, code *areas*) that *talk* to other libraries and code bases developed by other teams. In a sense, there's almost a one-to-one mapping between teams and the set of code assets they work on. This can be a valuable factor that influences where module boundaries are drawn and how modules designs begin to separate from one another. Each team works on one or more modules, and so all the code that a given team would work on becomes a part of their set of modules.

This is useful for a variety of reasons. Teams can work on their code and ship out functionality independent of other teams. They are assigned *ownership* of modules, so they can handle bug fixes or code maintenance. Additionally, when starting out a new project, when two teams need to work on modules where one depends on the other, both teams can together come up with an *API contract* that they agree with. Then, each team can work on their modules separately and in parallel, although the dependent modules are not yet available.

Reusability

One of the tenets of modularity is reusability. We earlier used the analogy of building blocks to describe modules. The idea of plugging in reusable modules together to create different applications is very powerful indeed! In order to make modules reusable, they should ideally have the following characteristics:

- They should have some specialized and limited responsibility. A module that does too many things is hard to reuse effectively.
- They should be independent--If a module depends on a whole lot of other modules to function, it becomes harder to reuse the module itself.
- It should be configurable--If the module is tweak-able and can be made to work for different use cases, it makes the module more amenable to reuse.

These characteristics do come with some trade-offs though! Here are a couple of them:

- Having smaller *specialized* or *single purpose* modules sometimes results in very small and fragmented modules, often requiring multiple modules to get anything done.
- Configurable APIs in modules often results in more complicated APIs, since the consumers have to deal with more knobs and levers to tweak and operate in order to work with your module. One way to get around this problem is to provide sensible defaults and provide configuration just as an override.

Modularizing by concerns

When designing modules, it'll be quickly apparent to you that not all modules are alike. Modules can be classified into multiple different types depending on various characteristics. One such classification can be achieved by their functionality or the concerns they address. At the highest level, you can classify modules into two different types:

- **Vertical concerns**: Business and application specific functionality. Solves a specific problem in the business domain. For example, the accounts module in a banking application.
- **Horizontal concerns**: Crosscutting functionalities that are not business or application specific. Instead, they provide low level functionality or framework that's business-agnostic. For example, logging or security modules.

When designing modules, a good rule to try and follow is to not mix these two concerns. If you design modules specifically for one of the two concerns, it improves clarity and reuse. For example, in the address book application, the module `packt.sortutil` provided generic sorting ability while being completely agnostic of what it's sorting, thereby addresses a horizontal concern. The module `packt.addressbook` deals with specific address book application functionality, thereby addressing a vertical concern.

As you can imagine, the type of module influences its design. For instance, reusability wouldn't likely be a primary focus when designing a module addressing a vertical concern, but it's vital when designing a module with cross-cutting concerns.

Modularizing by layers

Another useful factor that can help us draw module boundaries is application layers. A typical application involves layers or tiers of functionality like the UI layer, business layer, data layer, and so on. That's a great way to draw some initial module boundaries before then looking at other categories to modularize further. A module should ideally not be a part of multiple application tiers. Sometimes, different tiers are deployed on different physical hardware. So, having tier separations guide module boundaries make logistical sense as well when it comes to deployments.

Modularizing by change patterns

An approach that I've found helpful to verify module boundaries is analyzing patterns of new feature additions to your application. If most of the typical changes you make to your code base involves having to modify multiple modules, that might be a clue that your modules are too fragmented or the separation of modules could be better. It's OK if you are modifying multiple low-level modules (that is, with horizontal concerns) for an average code change or enhancement. But if each change or enhancement to your application requires you to modify too many modules with vertical concerns, you might want to re-look at the module boundaries and see if those different modules contain code that should ideally be together in the same module.

Designing API

We've looked at some guidelines and tips for drawing module boundaries and creating modules. How about the process of creating APIs? This might seem obvious, but the standard best practice of a separate public API and private implementation still applies here.

The goal when designing the module API is to expose a standard, consistent, and possibly unchanging programming interface as the **public** API of the module. The details of implementation that are internal to the module should be encapsulated. This is, in principle, no different from method and member variable encapsulation for classes. Design a public API for your modules that you want the consumers to work with. The implementation details are hidden in encapsulated packages and serve two purposes:

- To reduce and simplify effort for the consumer so that they don't have to know the internals
- To allow the module to change and evolve the implementation without having an impact on the consumers of the module

Java modules coding patterns and strategies

We've so far looked at some general higher level, almost common-sensical patterns, that apply to modularity in Java. Now let's dive into code. Let's look at some code patterns and strategies that can help you as you as you start designing modules and their APIs. Each of these strategies are presented with explanation about the pattern, why and when you should consider using them. Many of them have accompanying code examples for you to refer to. Some of these might be obvious. In fact, we've even applied some of the patterns when building the sample address book application we've worked on in this book. I hope this consolidated list provides you with a good reference to these patterns when designing and building modular applications.

Pattern 1 - Public interface, private implementation, and factory class

Separate the public API from the internal encapsulated implementation (we've already seen this strategy implemented in the sorting utility module of the address book viewer application earlier in the book). Also, expose a factory API method that creates new instances of the interface.

Here's how it works:

- The exported types are interfaces or abstract classes that are as lightweight as possible.
- The classes that contain the actual logic implement the interfaces in the exported packages. These types are not exported. Thus, all the implementation details are safely hidden away.
- There are factory classes in the exposed packages that form the APIs. These create a new instance of the right implementation class. The return types of these factory APIs deal with interfaces only.

Example

A sample implementation of this pattern is available in the folder `09-module-patterns/01-seperate-interface-impl`. The module `pattern.one` has the interface `PublicInterface` exposed in the `pattern.one.external` package, while the implementation classes `PrivateImplA` and `PrivateImplB` are in the encapsulated `pattern.one.internal` package:

```
module pattern.one {
   exports pattern.one.external;
}
```

We'd like the consuming modules to access the private instances through the public interface type. To facilitate this, there's a factory class `Factory` exposed by the module. This class has a public method `getApiInstance` that takes in an argument and then based on the value, returns the right implementation class. In the sample code, there's a simple `boolean` flag that affects whether one implementation instance is returned over another, but in a real-world module, this selection criteria would be more meaningful to what's returned, as this is how the consumer picks the right API instance based on their requirements. The return type of the factory method is an instance of the public interface. Thus, the consumer module doesn't know about the implementation details:

```java
public class Factory {
   public PublicInterface getApiInstance(boolean selector) {
      if (selector) {
         return new PrivateImplA();
      }
      return new PrivateImplB();
   }
}
```

Benefits:

- Hides the details from the consumer so that they don't have to know the internals
- Allows you to change the implementation or add new implementation types without the consumers having to change the way they interact with the module

Pattern 2 - Services for multiple dynamic implementations

An alternative way to abstract implementation types is to use them as services. This is an extension of the previous pattern, but while ensuring more loosely coupled and dynamic implementations.

Here's how it works:

- There's a service interface module that exposes the service interface type.
- One or more *service* implementation modules provide implementations for that service using the `provides` clause in the module definition.
- The consumer module does not directly depend on the implementation modules. It `requires` only the service interface module and declares that it `uses` the service.
- Code in the consumer module looks up service instances using the `ServiceLoader` API.

Example

The sample code implementation is available at `09-module-patterns/02-services`. The `pattern.two.service` module exports the `PublicInterface`. It doesn't contain any implementation classes of its own:

```
module pattern.two.service {
  exports pattern.two.external;
}
```

Two implementation modules `pattern.two.implA` and `pattern.two.implB` both contain implementations of the service that are declared using `provides` in the module declaration. Both implementation modules `require` the service module `pattern.two.service` to access the interface. Here's how the module definition for one of the implementation modules looks like:

```
module pattern.two.implA {
  requires pattern.two.service;
  provides pattern.two.external.PublicInterface with
   pattern.two.implA.ImplA;
}
```

The consumer module also depends on the service interface module, and *not* on the implementation modules. The `uses` clause in the module definition indicates that the module will need to look up the service:

```
module consumer {
   requires pattern.two.service;
   uses pattern.two.external.PublicInterface;
}
```

Benefits:

- Provides an additional layer of abstraction between the service consumer and provider logic.
- Completely loose coupling between consumer and implementation modules. There's no hard-wired `requires` dependency on the implementation modules.
- Flexibility in the implementation options available. Modules can be dropped in the module path at runtime, and as long as they implement and provide the service interface, they can be plugged in to the application.

Pattern 3 - Optional dependencies

We've seen how Java did not have an option for reliable configuration up until Java 9. You could add or remove certain classes and JARs from the classpath before running and the application would still execute (or at least, starts executing)! There are some utility libraries and frameworks in Java that have made good use of this flexibility.

Consider the Spring Framework. Spring is a popular application framework that uses and orchestrates functionality across a lot of other dependent libraries and frameworks by scanning the classpath for available libraries that it can work with. If you'd like Spring to use some of these supported libraries, just dropping certain necessary jars into the classpath is enough for Spring to pick it up and use its functionality. And if you don't, the Spring framework can still function without them, albeit without the optional functionality.

This flexibility plays an important role in the ease of use of these frameworks. Now, with Java 9 and strict requirements for module dependencies, wouldn't we be losing this flexibility? There's no optionally dropping jars into the classpath anymore! Things are much more strict and controlled now. Every module that a given module needs should be explicitly specified with a `requires` clause in the module definition. Given this new state of affairs, how could you build such modules that are optional and with *drop-in* flexibility?

The answer is optional dependencies. In Java 9, you can specify a given module dependency as optional by using the `requires static` qualifier. The syntax is:

```
module <module-name> {
   ...
   requires static <optional-module-dependency>;
}
```

The `static` qualifier tells the module system that the module `required` is optional. The module should still be available at compile time (because `javac` needs to compile the code and references after all!). But it is optional at runtime. If the module isn't available during runtime, `java` won't complain about the module's unavailability like it would with the `requires` only clause. It proceeds with execution assuming you know what you are doing. This new feature enables you to have modules with a bunch of `require static` optional dependencies, which can be freely dropped into the module path.

Here's how it works:

- When you have a module that optionally depends on one or more modules, use the `requires static` clause to establish optional dependency in the module definition. If *module A* optionally requires *module B*, you specify `requires static B` in module A's definition.

- During development and compile time, you don't *have* to do anything different. You could use the exported types from the optional dependencies just like a regular `requires` dependency. As always, the module(s) with the optional dependency needs to be available at compile time for the code to compile.

- At runtime however, things are different. This time, you can execute your application irrespective of whether the module with the optional dependency is available or not. If the module is available, it gets picked up fine. But if it isn't, you get a `NoClassDefFound` error. While it's not mandatory, it's a good idea to write code to handle this error scenario, in case the module you optionally require isn't available.

Example

Consider the sample code at `09-module-patterns/03-optional-dependencies`. The `pattern.three` is a module that optionally requires `pattern.three.optlib`. It uses the optional library if available, but the module is perfectly happy if it isn't available at runtime. To establish this optional nature of this dependency, `pattern.three` uses the `requires static` clause:

```
module pattern.three {
   requires static pattern.three.optlib;
   exports pattern.three.external;
}
```

The `pattern.three.optlib` has a simple library class that prints a message to the console. Nothing surprising here:

```
public class LibImpl {
   public void publicApi() {
      System.out.println("Called API method in LibImpl");
   }
}
```

Now, the code in the module `pattern.three` can directly import and use the exported types of the optional module (in this case, `LibImpl`). But this is not a good idea. By specifying that a dependency is optional, you are essentially asking the platform to let go of its reliable configuration guarantee and to *not* check and ensure that the module is available. This opens the possibility that this dependency is not satisfied at runtime. For this reason, it's the responsibility of the module now to be able to handle both the presence and absence of the module. Rather than have the `NoClassDefFound` error thrown to the user, we can be smart about using the optional types only if they are available. We can use the `Class.forName` API to examine if the class does exist.

This is the code in the `Util` class in module `pattern.three`. This is one way to reflect and use the types from optional dependencies:

```
try {
   Class<?> clazz = Class.forName("pattern.three.lib.LibImpl");
   LibImpl impl = (LibImpl) clazz.getConstructor()
                  .newInstance(); // Create new instance
   impl.publicApi(); // Call the API
} catch (ReflectiveOperationException e) {
   System.out.println("Did not find the Impl class module");
}
```

As with the previous examples, we have a `consumer` module that requires `pattern.three` and has a `Main` type that calls the module's API. Before executing the application, here's another important thing for you to know about optional dependencies. They don't get picked up in the module resolution process! So, we'll have to explicitly add the module to the execution process.

In `Chapter 8`, *Understanding Linking and Using jlink,* we discussed the module resolution process and how the Java Platform resolves the tree of dependencies by recursively fetching all dependent modules that are required in the module definition. It doesn't do that for optional dependencies! During the module resolution process, if the runtime encounters the `requires static` dependency, it does not resolve that module and its dependencies. These optional modules could be compiled and ready, sitting in the module path along with the other modules, but the runtime still doesn't see it. This brings up an interesting problem. How does the Java runtime know that these optional modules exist in the module path if it doesn't even look it up?

The solution is to add the modules manually into the module resolution process. Remember the `--add-modules` option we passed to `jlink` in `Chapter 8`, *Understanding Linking and Using jlink*? We used that flag to have `jlink` include modules to the resolution process.
The `java` command too has that flag available to include modules. So, to have the runtime *see* and use the optional modules, we'll need to add it using the `--add-modules` flag.

You can compile the example code with the `javac` command as usual. No changes here:

```
$ javac --module-source-path src -p src -d out $(find . -name '*.java')
```

When running, however, you need to add all the modules that are optional dependencies using the `--add-modules` flag. Here, `pattern.three.optlib` is the optional dependency. So, here's the command you use to execute the `Main` class in the `consumer` module and the resulting output:

```
$ java --module-path out --add-modules pattern.three.optlib -m
  consumer/app.Main

Called API method in LibImpl
```

Try removing the compiled `pattern.three.optlib` module from the `out` directory and run it again without the `-add-modules` option:

```
$ java --module-path out -m consumer/app.Main

Did not find the Impl class module
```

This time, you get the *fallback* code executed because the necessary class isn't available. The important distinction here is that the code still runs. It wouldn't have if the dependency wasn't optional.

> The `--add-modules` parameter is sensitive to the order, in that it should appear *before* the `-m` parameter. So, the following command will not work:
>
> ```
> java --module-path out -m consumer/app.Main --add-modules
> out/pattern.three.optlib # Doesn't work
> ```

Benefits:

- Allows you to create libraries that are *plug-and-play*. You can create a *main* library module that depends on additional modules optionally, thereby providing runtime flexibility in the modules and functionality that are actually a part of the execution.

Pattern 4 - Optional dependencies using services

While reading about optional module dependencies, a thought might have occurred to you--how about using services? We've learned in `Chapter 7`, *Introducing Services*, about how using services in Java modules provides a flexible and loosely coupled way of having modules work with each other. With services, you don't have to specify a readability relationship with `requires`. Modules that provide services are optional, not just in runtime, but also during compile time! So aren't services already better than optional dependencies?

The simple answer is yes. Services are definitely the preferred way of decoupling modules and removing *hard* dependencies. This is what we'll examine in this pattern. However, they do have a problem and won't work as well as you'd imagine. Let's explore why.

Here's how it works:

When using services, you typically achieve abstraction by creating two types--the interface (which *is* the service) and the implementations of the interface (which are the providers of the service). You don't *have* to do this, of course. You can have a Java class itself be the service type. But what we are discussing now applies to that too.

Given two modules A and B, if you'd like module A to optionally depend on B, you could use the previous pattern and use `requires static B` in the module definition of A. However, if you'd like to use services, you'll need to assign one or more Java interfaces or classes as *service types*. The `module A` needs to specify that it `uses` these types:

```
module A {
   uses <service-type>;
}
```

And `module B` needs to `provide` the services:

```
module B {
   provides <service-type> with <implementation-type>;
}
```

Now, B is technically optional. The application can run irrespective of whether module B exists in the module path or not! Seems simple enough, doesn't it? But there's a catch! Which module should the service type reside in? Is it module A or module B? It cannot be module B, because in that case, module A would need to *require* module B to access the service type in B, which defeats the whole purpose of making B optional! It could reside in module A, but now module B should depend on module A to access the service type. Thus module B `requires` A and module A `exports` the package containing the service type.

But wait! Our original goal was to make module A optionally depend on B. What we've ended up with now is module B depending on A! That seems the wrong way around, but if you think about the service dynamic, A is still using the implementation provided by B, and B is only dependent on A to get the service type. It is still confusing and it's not obvious what's going on just by looking at the module definitions. One way to solve the problem is to move the service types to a third `module C` which is required by both A and B. Now both A and B have access to the service types, and thus, are fully decoupled. This option might not always be feasible, and it is awkward to have a separate module just to solve this problem. But when it *is* possible, this approach of using services is one of the best ways to achieve flexibility and the *drop-anything-you-need* mechanism that exists with some libraries and frameworks in Java 8 and earlier.

Example

Look at the sample code at `09-module-patterns/04-optional-dependencies-with-services`. We have two modules, `pattern.four` and `pattern.four.optlib`. We want `pattern.four` to optionally depend on `pattern.four.optlib` using the services pattern we've seen so far.

The module `pattern.four` contains a service type `LibInterface` that it exports. It also declares that it uses provider implementations of `LibInterface`, which is what essentially makes `LibInterface` a service type:

```
module pattern.four {
    exports pattern.four.external;
    uses pattern.four.external.LibInterface;
}
```

The module `pattern.four.optlib` provides an implementation of the `LibInterface` service type. It also depends on `pattern.four` to access the service type in the first place. This is the seemingly inverted relationship we discussed earlier:

```
module pattern.four.optlib {
    requires pattern.four;
    provides pattern.four.external.LibInterface with
     pattern.four.lib.LibImpl;
}
```

There's a class `LibImpl` in `pattern.four.optlib` that implements `LibInterface` as declared in the preceding module definition:

```
public class LibImpl implements LibInterface {
    public void publicApi() {
        System.out.println("Called API method in Service");
    }
}
```

The module `pattern.four` is now totally unaware of `pattern.four.optlib`. It uses the `ServiceLoader` API to get any available instances, and if the optional module is available, it's happy to use it:

```
public class Util {
    public void utilMethod() {
        Iterable<LibInterface> libInstances =
            ServiceLoader.load(LibInterface.class);
        for (LibInterface libInstance : libInstances) {
            libInstance.publicApi();
        }
```

```
        }
    }
```

Benefits:

- Extends the *plug-and-play* concept that the previous pattern solved and adds a new level of decoupling. Modules can be optional both at compile time and runtime!
- Extends the one-to-one dependency of `requires static` with the services providing one-to-many dependency. There could be multiple modules providing services that are optionally picked up by the module using the services.

Pattern 6 - Bundle model classes as separate sharable modules

It's common for many enterprise applications to deal with multiple layers and tiers. They usually need to communicate and share data among them, and a frequently used pattern is to exchange data using model objects or **Data Transfer Objects** (**DTOs**). They are an example of code that needs to be shared across multiple layers and modules.

A good pattern to follow is to create separate modules just for the model (or DTO) classes. These modules can then be read by any module that needs access to those types. This could be a lightweight module containing just the model classes and not much else.

Pattern 7 - Open modules for reflection

Reflection is an important feature in the Java programming language, allowing the ability to inspect and modify types dynamically at runtime. This is another feature that has been put to good use by frameworks such as Spring, Hibernate, and others. These frameworks use reflection to examine your classes for annotations and interface implementations to infer information about how to treat your code. You might use reflection in your own code to achieve this dynamic functionality.

How does reflection fit into the concepts of modularity we've learned so far? Like we've seen before, the default behavior of strong encapsulation that protects types in a module from static access offers similar protection for reflective access as well. A Java type can be accessed through reflection if it's in a module that exports it, and the type calling the reflection API is in a module that reads the other module.

This results in a potential problem because of how reflection has been traditionally used in Java, especially in many of the frameworks like we've mentioned earlier. Frameworks like Spring expect to scan through your entire code base looking for classes that are annotated with certain key annotations. A lot of reflection API usage in Java code bases over the years have been implemented with an implicit understanding that the classes being reflected on are available for them to access. Once you move those types into modules, all the encapsulated types are effectively sealed off and not available for reflection. One easy solution is to expose everything! So, every module exposes all types that need to be accessed reflectively. But this is not a good idea because of the concept of the module API we've discussed earlier. The type that a module exposes using the `exports` clause is the module API. By exposing an otherwise private type just because it contains an annotation for the Spring framework, Hibernate, JPA, or any other such framework that uses reflection, we are adversely impacting the API of the module and the purpose of string encapsulation is defeated.

To address this issue and to still provide an option of using reflection with such frameworks, the platform has introduced a concept called **open modules**. These are a type of Java modules that still encapsulate types like we are familiar with, but with one major difference. The encapsulated types in these open modules are available for reflective access at runtime, without you having to allow compile-time access that an `exports` declaration would have provided.

How do you make a Java module an *open module*? Very simple. Just add the `open` keyword in front of the module definition in `module-info.java`:

```
open module <module-name> {
}
```

With this, the contents of the module are still encapsulated (except for any packages that you `export` in the module definition). But all the packages in the module are now available for access at runtime using reflection by any module that reads this module.

 Remember that the `open` keyword doesn't make the module open for reflective access for all modules. A module that needs to access any such types using reflection will still need to *read* the module that contains the type using the `requires` keyword.

Not only entire modules, but even individual packages can be marked as open with the `opens` keyword followed by the specific package you'd like to open for reflection. This provides more fine-grained control when you know that there are only certain classes in the module that need to be reflected upon:

```
module modulename {
  opens package.one;
  opens package.two to anothermodule;
  exports package.three;
}
```

In the preceding example, the package `package.one` is available for reflection by all modules that read module `modulename`. The package `package.two` is available for reflective access only by module `anothermodule`, if it chooses to *require* it. And package `package.three` is available for both reflective and compile-time access because it is exported.

Example

In the sample code at `09-module-patterns/06-open-modules`, the module `pattern.six` contains the type `Contact.java` in the package `pattern.six.internal`. Let's assume we'd like for this class to be internal to the module and not exposed. However, we'd like to be able to access the `Contact` class reflectively from another module `consumer`.

Here's the code in the `consumer` module that is doing reflection:

```
try {
  Class clazz = Class.forName("pattern.six.internal.Contact");
  Constructor<?> ctor = clazz.getConstructor();
  Object object = ctor.newInstance(new Object[] {  });
  System.out.println("Successfully created object using
    reflection");
} catch (ReflectiveOperationException e) {
    System.out.println("Did not find the Impl class module");
}
```

The consumer module establishes a dependency on the module `pattern.six` first:

```
module consumer {
  requires pattern.six;
}
```

But that's not enough! The module `pattern.six` should either export the type or declare that it's an open module.

Here's how the module definition for `pattern.six` looks like:

```
open module pattern.six {
}
```

Notice that the contents of the module aren't technically exported, so the types in the module are still encapsulated for static access. However, since the module is open, the types are available for reflection. Running `Main` in the `consumer` module should work now.

Benefits:

- Allows selective exposing types for reflection only.
- Useful for situations where the types need to be *scanned* for annotations and implementations by application frameworks and libraries that use that approach. For example, packages in modules containing Spring or Hibernate annotations can be declared as open to make them accessible by such frameworks. You can now do that while still maintaining encapsulation for traditional access.

Remember that with the `open` and `opens` declarations, you are technically letting go of strict encapsulation by allowing packages to be accessed reflectively. This is still a good option, and at least, much better than exporting packages, when all you want to enable is reflective access. The intent is made clear to the consumers of your module.

Pattern 8 - Use tooling for version control

As discussed in `Chapter 3`, *Handling Inter-Module Dependencies*, one important feature of most module systems is conspicuously absent in Java modularity--that of module versioning and version management. If you've dealt with build and packaging tools in the Java ecosystem such as Maven and Gradle, you might have come across the fact that all their library artifacts have version numbers associated with them. With Maven or Gradle, when you establish a dependency on another artifact or library module (and I'm using the word module loosely here), you not only have to specify its name and coordinates, you also have to specify its version number.

With Java module dependencies, there's no way to specify version-based dependency. The `requires` syntax, `requires <module-name>;` just accepts the module name, and not the version. For example, you can specify that your module depends on the `google.guava` module. But you cannot specify that it depends on version `1.5.2` of `google.guava`. The Java Platform Module System specification clearly states that versioning isn't one of the goals of the module specification. The idea is to leverage the existing build tools and containers to solve this problem, which they have already done in earlier versions of Java.

If you are not familiar with what the build tools such as Maven or Gradle do, their job in *pulling in* dependencies can be classified into two parts. I am simplifying, of course, but at a high level, these tools do the following:

1. Provide a way for each project to specify what other libraries they are dependent on.
2. Pull in those libraries during build and adding the JARs to the classpath so that the project that needs them has the necessary libraries available to use. These JARs are typically downloaded from a central repository based on the dependencies and version numbers specified.

Because tools such as Maven and Gradle does #2 above, it is essential for them to have all the details--not only which library to download, but also which version of the library to download. Remember, it needs to download the right jar from a repository with thousands of libraries with multiple versions of each. The Java module system does #1 but not #2, but not for the purposes of fetching or downloading artifacts from somewhere. It just assumes the modules are already there! This is why versions do not apply here. The version of the module you have in the module path is the version that will be used.

This is where something like Maven fundamentally differs from JPMS. The build tools deal with build artifacts--downloading and assembling packaged jar file distributables. A Java module is not a build-time artifact, but a compile time and runtime artifact. Maven concerns with making sure the right dependencies are assembled. The Java Module system is concerned with compile and runtime integrity of binaries that have already been assembled.

This allows the option of using build tools such as Maven or Gradle to download the right versions of modular JAR files and dependencies, thereby leaving the fully prepared set of modules available in the module path for the module system to then take over and use.

We'll look at Maven integration with Java 9 modular applications in much more detail in `Chapter 12`, *Using Build Tools and Testing Java Modules*.

Do not use version numbers in your module names. It is very tempting to create multiple modules with the version numbers trailing the names-- with module names such as `my.module.v1`, `my.module.v2`, and so on. This is not recommended because this does not provide any indication about the relationship and the similarities between two different versions of the same module, and is essentially a *hack* to get versioning to work with Java modules. A much better way is to let a build system bring in the right version of modules as discussed, and the platform does not have to deal with versioning.

Pattern 9 - Design for changes

As with building any API, you have to keep your users in mind when you'll eventually plan to change it. Thus, you'll have to keep possible future changes in mind when you design it! The exported packages in your module are the public API, so your users could be accessing any of them. This means that changing any types in the exported packages of your module will need to be approached with caution, as it could potentially break any consumers of your module.

Of course, this depends on the change itself. If you are adding a new type to an exported package, or are adding new member variables or methods to existing exported types, the changes are still backward compatible. But if you want to remove member variables from exported types or change method signatures, you end up breaking code that uses those APIs.

Here are some guidelines that help minimize possible changes to module APIs:

- Keep the exported types as lightweight as possible. We've already seen how you can expose interface types that are backed by encapsulated implementation types. Having lesser moving parts in exposed types makes them less likely to change in future.
- When you plan to make backward incompatible changes, plan to give your module consumers a heads up. This could be in the form of the `@Deprecated` annotation on the methods that you plan to remove, for example. If possible, try to provide both the old and new APIs together (with clear deprecation notices on the old APIs) so that the consumers of your module have enough time to switch their code to use your new APIs.

The `@Deprecated` annotation in Java 9 can be used on a module declaration too! This is very handy when you want to mark a complete module for deprecation. Here's an example:

```
@Deprecated(since = "9", forRemoval = true)
module mymodule {
}
```

This marks the module as deprecated from Java 9 onward, and also that it could be a removed in any future release. If any module tries to use your module with a `requires`, the compiler will issue a warning about the deprecation.

Pattern 10 - Protect against dependency leakage

In `Chapter 5`, *Using Platform APIs*, we've looked at how dependent types can be leaked by an API and it may not be very obvious it's doing so. The best practice to follow is to make the usage of your module as lightweight as possible. Ideally, using your module should be as simple as adding a `requires` clause for the module and then just using it!

Here are some guidelines to follow:

- Make sure your module is self-sufficient. You shouldn't need to depend on another module to use it.
- If your module's APIs need to return types that are a part of another module, try to encapsulate them into types that are exposed in your own module. If your APIs could throw exceptions that are a part of another module, try to catch them and re-throw custom exceptions that are exposed by your module.
- If using your module's APIs requires usage of types in other modules and cannot be wrapped like mentioned previously, make sure those modules have transitive dependency so that the consumers of your module automatically get them.

As the third guideline implies, sometimes you may want to enable transitive dependencies and allow types from other modules to be a part of your module's APIs. As with most best practices, you will need to examine this on a case-by-case basis as there is no right answer that applies in all situations.

A note of caution, however. Once you establish a transitive dependency in your module on another module, it is very easy for those types to creep into your APIs. For example, let's say you are working on module **A** that exposes a bunch of different APIs. Assume that the usage of one of those APIs requires a type from module **B** and it just cannot be avoided. The solution is to have a transitive dependency on module **B**, so that any consumer of your module also gets the type from **B**:

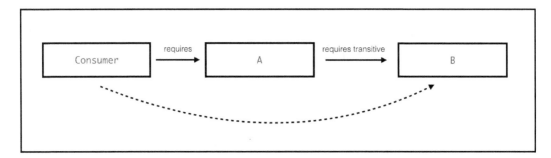

Now, once the transitive dependency is established, you can very easily build new APIs in module **A** that also require types from **B**. **B** is transitive anyway, so the consumer already has access to those types. So, there's no need to prevent that or wrap those types from **B** anymore, is there? Well, this is a slippery slope! The more types of a transitive module you use, the more coupled that module becomes to your own. It's harder to decouple it if you choose to refactor module **A** in the future, perhaps to remove the dependency on **B**. This is why I would still recommend wrapping types and preventing leakage of dependent types in your APIs even if those types are transitively available to the consuming module. The primary goal in designing a module should be to establish a purpose and an API for a module, and not to blindly add whatever `requires` declarations it takes just to get things to work!

Pattern 11 - Aggregator and facade modules

We've looked at aggregator modules in Chapter 6, *Module Resolution, Readability, and Accessibility*. Aggregator modules allows us to create modules that consolidate a set of libraries that are commonly used so that the consumers can require just one aggregator module rather than the more tedious process of finding the right list of modules to require. Using aggregator modules is a good pattern to use when you have multiple modules in your application that need a standard set of dependencies to be *required*. This not only makes the process of establishing dependencies on new modules easier, it also allows you to change and update that list of dependencies in one place and have it reflected across all other modules in your application or organization.

Following is an example aggregator module that provides transitive dependency on three other modules:

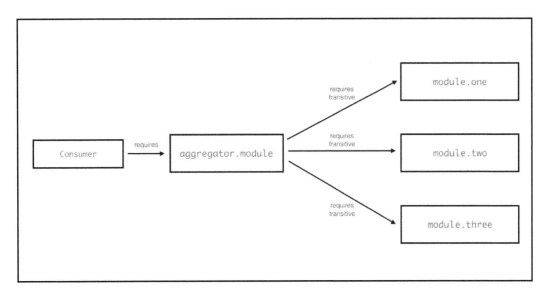

There's another pattern that's closely related that I like to call *facade modules*. These are an extension of aggregator modules in that they do offer dependencies to a group of modules using transitive dependencies, but they might also contain logic that deals with types from multiple modules. While aggregator modules just do transitive dependencies and do not necessarily contain logic of their own, the *facade module* might contain logic to do things like choose an API from one of the modules based on certain criteria, co-ordinate and synchronize calls across multiple module APIs, and so on.

Both aggregator and facade modules are designed for special use cases and act as *wrappers* around the underlying modules. Since they perform consolidation of modules for this reason, they may not offer the best reuse opportunities. But that's OK! Like we've discussed before, the best modules to facilitate reuse are simple single-purpose modules. However, aggregator and facade modules provide a middle ground between extremely fragmented modules that are pain to use and specialized modules that are easier to use but lack flexibility. A very handy pattern to use in such cases, when you are trying to strike that balance.

Example

In the sample code at 09-module-patterns/09-aggregator-and-facade-modules, the module pattern.nine.facade acts as an aggregator and facade module that consolidates two separate modules--module.one and module.two. It has a transitive dependency on both those modules, so any module that reads pattern.nine.facade also automatically reads those two modules:

```
module pattern.nine.facade {
   requires transitive module.one;
   requires transitive module.two;
   exports pattern.nine.external;
}
```

Not only does the module do that, it also has a thin *facade* API. There's a class it exports-- FacadeApi that has an example method to illustrate how a method can *choose* between two implementations. Here, the method chooses one of two implementations based on an input String value. But you can easily imagine facade APIs written in such a module that offer help around business rules or logic of your application that affects which libraries are used:

```
public void facadeMethod(String apiChoice) {
   if ("one".equals(apiChoice)) {
     apiOne.apiMethod();
   }
   else if ("two".equals(apiChoice)) {
     apiTwo.apiMethod();
   }
}
```

Now, the consumer module that reads pattern.nine.facade has two options. It can either access the library modules directly (And it can because of the transitive dependencies--it transitively reads both module.one and module.two). Or, it can call the API through the facade method to get help on which one to call. Both work perfectly fine, as you can see in the following code:

```
public static void main(String[] args) {
   FacadeApi facade = new FacadeApi();
   ApiTwo apiTwo = new ApiTwo();
   facade.facadeMethod("one"); // Calling the API through the facade
   apiTwo.apiMethod(); // Calling the other API directly
}
```

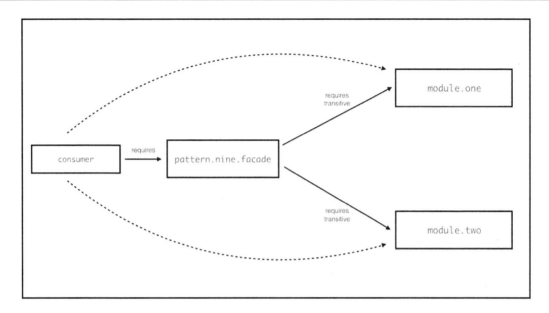

Summary

In this chapter, we've looked at some guidelines and best practices to create modules and identify module boundaries. When creating a new application or when migrating an existing legacy application to Java modules, it's always a good idea to have a map of the modules and their interactions designed in advance. We've looked at some best practices that let you figure out what a module should be made of and what would cause you to segregate logic into separate modules.

We then looked at a list of best practices and ideas to use in your code. Many of the best practices discussed previously come with simplified code examples. Each example is intentionally bare-bone with code that demonstrates just the pattern being discussed and little else, so that you can easily pick any of them up and tweak them further or apply them in your own code.

Now that we have these patterns in your tool belt, let's tackle a major challenge that Java developers will face when moving to Java 9, migration of existing code. There have been years and years of Java development and tons of legacy code of various complexities that has been built using earlier versions of Java. How do we approach moving them to take advantage of Java modules? Before that, would they even work with Java 9? Let's begin to answer those questions, as well as understand what it takes to get your code read for such a migration in the next chapter.

10
Preparing Your Code for Java 9

In the last chapter, we looked at several patterns and best practices to use when building Java 9 modular applications. They are an extremely handy set of rules to remember when building new applications. But it's not always that developers have the opportunity to work on greenfield projects where they have the freedom to think about and build application architecture from scratch. What if there's already a lot of code built using Java 8 or earlier? How do we migrate such code to Java 9?

In this chapter, we'll be covering:

- Working on legacy code and getting it ready to be run in Java 9
- Compiling legacy code in Java 9 and executing pre-Java 9 compiled code in the Java 9 runtime
- Classpath behaviors in Java 9 and the unnamed module
- Handling errors and non-standard API access and using the jdeps tool
- Using override switches to work around tricky code and APIs

Beginning Java 9 migration

You probably have some Java 8 (or earlier) code on your hands. And you are probably wondering what you'll need to do to get this to work with Java 9. When the Java 9 specification was going through the **Java Community Process** (**JCP**), there was some concerns in the developer community about just this. Will the legacy Java code work as-is in Java 9? If there are changes to be made, how much time and effort would they consume? Fortunately, Java has a great track record of maintaining backward compatibility, and that continues even with such major changes that have been brought into the language with the new modularity features. However, since Java 9 is one of the biggest overhauls to the Java internals, there might be some work that needs to be done. The amount of work depends primarily on two factors--the nature of migration you are trying to perform and the way the code itself is written.

Now what do I mean by *nature of migration*? When tackling Java 9 migration, it's useful to think about the effort in stages. At a high level, you could move your existing pre-Java 9 code through the following two stages:

1. Getting your code to compile and execute in Java 9 as-is.
2. Refactoring the structure of your code to use the modularity features.

Step 1 involves using the `javac` and the `java` commands on your existing code base just like you have done all along, but with the new Java 9 version of the compiler and runtime. In this phase you'd like to make as little changes to the code as possible! **Step 2** involves refactoring or rewriting your code to use modularity features, including the things we've learned so far in this book--breaking down the code base into modular units, creating `module-info.java` for each of those modules and then establishing relationships between the modules.

Are both these steps necessary for migrating to Java 9? Well, **Step 1** is. For any application that you plan to run and use in the foreseeable future, it's worth getting it to at least work with the new Java 9 runtime. That way, you are ready for whenever Java 8 becomes *end-of-lifed* in the future. This type of migration should be relatively easy, except for a few things to look out for that we'll cover in this chapter.

After you've done that, and your applications now work with Java 9 compiler and runtime, you do have an option of refactoring your code to use all the cool new modular features you've learned. But that may not always be valuable. If you have code that you don't plan to modify or enhance over time, and you just need to *maintain* it to run the business, you aren't going to get a lot of value by refactoring it to use Java 9 modules.

However, if you anticipate making changes and actively working on the code base, there is benefit to refactoring the code to use modules. The next chapter deals with migrating code that involves using the rich JPMS features we now get with Java 9.

 We'll be covering **Step 1** in this chapter. **Step 2** is covered in `Chapter 11`, *Migrating Your Code to Java 9*.

Introducing the sample Java 8 application

We will be using a sample Java 8 code base to try migrating to Java 9. It's a command-line `shopping bag` utility. When you run the application, it prompts you to add items to your shopping bag. Once you've added all the items and you are done, you type `end`. The application then displays a consolidated shopping list of items that you've added. The application is intentionally simple, but it gives us a good starting point to work through the migration.

Here's a screenshot of the application in action:

```
Jul 23, 2017 4:14:59 PM com.packt.sortstrings.app.App main
INFO: Shopping Bag application: Started
Enter item (Type 'end' when done): Processor
Enter item (Type 'end' when done): Motherboard
Enter item (Type 'end' when done): RAM stick
Enter item (Type 'end' when done): Liquid CPU Cooler
Enter item (Type 'end' when done): RAM stick
Enter item (Type 'end' when done): RAM stick
Enter item (Type 'end' when done): SSD card
Enter item (Type 'end' when done): Mid Tower Case
Enter item (Type 'end' when done): end

Shopping Bag Contents
-----------------------------
Processor    1
-----------------------------
RAM stick    3
-----------------------------
Motherboard    1
-----------------------------
SSD card    1
-----------------------------
Liquid CPU Cooler    1
-----------------------------
Mid Tower Case    1
-----------------------------
Jul 23, 2017 4:16:15 PM com.packt.sortstrings.app.App main
INFO: Shopping Bag application: Completed
```

The application consists of three classes in three different packages:

- The ShoppingBag class: It contains a method to add items to a shopping bag, and one to pretty print the contents of the bag. The class uses the Bag data structure from the Apache Commons Collections library. Think of this data structure as something similar to a Set, but with duplicates allowed:

```java
public class ShoppingBag  {
   public static String END_TOKEN = "end";
   private Bag<String> bag = new HashBag<>();
   public boolean addToBag(String itemName) {
      return (END_TOKEN.equals(itemName)) ||
       this.bag.add(itemName);
   }
   public void prettyPrintBag() {
      ...
   }

}
```

- The UserInputUtil class: It contains a method to prompt the user for an input. It also contains a public close method to close the input stream when done:

```java
public class UserInputUtil {
   Scanner scanner = new Scanner(System.in);
   public String getUserInput(String prompt) {
      System.out.print(prompt);
      return scanner.nextLine();
   }
   public void close() {
      scanner.close();
   }

}
```

- The App class: Putting it all together. This class has the main method. It uses the UserInputUtil to prompt the user to enter items into the shopping bag. It adds each item to a ShoppingBag instance, and it then prints the bag when done:

```java
public class App {

   private static final Logger logger =
      Logger.getLogger(App.class.getName());

   public static void main(String[] args) {
```

```
        logger.info("Shopping Bag application: Started");

        ShoppingBag shoppingBag = new ShoppingBag();
        UserInputUtil userInputUtil = new UserInputUtil();
        String itemName;
        do {
          itemName = userInputUtil.getUserInput("Enter item (
            Type '" + ShoppingBag.END_TOKEN + "' when done): ");
          shoppingBag.addToBag(itemName);
        } while (!ShoppingBag.END_TOKEN.equals(itemName));
        userInputUtil.close();
        shoppingBag.prettyPrintBag();
        logger.info("Shopping Bag application: Completed");
      }
    }
```

In addition to the application code, there's a `lib` folder with the Apache Commons Collection library JAR file--`commons-collections4-4.1.jar`. The code depends on this library JAR file. We'll need to add this JAR file to the classpath when compiling and running the code.

 I recommend looking at the included source code at the location `-10-migrating-application/01-legacy-app`and getting familiar with it. We'll be using this application as we work through the migration process.

Using the Java 9 compiler and runtime

Let's get started with the first step--compiling and running an old code base using the Java 9 compiler and runtime. It'll be great if things work as-is. If changes are required, we'd like to make as few of them as possible.

First, make sure you are using Java 9 using the following command. If you have a different version, you'll need to switch, as covered in Chapter 2, *Creating Your First Java Module*:

```
$ java --version
```

From the project folder, create a new out directory for our compiled classes and run the following Java compiler command to compile all the `.java` files:

```
$ mkdir out
$ javac -cp lib/commons-collections4-4.1.jar  -d out $(find . -name
  '*.java')
```

In the preceding `javac` command, we are adding the commons collections JAR file to the classpath using the `-cp` option, specifying the output directory for the compiled classes using the `-d` option and then specifying all the `.java` files in the following directories recursively using `$(find . -name '*.java')`.

The compilation step should go through fine without any errors. Great! Let's try to run it:

```
$ java -cp out:lib/commons-collections4-4.1.jar
  com.packt.sortstrings.app.App
```

In the preceding `java` command, we are specifying two paths in the classpath `-cp` option-- the `out` directory that contains the compiled classes and the common collections JAR file. Following that is the fully qualified class name of the class with the `main` method.

 Notice that we are still using classpath and not the concept of module path. Java 9 still works with classpath, and with the same `-cp` option as did the previous Java versions. More on that shortly.

Running the command should result in success, with the prompt being displayed as expected. And there you have it! A Java 8 application has compiled and executed using Java 9, and not a single line of code needed to be changed! As much as I'd love to tell you that all legacy code will work just as easily as this, it is unfortunately not true. There are some cases that need more effort. However, the good thing is that in the majority of the cases, this process *should* be this effortless. We'll look at some of the cases where you might run into problems, and how to address them in the next section. But first, knowing what we now know about Java 9, isn't it surprising that everything worked well? If you think about it, both the compilation and execution should have failed! Why? Here are a couple of reasons:

- We learned that Java 9 is moving to a module system and that *everything*, be it the application code or the platform, should be in a module! Our Java 8 code is obviously not in a predefined module. That's fine in Java 8, but shouldn't that have caused an error in Java 9?
- Notice that `App.java` is using the Java logging API. We've learned in `Chapter 4`, *Introducing the Modular JDK* that the logging APIs have been bundled into a separate platform module called `java.logging`. And all code that accesses any module that's not `java.base` should require it explicitly. That's clearly not happening in the code here, because this is Java 8 code, and there's no `module-info.java` module definition to begin with.

This begs the question--how did compiling and executing this code in Java 9 still work? It all works thanks to some special features introduced in the language to support this very process--executing legacy code in Java 9. The specific feature that's working for us here is called the **unnamed module**.

The unnamed module

Well, we weren't wrong. All code in Java 9 *needs* to be in modules. And all modules need to have the right readability and accessibility relationships for applications to work. But that might be problematic! Because, as with every new Java release, there are thousands of developers trying to run their legacy Java code bases using the new Java version. If we were to expect each legacy Java code base to be wrapped into modules before it can even run in Java 9, which would introduce a significant cost of effort in the developer community. Thankfully, there's a way out. When you are using Java 9 to compile or run legacy module-less Java code in the classpath, you *don't* have to manually create module wrappers yourself. The platform automatically creates a single module that comprises of everything you have in your classpath. This module doesn't have a name and so, is referred to as the *unnamed module*.

With all the Java 9 code we've compiled and executed so far, we've not been using the classpath at all. Here's a schematic of the modules in our Java 9 application as we've been running it so far:

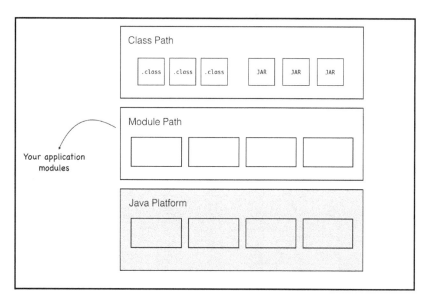

We've so far had the whole runtime work with built-in platform modules in the JRE along with your application modules from the module path. These together form the complete set of observable modules. Now what happens if you throw in the classpath in there? When running with the classpath option, here's how the picture looks like:

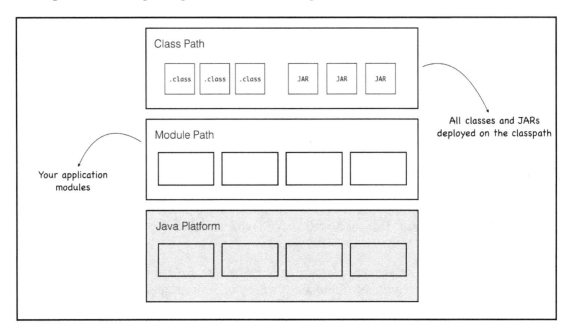

And here's where we would have violated the *all-code-needs-to-be-in-modules* rule. Thanks to the automatic module feature, we haven't. The Java 9 platform automatically wraps all the classes and JARs in the classpath into one unnamed module:

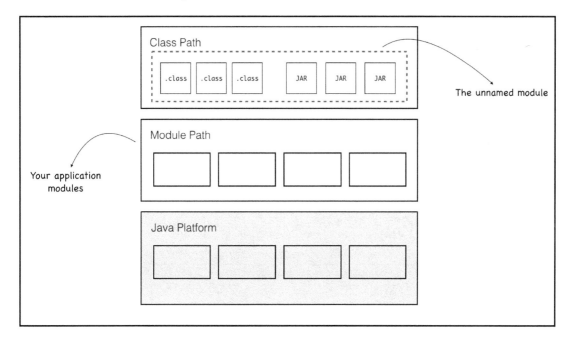

This is exactly what's happening to the shopping bag application. All the application code, including the common collections jar is a part of the single unnamed module. OK, that addresses one of the concerns. How about the second one? How did the code get access to the Java logging API? Shouldn't the unnamed module declare requires `java.logging`? But how could it? The unnamed module doesn't have a `module-info.java` file anyway! Because the platform cannot really tell for sure what the classpath code needs, the unnamed module is automatically given readability access to *all* observable modules. In other words, it mimics the *free-for-all* behavior of code in the classpath pre-Java 9--it `requires` everything, because that's the only way the platform can maximize the chances of any legacy code working as-is in Java 9. If you were to draw a module graph, it would look like the unnamed module has readability relationship to every module in the set of observable modules, as represented in the following diagram:

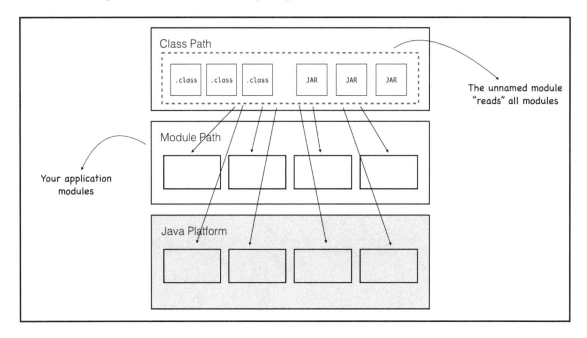

This diagram is very messy, so we'll not draw this again. From now on, we'll just simplify all the readability edges coming out of the automatic module into a single arrow to keep things legible.

The automatic module feature was built into the platform specifically for migration purposes, and as you can see, it's the reason why our Java 8 code was able to compile and run in Java 9 without any errors. To summarize:

- Every time you supply the `-classpath` option to compile or execute code in Java 9, the platform creates an unnamed module. All classes and jars in the supplied classpath are bundled into this unnamed module.
- The unnamed module automatically *reads* every observable module. Thus, not only does it read all the Java 9 platform modules, it also reads all your application and library modules in the module path (if you've supplied the module path argument to the command, in addition to the classpath.

 Every time you use the Java compiler without any module path options, you runs the compiler in what's referred to as a *single module mode*. In this mode, like we've seen, we are dealing with the single unnamed module. The code is expected to be organized into the traditional package-based directory structure, and there are no module folders.

Handling non-standard access

Wait! There's a catch! The unnamed module reads all Java platform modules and because of that, I mentioned it mimics the *free-for-all* behavior of the pre-Java 9 platform. But that's not exactly true. Pre-Java 9, the entire platform, and all the classes in it were accessible to your application code. With Java 9 platform modularization, there are several internal types in platform modules that are not exported, thus making them encapsulated. It's a good thing that the unnamed module automatically reads all platform modules by default, but is that enough? Not really, because it just enables the code in the classpath to access only the types *exported* from the modules. But what if your legacy code uses a type that is now encapsulated in a platform module in Java 9? Just having the unnamed module read all the platform modules is not enough, because the encapsulated types would still not be available. The same problem exists for code that accesses types that are removed. Yes, there are certain types in JDK 8 and earlier that are no longer available in Java 9. And any legacy code that uses such types will fail to compile and run in Java 9.

The code at `10-migrating-application/02-non-standard-api` is an example of a code with such access of internal types. The class `App.java` uses two types:

- `Base64Encoder` that was available in previous versions of Java, but now with Java 9, has been completely removed
- `CalendarUtils`, which is encapsulated as an internal type in the `java.base` module in Java 9

Even if you were creating a new Java 9 module, there's no platform module that your code can require to access it. The type is not exported from the module and so is effectively sealed. Thus, even the unnamed module would not be able to access them.

Here's the sample code. The code itself is completely non-functional as it is just an attempt to try using these two types:

```
package com.packt.app;
import sun.misc.BASE64Encoder;
import sun.util.calendar.CalendarUtils;

public class App {
  public static void main(String[] args) {
    BASE64Encoder enc = new BASE64Encoder();
    CalendarUtils.isGregorianLeapYear(2018);
  }
}
```

Switch to Java 8 compiler and compile the code:

```
$ export JAVA_HOME=$(/usr/libexec/java_home -v 1.8)
```

Notice that while the compilation goes through, you do see warnings!

```
$ javac -d out $(find . -name '*.java')
./src/packt/app/App.java:4: warning: BASE64Encoder is internal proprietary API and may be removed in a future release
import sun.misc.BASE64Encoder;
               ^
./src/packt/app/App.java:5: warning: CalendarUtils is internal proprietary API and may be removed in a future release
import sun.util.calendar.CalendarUtils;
                        ^
./src/packt/app/App.java:10: warning: BASE64Encoder is internal proprietary API and may be removed in a future release
        BASE64Encoder enc = new BASE64Encoder();
        ^
./src/packt/app/App.java:10: warning: BASE64Encoder is internal proprietary API and may be removed in a future release
        BASE64Encoder enc = new BASE64Encoder();
                                ^
./src/packt/app/App.java:11: warning: CalendarUtils is internal proprietary API and may be removed in a future release
        CalendarUtils.isGregorianLeapYear(2018);
        ^
5 warnings
```

For quite a while now, developers have been warned about such usages of internal types! For someone working on such code, it should not come as a surprise that these APIs don't work in Java 9.

Let's switch to Java 9 and compile this code. Use the following command on macOS or Linux:

```
$ export JAVA_HOME=$(/usr/libexec/java_home -v 1.9)
```

On Windows, follow the steps outlined in `Chapter 2`, *Creating Your First Java Module*.

After switching the Java version to 9, run the compile command on this code. This time, you don't get warnings. You get errors and the code doesn't compile:

```
$ javac -d out src/packt/app/App.java
src/packt/app/App.java:4: error: cannot find symbol
import sun.misc.BASE64Encoder;
               ^
  symbol:   class BASE64Encoder
  location: package sun.misc
src/packt/app/App.java:5: error: package sun.util.calendar is not visible
import sun.util.calendar.CalendarUtils;

  (package sun.util.calendar is declared in module java.base, which does not export it)
src/packt/app/App.java:10: error: cannot find symbol
                BASE64Encoder enc = new BASE64Encoder();
                ^
  symbol:   class BASE64Encoder
  location: class App
src/packt/app/App.java:10: error: cannot find symbol
                BASE64Encoder enc = new BASE64Encoder();
                                        ^
  symbol:   class BASE64Encoder
  location: class App
4 errors
```

Notice that there are two different errors, one for each type:

- The error for `CalendarUtils` indicates that the type is now encapsulated (that is, not exported) from `java.base`.
- The error for `BASE64Encoder` mentions that the compiler just doesn't find it. The type has been removed from Java 9.

When compiling and running legacy code in Java 9, these are two of the most likely errors you could get because of the modularity changes. Fixing either of these errors requires changing your code. You'll have to either find an equivalent class or API in the new platform that does what you need. Or find an external library that has the APIs you need. What's tricky is that the problematic code may not necessarily be in your application code. It could be in a library or a framework that you use. Even in that case, your application won't compile or run in Java 9, until you remove the dependency or the library is updated.

There is some help that the platform provides to help you identify such problems with your application and its dependencies. It's a tool called `jdeps`.

`jdeps` was first shipped with Java 8 to help developers identify and fix internal API access. With Java 9, it's much more helpful and detailed.

The jdeps tool

The **Java Dependency Analysis Tool** (**jdeps**) is a utility that can statically examine your application and library classes to identify if there are any uses of the JDK internal APIs that no longer work with Java 9. You can run `jdeps` on your compiled class files or JARs, and have it list out all such references. For each reference, `jdeps` will highlight usages of internal types that are no longer available for your code to use. It even suggests replacement APIs if they are available.

The command syntax looks like this:

```
$ jdeps -jdkinternals <jar-files>
```

If you have a bunch of classes compiled and you want to run `jdeps` on them, you can even provide a classpath parameter:

```
$ jdeps -jdkinternals -cp <class-paths>
```

Let's try this with the `02-non-standard-api` project. We've already compiled the project (albeit with warnings) with the Java 8 compiler, and the classes now exist in the out directory. Running `jdeps` on them yields the following output:

```
$ jdeps -jdkinternals -cp out/
out -> JDK removed internal API
out -> java.base
   com.packt.app.App                   -> sun.misc.BASE64Encoder              JDK internal API (JDK removed internal API)
   com.packt.app.App                   -> sun.util.calendar.CalendarUtils      JDK internal API (java.base)

Warning: JDK internal APIs are unsupported and private to JDK implementation that are
subject to be removed or changed incompatibly and could break your application.
Please modify your code to eliminate dependence on any JDK internal APIs.
For the most recent update on JDK internal API replacements, please check:
https://wiki.openjdk.java.net/display/JDK8/Java+Dependency+Analysis+Tool

JDK Internal API                       Suggested Replacement
----------------                       ---------------------
sun.misc.BASE64Encoder                 Use java.util.Base64 @since 1.8
```

`sun.misc.BASE64Encoder` is indicated as a *JDK removed internal API* while `sun.util.calendar.CalendarUtils` is indicated as a JDK internal API from `java.base`. In the case of `BASE64Encoder`, the tool provides a helpful suggestion to use an alternative API (`java.util.Base64`) that has been available in Java since version 1.8.

`jdeps` can also be run on JARs as previously mentioned. If we were to run the tool on the included `01-app-migration` project for example, we'll get no output. Which is a good thing because that means there are no JDK internals being used, and the JAR is good to use for Java 9:

```
$ jdeps -jdkinternals commons-collections4-4.1.jar
```

 `jdeps` is a *static* code analysis tool, with emphasis on the word *static*. It looks at the code to identify illegal API use. It cannot identify dynamic runtime use through reflection, for example. Thus, there is a chance that `jdeps` gives you the all-clear for a code base, but when you run it, you might still end up with an `IllegalAccessException` because the code uses reflection to access an internal type that's no longer available.

To summarize, `jdeps -jdkinternals` is a great tool to use to check your pre-compiled application and library classes and verify any incompatibilities with Java 9. It is especially helpful that the tool recommends alternative options to use when possible.

Overriding module behavior

`jdeps` is great at identifying internal API access and suggesting fixes. They come in handy when fixing your own application code that contains such problems. But what if `jdeps` reports problems with some code in a library or a framework you are using? In such cases, you have lesser control over the code. Even if the framework itself is open source, the scale and complexity of the library may not make it feasible for you to implement the fix yourself. This does present a very clear risk for applications moving to Java 9--your app won't run in Java 9 until all your libraries are updated to work in Java 9. It's very likely that most library developers have either already heeded to the scores of warnings in Java 8 and fixed their code, or they will soon, because of their code breaking in Java 9. But if they don't, this could mean that your migration plans are at the mercy of the library authors.

Thankfully, the platform comes with some override features to get around this problem. The override features we'll look at here apply not just to legacy Java code being compiled in Java 9, they also work on Java 9 modules. But since they are primarily designed to assist migration, they should be used in the context of migration only, and other uses should ideally be avoided.

What are these override features? Remember that a Java 9 module has a *module definition* that specifies what it `requires` and what it `exports`. These individual module definitions that are specified in the `module-info.java` file at development time essentially control the accessibility relationship between modules during compilation and runtime. However, it turns out, both the compiler and runtime has override options for these module relationships that allow you to change what any given module `requires` or `exports` by specifying command-line arguments.

There are three command line flags to `javac` and `java` to override specific module configurations:

- `add-reads`: The `--add-reads` option allows you to specify additional readability relationships that may not already be available for a module as per the module configuration. The syntax is:

```
--add-reads <source-module>=<target-module>
```

Adding this option to the `javac` and `java` command line creates a new readability relationship only for that command execution you use the argument for. For example, let's say you have modules `moduleA` and `moduleB`, and you want to have `moduleA` read `moduleB`. You can either edit the `module-info.java` file in `moduleA` and add the line `requires moduleB;`, or add the following argument to the compiler and runtime, as shown in this following truncated command:

```
$ java ... --add-reads moduleA=moduleB
```

- `add-exports`: The `--add-exports` option allows you to add additional exported packages from a module, thereby breaking or overriding encapsulation. The syntax is:

```
--add-exports <source-module>/<package-name>=<target-module>
```

- For example, if `moduleA` needs package `pack.internal` from `moduleB`, but `moduleB` does not export the package, you can add the following override to have `moduleB` export the required package for `moduleA`, as shown in this truncated command:

```
$ java ... --add-exports moduleB/pack.internal=moduleA
```

- `add-opens`: The `--add-opens` option lets you override the `opens` relationship between modules to allow reflective access. This is an override that simulates the `opens` keyword configuration in the module definition. The syntax is:

```
--add-opens <source-module>/<package-name>=<target-module>
```

- Following the same example, if `moduleA` needs runtime-only reflective access to the package `pack.internal` in `moduleB`, you would run the `javac` or `java` command with the following option:

```
$ java ... --add-opens moduleB/pack.internal=moduleA
```

Note that the overrides are always *qualified*, that is, you specify them for a specific target module. For example, you don't use the `--add-exports` flag to export a package to every other module. You explicitly specify one or more target modules that the override applies to from the source module. That's a good thing because every override is made consciously and it's easy to track what is needed to get the application to work.

There is another way to provide these overrides in addition to command line arguments. You can specify them inside JAR file manifests. Let's say you have an executable JAR file that needs some overrides to work with platform modules in Java 9. To avoid having to specify these overrides everytime as command line arguments, you could just specify these as manifest attributes in the `MANIFEST.MF` file in your JAR file. As with all manifest attributes, the value should be specified following a space after the attribute name in the `MANIFEST.MF` file. The manifest attribute `Add-Exports` corresponds to the `--add-exports` argument. The attribute `Add-Opens` corresponds to `--add-opens`. There's no manifest attribute equivalent for `--add-reads`.

In addition to these overrides, there's a master *kill switch* for any modularity related encapsulation for classes in the classpath--the `--permit-illegal-access` flag. Unlike the previous three options, this option works only on code in the classpath. This flag, when passed to `javac` or `java` effectively disables *all* readability and accessibility restrictions, thus making any type accessible to any other type in the classpath. It's almost as if there are no Java modularity features, and everything in the classpath works as if you are running in Java 8 or earlier. As you'd expect, it's not a good idea to use this flag, especially if you are running code in production. This is provided to help developers migrate their classpath applications, and could very well be removed in the future. Think of this as a *last resort* option to get things to work as you work on migration.

Now that you've learned these override options, how can you apply them to solve the problem we started discussing this section with libraries or classes in your Java 8 code that use encapsulated APIs, and thus no longer work in Java 9? If the code is not in your control and you cannot fix it to *avoid* using the encapsulated types, you could use the override switch to manually add the required exports! For example, our code in the 02-non-standard-api used an internal non-exported type CalendarUtils from java.base. Since we obviously cannot change the module descriptor for the java.base module, what we could instead do is pass the --add-exports option to the module and have it export the required packages.

But here's a problem. Note that the syntax needs the source and target module names. The source module name is java.base of course. What is the target module? It's the unnamed module, because it's the classes in the classpath that needs this package. This brings up an interesting question--what is the name of the unnamed module? The unnamed module doesn't have a name (or indeed it wouldn't be called that!), but there's a special token called ALL-UNNAMED that you can pass to the override arguments that let the platform know that you are referring to the unnamed module:

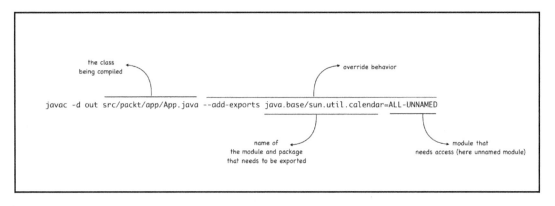

This command should solve the problem of the CalendarUtils access in our code. There's still the missing BASE64Encoder type. There's no command-line argument to fix that one. Like we've seen, the type simply doesn't exist in Java 9. We'll have to replace it with something that does. Taking the suggestion provided by jdeps, the class AppFixed.java has the updated code that uses the Base64class instead:

```
$ javac -d out src/packt/app/AppFixed.java --add-exports java.base/sun.util.calendar=ALL-UNNAMED
src/packt/app/AppFixed.java:6: warning: CalendarUtils is internal proprietary API and may be removed in a future release
import sun.util.calendar.CalendarUtils;
                        ^
src/packt/app/AppFixed.java:12: warning: CalendarUtils is internal proprietary API and may be removed in a future release
        CalendarUtils.isGregorianLeapYear(2018);
        ^
2 warnings
```

This time, you don't get errors and the compilation goes through. You still see the warning about using an internal type. The compiler still reminds you that it's not an ideal situation, but since you've added the override, it trusts that you know what you are doing.

If the code was complied in a previous version of Java and you were running it in Java 9 *and* the problem was only with accessing encapsulated types, you can add the same override arguments to the `java` command and have it run. However, if the compiled classes are referring to unavailable types, like the `BASE64Encoder` type we just looked at, you have no choice but to edit the code and recompile first.

Understanding the impact

Now that you know what are the possible problems you could face when compiling or running legacy code in Java 9, as well as how to solve those problems when they occur, let's spend some time understanding the scope of these problems. How worried should you be about having to encounter and fix these issues in your legacy Java code?

We can classify backward-incompatible APIs into the following broad categories:

- **APIs with replacements**: This link (also the link provided in the output of `jdeps --jdk-internals`) provides a complete list of APIs that need replacements in Java 9: `https://wiki.openjdk.java.net/display/JDK8/Java+Dependency+Analysis+Tool`.

- **Encapsulated APIs**: When you run `jdeps`, you might see errors about usage of internal JDK types that do not have replacement suggestions. They could just be types that were formerly available pre-Java 9 but are now encapsulated in a platform module. These are fixable by using the right command line overrides to the `javac` and `java` invocations.

On the other hand, there are certain APIs that were originally meant for removal, but they still happen to be available. While the intent has been to encapsulate all the internal JDK APIs, there have been a few APIs that have been so widely used in the Java developer community and for which there are no suitable replacements that encapsulating them would add so much more difficulty to the migration process. Remember the widely used `sun.misc.Unsafe` API we discussed in `Chapter 1`, *Introducing Java 9 Modularity*? Such APIs continue to be accessible in Java 9. But in order to make these APIs easier to deprecate later, they have been moved into a separate module called `jdk.unsupported`, from which these types can be accessed.

Running `java -d` on the `jdk.unsupported` module shows us the *unsupported* APIs that are still accessible for now:

```
$ java -d jdk.unsupported
jdk.unsupported@9
exports com.sun.nio.file
exports sun.misc
exports sun.reflect
requires java.base mandated
opens sun.reflect
opens sun.misc
```

A word of caution. The `jdk.unsupported` module and the APIs are very likely to be removed from the next versions of Java, so don't plan on relying on this module for too long.

Recommended strategy

Let's wrap up by outlining the recommended strategy for compiling and running your legacy code in Java 9. Here are the steps you'd ideally follow:

1. Run `jdeps --jdk-internals` to verify if your code has any internal API access. If there are no errors, just try compiling and running your code in Java 9. For the vast majority of cases, where there are no accesses to internal JDK APIs, the code should simply just work.
2. If there are errors and they are caused by your application code that you can change, follow the `jdeps` recommendation and fix those errors.
3. If the errors are caused by libraries that are not in your control, check if there are updates published by the library authors and get the latest versions. Many libraries that use internal APIs are being updated to work with Java 9, and the fix for your libraries might have already been done and published.
4. If none of the previous steps work, consider using the override options `--add-exports` or `--add-opens` to the platform APIs that you need internal access to. This is a short-term stop-gap arrangement until the offending code or library is fixed.

5. If none of these work, as a last resort, turn off all modularity features with the `--permit-illegal-access` kill switch. While it is not recommended (and you certainly don't want to deploy an app with this switch in production), it's a handy way to get started if you are being overwhelmed with compatibility issues. A cool feature of this switch is that when you run your code that makes any *illegal access*, it prints out a warning message. It can be very helpful to consolidate this information and plan to fix them later.

Summary

This chapter covered the first of the two phases of code migration to Java 9-- the process of compiling or running your pre-Java 9 code in Java 9. We used a sample Java 8 project (without any internal API access) in order to compile and execute it in Java 9. We then looked at a class with a couple of deliberate internal API access instances and saw what the error we'll encounter looks like. We learned about the `jdeps` tool and how to use it to statically scan your code base and identify such instances.

Once the instances have been identified, we covered a couple of ways to solve the problem-- using the suggested replacement APIs or using command-line flags to temporarily overcome the problem. We used both these options to get the previously failing code to compile and execute fine in Java 9. We then looked at a high level strategy to follow in order to complete the process of getting your legacy code to run in Java 9.

If you are working on code that you just need to maintain and are not likely to build on, this is where you could stop your migration journey. But, if you need to actively evolve the code, it's a good idea to go further than that. In the next chapter, we'll learn how to get it through the second phase of the Java 9 migration--to refactor it to use the Java 9 modularity features.

11
Migrating Your Code to Java 9

In the previous chapter, we looked at what it takes to start with a pre-Java 9 code base and have it compile or run with minimal changes in the new Java 9 platform. We also looked at some problems you could face with your legacy code and how to solve them.

If you are working on a code base that you expect to make many changes or enhancements to, then you'll want to do more than just run it in Java 9. You'll want to take advantage of the modularity features that Java 9 provides. Of course, you shouldn't always blindly rewrite your application to use modules just because you can! The advantages of modularity--strong encapsulation and reliable configuration--are the most useful in applications where there is a large code base with clear boundaries and multiple teams working on it. In this chapter, we'll take a look at how you can use those new modularity features and gradually introduce them to your pre-Java 9 codebase.

These are the topics we'll be covering in this chapter:

- Migration strategy for codebases
- Automatic modules
- Library migration
- Multi-release JARs

We'll be working on the shopping bag example that we've looked at in the previous chapter. We've got it compiling and running in the Java 9 platform. We'll now be adding modularity features to the code.

Now, how do you go about doing something like that? In the case of a small application, like the example code we are looking at, it is trivial to make a complete change across the application--you can split a small codebase into modules based on the roles that different types in your code performs. And then wrap the individual modules in modules with the right module definitions. Easy!

Unfortunately, most real-world applications are much larger and more complex. Thus, they cannot be modularized with a **big bang** approach. You'll have to gradually chunk away at it, moving portions of the application into modules. How would this work in an application where a portion of the code is modularized while the rest isn't? In addition, most applications, especially enterprise Java applications, use some kind of a framework or library to handle application infrastructure. What does Java 9 migration mean in those cases? Would the libraries need to be rewritten to use modules as well? Could you modularize your application while the libraries are not yet modularized? Before we answer these questions, let's first understand what the migration goal is. What are we trying to achieve?

Understanding the migration goal

Let's assume you are done with the steps in the previous chapter and your legacy code now complies or runs in Java 9. You are ready for the next step--to migrate your code to use Java 9 modules! What does that look like?

Here's a very high-level picture that shows the different elements of a typical pre-Java 9 application running on a Java 9 platform:

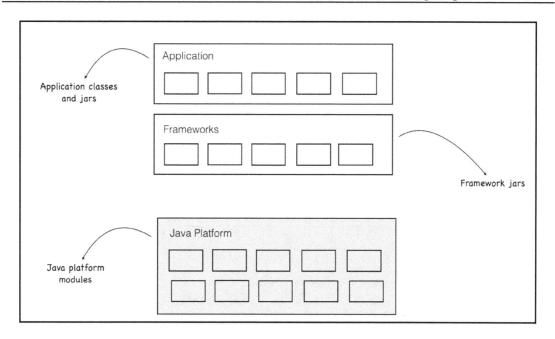

You can break a typical application down into three distinct layers. At the very top layer are the **application classes and jars**. Typical applications have a combination of **application classes and jars** along with any internal libraries, such as shared utility components. All of these are application specific. Since the application is yet to be migrated to Java 9, this layer consists of classes and jars in the classpath.

The second layer denotes any **frameworks** that the application might be using. It's very rare to find Java applications these days that do not use an application framework of some sort. Frameworks such as Spring, Vaadin, JSF, and Hibernate are very commonly used. These are typically bundled into the application as .jar files, either downloaded manually or through a dependency management utility such as Maven or Gradle. Will the libraries be in the classpath or the module path? It depends on the library, and if the authors have migrated it to Java 9. If the libraries are already migrated, all you need to do is simply add them to the module path! However, for the sake of this chapter, let's assume that the libraries are still not migrated, so that you know how to tackle the more complex scenario.

The third layer is the underlying **Java Platform** that powers it all. This, as we've seen in this book, is a fully modularized platform as of Java 9.

Since we are assuming that none of the application code or the libraries are Java 9 modules, they are primarily running in the class path, and the module path is completely empty. This is just the way we left our code at the end of the previous chapter. Here's the *before* picture:

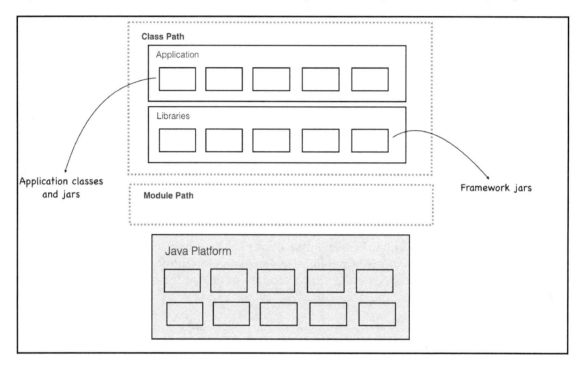

The goal is to create modules and move everything from the **classpath** into the **module path**. Once we are done, the **classpath** will be empty and everything that the application needs will run from the **module path**. Here's the ideal *after* picture:

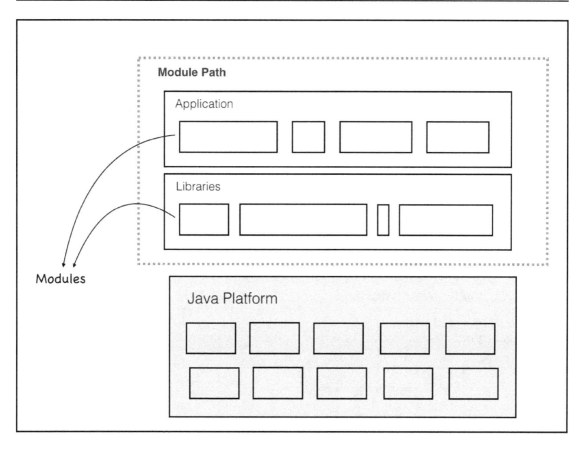

Notice that in the *after* picture, we aren't even using the **classpath** anymore. All the code and binaries we need are now converted to modules and made available in the **module path**. Thus, in an ideal world, there is no need to even pass the classpath argument! Also, notice that I have intentionally changed the representation of modules to random sizes. This is to highlight that there might not be a one-to-one mapping between the JARs and classes in the classpath to the converted modules. You might break a single JAR in your Java 8 application into multiple modules in Java 9 or merge multiple JARs into a single module.

Now that we have an idea about what the end goal is, let's look at the migration strategy.

Beginning the migration

Let's go through the migration process by working on the sample shopping bag application. It's a simple app that contains three classes--one to read user input, one to provide a shopping bag functionality, and one class with a main method to drive execution-- iteratively taking in user input, adding it to the shopping bag, and then printing the contents of the bag. The application has a dependency on the commons collections JAR file for the Bag data structure. It also calls the Java logging API to log the start and end times to the console.

 The shopping bag application has code that is referred to as a *monolith*. That is, all the code that forms the app is in one code base. This is really a simplification, and does not represent a real-world application that could span multiple projects and have different build artifacts that are bundled together. We'll keep things simple and run through the migration process with the simplified monolithic code base first and then expand it to a multi-project setup.

We are starting with the code in the `01-legacy-app` folder. The application code is in the `src` folder and the commons collections JAR in the `lib` folder:

```
src
└── packt.shoppingbag
    └── com
        └── packt
            └── shoppingbag
                ├── app
                │   └── App.java
                ├── data
                │   └── ShoppingBag.java
                └── input
                    └── UserInputUtil.java
```

The first step to modularizing this application is to create one big module that wraps around the entire application. We've run this application in the classpath in Chapter 10, *Preparing Your Code for Java 9*. The platform helped us there by creating an unnamed module that housed all of our code, which was an automatic process. This time, we'll do this ourselves by creating a module for our application called packt.shoppingbag.

First, just like before, let's assign a module source folder where the source of all the modules resides. You can either create a new folder or use the existing src folder. I'll choose the latter. In the src folder, create a module room folder, packt.shoppingbag, and a module-info.java file within it:

```
module packt.shoppingbag {
}
```

It's just an empty module descriptor for now. We'll get back to this in a bit.

Now that we have a module root, you can move the entire source (with the package name folder hierarchy) into the module root folder. The source code in the 11-migrating-application/02-migrating-to-one-module folder represents this state of the code base:

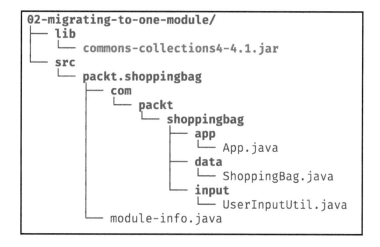

What we have now is far from a *modular* Java application. However, it does technically have one module. So, the way to compile and execute this application needs to be similar to what we've done so far in this book. That is, use the module source path argument for the source location containing the module root and the module path argument to point to the location of the compiled modules.

Let's try compiling this application. We'll first create a folder called out to contain the compiled classes:

```
$ mkdir out
```

Here's the javac command we've used all along:

```
$ javac --module-source-path src -d out $(find . -name '*.java')
```

If you run this, you'll get the following error:

```
$ javac --module-source-path src -d out $(find . -name '*.java')
./src/packt.shoppingbag/module-info.java:3: error: module not found:
commons.collections4
requires commons.collections4;
                            ^
1 error
```

The compiler is unable to find the commons collections dependency. Makes sense! The JAR in the lib folder and we never told the compiler about it. Now, can we add this JAR to the class path and compile again?

```
$ javac --module-source-path src -cp lib/commons-collections4-4.1.jar -d
out $(find . -name '*.java')
./src/packt.shoppingbag/module-info.java:3: error: module not found:
commons.collections4
requires commons.collections4;
                            ^
1 error
```

Nope, that won't work either. Why is that? Here's a picture of the application we have now:

We've moved the application code into the **module path**, but the library (in our case, a single JAR file) still exists in the **classpath**. And, since it is in the **classpath**, it is a part of the automatically created unnamed module. We've already seen how the unnamed module reads all resolved modules by default. Thus, any code in the unnamed module can access types in the **module path**. This is what we did in Chapter 10, *Preparing Your Code for Java 9*:

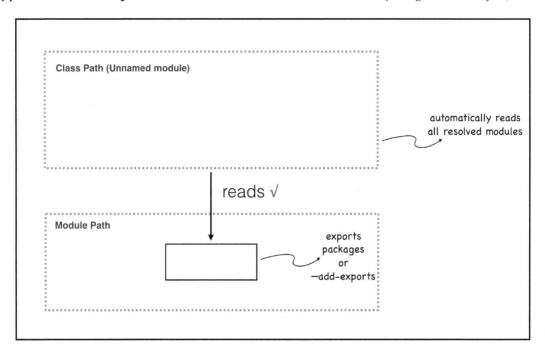

However, what we are trying to do here is the other way round. We want a module in the **module path** to access types from the **unnamed module**, and there's the problem. It turns out that no other module can read the **unnamed module**!

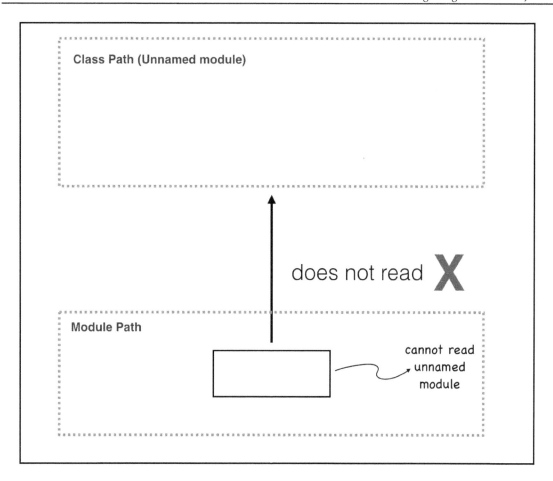

This is an intentional restriction. Every module needs to meet the requirements of strong encapsulation and reliable configuration. If a module were to read the class path, we'd basically be tossing reliable configuration out of the window! Since the class path does not have reliable configuration, there's no way the platform can verify if the module has everything it needs. So, preventing explicit Java 9 modules from accessing the classpath is a Good Thing™.

It does cause a major problem with migration though. Moving code from the class path to the module path is taking it down a one-way street. Once the code is crossed over to the module path, it cannot access anything from the class path. It's not so much an issue for your application code. Like we've seen, you can take your entire code base and put it in a giant named module, like we did with the shopping bag app. And now, none of your code is in the classpath. Great! However, what about libraries? Almost every Java application has third-party libraries and frameworks that are mostly JARs pulled in from the internet and bundled into the classpath. Since we don't control or maintain the library code, we cannot put their code in a module and wrap them with a module descriptor. So, until the authors of your libraries get to migrate their code to Java 9, you are stuck with non-modular libraries. How can your types access them? Do you have to hold off on modularizing your code until the very last library you use has its code migrated to Java 9?

Thankfully, that's not the case. The platform helps, once again, with the ability to create modules from JARs automatically. These modules are called **automatic modules**.

Automatic modules

In order to avoid the problems with third-party library dependencies, which we just discussed, the Java platform has a mechanism to automatically create modules from JAR files. You don't need to access the library code or even create a module descriptor. All you need is the JAR file. This works great because, for any third-party library, the one thing that you are sure to have is the JAR file!

Okay, what does it take to convert a JAR file into an automatic module and drop them into your application? The answer is--nothing! All you need to do is drop any JAR file into the module path. The platform automatically converts it into a module. Here are the things that the platform does to every JAR that it encounters in the module path:

- It automatically converts the JAR into a module and gives it a name
- It sets up the module definition--What the module reads and exports

And since they are now modules with a name (albeit automatically created), your code can depend on and require them just like any other module.

Let's examine the preceding two options in detail.

Automatic module naming

Given a JAR file, how does the platform know what to name it? For instance, if I were to drop the JAR file we are currently working with--`commons-collections4-4.1.jar`--into the module path, what would be the name of the module that gets created from it?

Naming of an automatic module is based off of the name of the JAR file, without the `.jar` extension. For example, if your JAR is named `foo.jar`, the name of the automatic module is `foo`! But, wait! What about invalid characters? It's very common to have the – character in the JAR name, but it's not allowed in module names. In such cases, the – character is automatically replaced by the `.` character. So, if the JAR file's name is `my-lib.jar`, the name of the automatic module would be `my.lib`.

While this naming works, it can be a hassle. It's because most JARs (especially ones from Maven or Gradle build systems) commonly have the version number in the name. This means that every time you get a new version of the JAR, the name of the module changes! To prevent that, and to make the library module names consistent, the automatic module name drops the version number from the name.

In summary, given a JAR file name, the automatic module naming does the following:

- It drops the `.jar` file extension
- It replaces – characters with `.`
- It removes the version string

Thus, the JAR, `commons-collections4-4.1.jar`, gets the automatic module name--`commons.collections4`.

Here are a few more examples:

JAR file name	Automatic module name
`commons-lang-1.2.10.jar`	`commons.lang`
`spring-core-4.3.10.RELEASE.jar`	`spring.core`
`guice-4.1.0.jar`	`guice`

Automatic module definition

What does the automatic module *require* and *export*? The answer is--everything! Remember that the platform creates the module descriptor automatically, so it has no idea what the module needs or what it will be used for. To make sure things work, it creates the least restrictive module definition possible.

- It `requires transitive` all resolved modules
- It exports all modules
- It reads the unnamed module (that is, all code in the classpath)

I hope you agree that this is the worst module definition you can possibly create for a module. However, this is required to ensure that the libraries in the Java ecosystem work seamlessly as automatic modules. This is not the ideal end state. We'd like to move to an environment where all the libraries are modularized too, and we work with actual modular JAR files with well-defined `requires` and `exports` definitions in the module path. Until that happens, automatic modules help get us going with the migration.

Note that the automatic modules `requires transitive` all resolved modules. You read that right! When you depend on an automatic module, you read *everything*, whether you want it or not! Be very cautious about what dependencies you use. Just because you get readability to any module doesn't mean it's okay to use it. Always keep the module definition in mind. Automatic modules are just a stop-gap arrangement. You don't want to take the readability relationship you get for granted. Remember that when the automatic module goes away, the transitive readability goes away with it.

Migrating with automatic modules

With this knowledge of automatic modules, let's resume the migration of the shopping bag application. We need to get the commons collection JAR out of the classpath and made into an automatic module. To do that, rather than moving the JAR, we'll just supply the `--module-path` argument with the path to the JAR (the `lib` folder), thereby making the JAR file in the module path. (Unlike the classpath, you don't have to specify the file name. Just the folder location will do.)

Here's the compiler command:

```
$ javac --module-source-path src --module-path lib -d out $(find . -
name '*.java')
```

We will get the following different errors now:

```
./src/packt.shoppingbag/com/packt/shoppingbag/app/App.java:3: error:
package java.util.logging is not visible
import java.util.logging.Logger;
                ^
(package java.util.logging is declared in module java.logging, but module
packt.shoppingbag does not read it)
./src/packt.shoppingbag/com/packt/shoppingbag/data/ShoppingBag.java:3:
error: package org.apache.commons.collections4 is not visible
import org.apache.commons.collections4.Bag;
                 ^
(package org.apache.commons.collections4 is declared in module
commons.collections4, but module packt.shoppingbag does not read it)
./src/packt.shoppingbag/com/packt/shoppingbag/data/ShoppingBag.java:4:
error: package org.apache.commons.collections4.bag is not visible
import org.apache.commons.collections4.bag.HashBag;
                    ^
(package org.apache.commons.collections4.bag is declared in module
commons.collections4, but module packt.shoppingbag does not read it)
3 errors
```

This fix should be a bit more obvious. The compiler is complaining that the
packt.shoppingbag module does not *require* the modules whose types it uses. It uses the
logging API (in module java.logging) and the Commons Collections API (from the now-
created automatic module called commons.collections4). Let's add them both as
dependencies in module-info.java. Note that we are using the automatic module name
to establish read relationships just like any other Java 9 module:

```
module packt.shoppingbag {
    requires java.logging;
    requires commons.collections4;
}
```

In this sample application, we are using just one JAR file. It is far from a
realistic scenario. Most real-world applications have multiple JARs. So,
this step would involve converting all the necessary JARs into automatic
modules by adding them to the module path and then adding the
right requires declaration in your module definition files.

When compiling again, things should work without any errors. To execute, we'll use the same `java` command with the `--module-path` flag that we've used before, with one minor change. We need to add the `lib` folder to the module path, because we, again, want the commons collections JAR to be treated as an automatic module.

```
$ java --module-path out:lib -m
packt.shoppingbag/com.packt.shoppingbag.app.App
Aug 02, 2017 2:47:45 PM com.packt.shoppingbag.app.App main
INFO: Shopping Bag application: Started
Enter item (Type 'end' when done):
```

We use the delimiter (`:` for macOS/Linux and `;` for Windows) to separate the two module paths--`out`, which has the compiled modules, and `lib`, which has the JAR. Everything should work as expected.

There is one potential problem that could result from automatic modules that you need to watch out for. Remember the split package problem that we discussed in `Chapter 6`, *Module Resolution, Readability, and Accessibility*? It is not possible for a single package to exist in two different modules in Java 9. However, it is possible for a package to exist in two different JARs. Now what happens when you take two such JARs that share a package and make them as automatic modules? They don't work, because they result in the split package problem. If you encounter this problem with any library of yours, there is unfortunately not much you can do. You'll either have to move things back to the classpath, or bug the library developers to have them fix their code. Or both!

Using jdeps to outline module relationships

We used `jdeps` to identify the usage of internal JDK APIs. The tool can do much more than that! One feature that comes in handy when migrating code to Java 9 is the `-summary` option. What this does is go through your compiled modules and identify the relationships between different modules. This makes sure that you get the right `requires` relationship specified in your modules, including the automatic modules.

Run the following `jdeps` command in the `11-migrating-application/02-migrating-to-one-module` folder:

```
$ jdeps -cp lib/commons-collections4-4.1.jar -recursive -summary out
commons-collections4-4.1.jar -> java.base
out -> lib/commons-collections4-4.1.jar
out -> java.base
out -> java.logging
```

The `-recursive` flag instructs `jdeps` to recursively navigate subfolders and list the dependencies of modules found in them too.

Notice that you get a really helpful output listing what module reads what. This is very handy when you have a bunch of JAR dependencies that were compiled in Java 8 or earlier, and you are trying to add them as automatic modules; rather than guessing what modules need to read these automatic modules, you can just run this command and get a good overview.

Refactoring into smaller modules

Now that you have your codebase in the module source path, the next steps would be to gradually break it down into smaller modules. This effort depends on the size of your codebase and how much of it you want to tackle at a time. You can choose to leave the single module as is and only create modules for any new code that you write. Thus, the legacy code does not get the benefit of modularity concepts, but any new code does. However, it is highly recommended to do the following two steps at this point:

1. Find modular versions or equivalents for your libraries and move the JARs out of the module path.
2. Break down the module into smaller modules.

Step 1 removes the broad transitive dependencies that automatic modules give you, so that you can get more fine-grained control over your dependencies. This depends on the libraries you use and if the authors have gotten to migrating them to Java 9. Once a library gets updated to Java 9, the updated version can still be placed in the module path, but this time, since they'll have a proper module descriptor, the platform will not need to convert them to automatic modules. You might have to check if the new name of the Java 9 modules in those libraries are different from the automatic module names you had previously used, and if they are, update your module descriptors to use the new library module name.

Step 2 makes sure that the legacy code also gets the benefits of strong encapsulation and reliable configuration. Since unlike step 1, we can control step 2, let's do just that for the shopping bag application.

Let's say we'd like to split the code into the following three modules:

- User Input module
- Bag module
- App module

I know this is an overkill for this small application. However, it helps as an example, illustrating the next step in the migration.

The `11-migrating-application/03-splitting-modules` folder contains the state of the application after separating the code into multiple modules. Note the module descriptors in each module narrow down the dependencies, making it clear which part of the code needs those external APIs. The `java.logging` is required just by the `packt.app` module. The commons collection is required by `packt.bag`.

Handling larger codebases

The sample application we modularized is very simple and not a representation of most real-world applications. Here are a couple of characteristics in which most applications differ:

- They have a *broader* code base that spans multiple projects. These projects may reside in different source locations and may be hooked to a build system. The build of the main application then gathers the right dependencies together to form the final application build.
- They have many more framework dependencies that have more complex needs. Frameworks such as Spring or Hibernate require access to your application code to do reflection. They might scan your classes for annotations and do various things such as dependency injection and object-relational mapping. In that sense, it is not just your application code that needs access to libraries as automatic modules; even such automatic modules would need access to your application code.

Given such a large Java 8 code base, how do you even begin migrating? Here are some steps that you'd typically follow:

Step 1: Draw module boundaries and create a high-level module map:

In my opinion, modularizing existing code starts with having at least a rough high-level idea of the modules you need and how you plan to split the code base. We've looked at some strategies and tips to help you draw module boundaries in Chapter 9, *Module Design Patterns and Strategies*. Depending on the complexity of your code, you'll need to either look at the code in entirety or in high-level parts and come up with some module names and interfaces.

Once you have a rough idea about what your modules will be, you can create a module graph that represents the dependencies between these modules. Don't get too involved in the details. This is just a rough sketch and you may be inclined to make changes to either the modules or their relationships as you get into the weeds and start refactoring.

Step 2: Modularize the *main* application:

Among all the code projects that a large application consists of, there's usually one that can be classified as the *main* project. It is the one that perhaps starts the execution or the project that is built and deployed as the application. That would be a good place to start. You can follow the steps you learned in this chapter to bring that application over to the module path first.

Step 3: Use the module overrides for special library needs:

If you are using a framework like Spring or Hibernate, you are sure to run into problems when using them as automatic modules. That's because those frameworks typically need access to your code base to reflectively scan your classes for annotations. We know that automatic modules read all resolved modules. So, it technically reads your application modules that could have Spring annotations. However, if your modules do not *export* the packages, it'll still be unable to access them. You can get around this problem in a couple of ways:

- Add the `opens` declaration to the packages that contain such annotations in your module definition so that the libraries have access to reflect on the necessary classes
- Use the `--add-opens` command-line arguments to achieve the same result

Step 4: Leverage automatic modules for in-house build artifacts:

There's no reason why you should not use automatic modules even for your own application JARs. Let's say you are migrating a large Maven application with multiple artifact dependencies on other projects that are built in-house (or code that you own). Those in-house artifacts can be added to the module path and converted into automatic modules too. One thing to watch out for here is the split package problem. Since we are dealing with in-house code, there's a good chance that there are package overlaps between JARs. In such cases, you'll need to refactor your code to make sure there are no overlapping packages in JAR files. You can do this refactoring while using an older version of Java too.

Step 5a: Break down the *main* project into smaller modules:

Again, following the process we used in this chapter, start chunking away pieces of the monolithic module into smaller pieces. Establish clearer dependencies among the smaller modules as you go.

Step 5b: Migrate modules from the leaf up:

In parallel to **Step 5a**, you can also start migrating projects other than the main project too. Since you've built your module tree, the order of migration of modules becomes clear. You can make your migration significantly easier by ordering the modules you choose to migrate from the leaf of the module dependency tree and work your way toward the top. The ideal candidate for migration is a module that does not have any other application module dependency. Dependency on Java modules is okay though!

For example, let's say this is your target module graph for the code that you plan to achieve after migration. The graph includes just your application modules. Any dependency on platform modules is excluded in this graph:

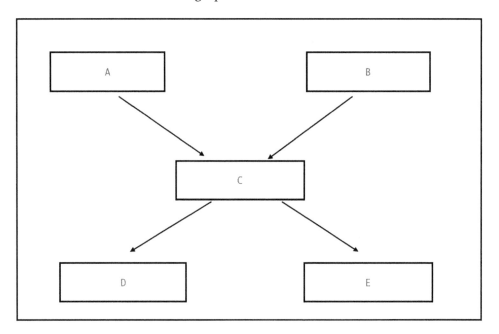

The first set of modules you should pick for migration are **D** and **E**. Once they are done, migrate **C**, then **A** and **B**.

Migrating libraries

We've looked at steps and strategies to follow when migrating applications to the Java modules. How about libraries? Let's say you are the maintainer of an open source library that is used by many people. Or, perhaps, you maintain a library that's used by multiple teams in your organization. How would you migrate such a code base? Wouldn't that require you to follow the same steps we've covered to migrate applications? Well, mostly yes. However, there are certain things you need to do differently with libraries. This section covers those details.

What's perhaps the biggest difference with libraries is that you no longer work in the *context* of an application. A library could be used by multiple applications. These applications could be using multiple versions of Java. How could you create a single library JAR that could work for all those cases? Thankfully, there are some features in the platform that make this easier.

Before we get into those specific problems, let's look at what it takes to migrate library code to use Java 9 modules. Here are some high-level steps you need to follow as a library author:

1. **Eliminate the JDK internal API usage**: This is no different from what we did for applications. We need to make sure the library is a good Java 9 citizen. Calls to JDK internals or deprecated APIs are a no-no. Refactor your code to avoid the calls or use a replacement that our friendly `jdeps` tool with the `--jdk-internals` option suggests.

2. **Eliminate any split packages**: We've looked at how split packages cause problems with automatic modules. You'll need to make sure your JARs do not contain packages that could potentially exist in other JARs in your organization. If other teams own libraries whose packages conflict with yours, you'll need to work with them to streamline the package names

3. **Identify a name for your core library module**: As with any module, you need to come up with a name for the library. This is not that big of a deal when working with libraries that are used only in your organization. However, it's a much more important step when dealing with open source modules. Like we've covered in `Chapter 2`, *Creating Your First Java Module*, module names can follow reverse domain name convention. You can opt to go with a shorter name for strictly in-house libraries to ease readability and communication, because name conflicts are less likely in such cases.

4. **Start refactoring and converting your code into modules**: This involves moving your code into module root folders, adding module descriptors, and defining the `requires` and `exports` definitions for your modules. Be careful about any types that you encapsulate. If there are consumers of your library using those types, they'll not be able to use them anymore, unless they add the `--add-exports` overrides.

   As with application migration, I highly recommend that you survey your library code and come up with a high-level module diagram that outlines the relationships between modules before you start digging into the code and moving files around. It will save you a lot of time and work!

5. **Add transitive dependencies or wrap around dependency leakage**: There's a chance that your library code depends on other libraries. They may be other in-house libraries or open source JARs. These libraries may not be migrated to Java 9 yet, and we have the same problem we did for application dependencies. Here, again, you'll need to use automatic modules for the JARs that your library depends on. If using your APIs requires access to those libraries, it's a good idea to add require transitive on those libraries in your module definition. If possible, wrap around those types so that the code consuming your library doesn't have to be aware of this dependency.

Reserving library names

Let's say you are a library developer who is not ready to migrate your code to Java 9 yet. We know that's not a problem. Other Java 9 applications can still consume your library by dropping the JAR into the module path, thus making an automatic module out of it. They use the auto-generated module name from the JAR file name and use that in their module definition files. However, what if you have a really cool name for your module that you plan to use when you eventually get to migrating to Java 9? Does it mean that all the consumers will then have to go to all the module definitions that specify the auto-generated name and update them to the new module name? That can be tedious.

The Java 9 platform gives library authors an option to *reserve* a module name for their libraries, even before migrating their libraries to Java 9. So, you, as a library author, can specify what you want your Java 9 module name to be in the `META-INF/MANIFEST.MF` file in your JAR. You can do this in your Java 8 compiled JAR. Once you do that and bundle it into your JAR file, when it is dropped into the module path in a Java 9 application, the platform picks that name up as the automatic module name. It essentially overrides the automatic naming of modules from the JAR file name.

Here's how you specify your preferred automatic module name in your JAR file. Create a file called `MANIFEST.MF` file in the `META_INF` folder in the root of the JAR file. Add the following line to specify the preferred automatic module name:

```
Automatic-Module-Name: <my.preferred.module.name>
```

Once you've done this, the JAR is given this name instead of the name from the JAR file name when the platform converts it into an automatic module. And all the consumers have to refer to your JAR in the module path by using this preferred module name. Thus, when you do get to migrating your module to Java 9, you can use the preferred name in the module descriptor and the consumers of your library won't need to change their module descriptors.

Using jdeps to create module descriptors

Once you start breaking down your library JARs into modules, depending on the size of your library, you may have a lot of work to do. It's not straightforward to identify which modules you'll need to `require` and which you'll need to `export`. The `jdeps` tool has another trick up its sleeve. It can look at your JAR files and automatically come up with module descriptors for you to use.

The syntax is as follows:

```
$ jdeps --generate-module-info <output-location> <path-to-jars>
```

Let's try this for the commons-collections JAR file:

```
$ jdeps --generate-module-info out lib/commons-collections4-4.1.jar
```

The output should look like this:

```
writing to out/commons.collections4/module-info.java
```

As you can see, `jdeps` has generated a module root folder with the same automatic naming algorithm we've seen before. Inside that folder, it has created a `module-info.java` file that it has populated with the `requires` and `exports` declarations that it identified by scanning the classes in the JARs:

```
module commons.collections4 {
  requires transitive java.xml;
  exports org.apache.commons.collections4;
  ...
}
```

You can run this command and point to multiple JARs, and it'll do this for every single JAR, which also benefits from any relationships between the JARs. The generated `module-info.java` files for those related modules will include the relationship too!

> Remember to use this feature just as a starting point to define your module definitions. The platform cannot obviously guess the perfect module definition for your library just by looking at the code. It's your job as the author of the library to come up with what it requires and what it encapsulates or exports. There is also a technical limitation here. The `jdeps` does static code analysis, so it will not be able to catch any runtime reflective access that libraries may perform. If your library is using reflection, you'll need to manually add the `exports` or `opens` declarations to the right modules yourself.

Building libraries for multiple Java versions

When migrating applications, we had to deal with the scenario that the dependent libraries might not all be migrated to Java 9. When dealing with libraries, you'll need to tackle the opposite problem. The applications consuming your library may not all be Java 9. You'll have to support Java 8 (or perhaps even older versions of Java in some cases). How do you, as a library author, create library distributions for all those versions? Before Java 9, you used to have two options:

- You could create separate JARs for each Java version
- In your library code, you could use reflection to do a *feature check*. For example, you could reflectively access a platform API that was introduced in Java 8. If it works, you are in Java 8. If not, drop down to Java 7, and so on.

Both these options are tedious. There is a new alternative with Java 9, with a feature called *multi-release JARs*. The concept is simple. You create a special JAR file called a *multi-release JAR* that contains classes for all versions of Java you are targeting.

Here's how it works. Multi-release JARs have a special structure that holds the classes within it:

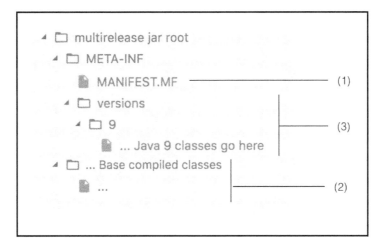

Here's what you'll find in a multi-release JAR file, corresponding to the numbering in the diagram:

1. There's a root `META-INF` folder with a `MANIFEST.MF` file that contains the following line:

   ```
   Multi-Release: true
   ```

   This tells the platform that this is a multi-release JAR and thus needs to be treated differently

2. The JAR root also contains a default version of the compiled classes, just like any other JAR. Remember, this JAR targets multiple Java versions and it could hold multiple target versions of the same class. The classes at the root folder are the *default* base versions that could potentially apply to multiple Java versions

3. There's a folder called `versions` inside `META-INF`. To target multiple runtimes, the JAR packages classes into sub-folders here. There's one folder for each Java version you want to target. Each such folder contains classes that have been specifically compiled for that release version. So, if the JAR is used in that version of the Java platform, the classes in the version folder override the classes in the `multirelease` folder and are picked up instead. If the JAR is used in a platform version that does not have classes in the `META-INF` folder, or the class needed doesn't exist in the version folder, the runtime falls back to the contents of the `multirelease` folder.

Notice that the default versions of the classes are in the root location in the JAR file. This is why you can use the JAR file with older versions of Java too. To older Java versions, a multi-release JAR file looks just like an ordinary JAR file--the root location is all the platform looks at, and the versions folder is ignored!

Let's try creating a simple multi-release JAR. The `11-migrating-application/04-multirelease-jars` folder contains an extremely simple library. It's called `mylib` and it has a class with a method that prints the contents of a list passed to it.

We'd like to create a multi-release JAR for this library targeting two different versions of Java:

- The base version of the library targets all pre-Java 9 versions. It contains code that performs a `for` loop and prints the contents of the list as follows:

```
public class PrintList {
  public void print(List<?> list) {
    for (int i = 0; i < list.size(); i++) {
      System.out.println(list.get(i));
    }
  }
}
```

- The Java 9 specific version of this library has two changes--it declares itself as a Java 9 module with `module-info.java` and it uses `forEach` and a function reference to print the contents of the list, as follows:

```
public class PrintList {
  public void print(List<?> list) {
    list.forEach(System.out::println);
  }
}
```

The two versions of the library are in two separate folders. Since there will be two separate versions of the same class, it helps to separate them this way.

Here's the structure of the code:

```
    ── base
    │    └── src
    │         └── packt
    │              └── mylib
    │                   └── PrintList.java
    └── java9
         └── src
              └── packt.mylib
                   ├── module-info.java
                   └── packt
                        └── mylib
                             └── PrintList.java
```

The first step to making a multi-release JAR is to add the MANIFEST.MF file that declares it. Add this file at the root of the project with a single line, shown next. Make sure you match the statement exactly without any extra spaces:

```
Multi-Release: true
```

Now, we'll create the folders that hold the compiled classes. We'll create a folder called out and have two subfolders--base for the base classes and 9 for the Java 9 version, as shown here:

```
$ mkdir out
$ mkdir out/base
$ mkdir out/9
```

Next, we will compile the classes into these two folders by setting the right release versions. The --release parameter to the javac command lets you target specific Java versions for your compiled classes:

```
$ javac --release 7 -d out/base base/src/packt/mylib/PrintList.java
```

The preceding command compiles the PrintList.java class with target release 7, and places the complied output in the out/base directory.

 Note that you don't need to have multiple versions of Java installed on your machine to achieve this. Java 9 has the ability to generate classes targeting different versions of Java by itself! This is analogous to the -target flag in Java that has been available in earlier versions of the Java platform.

Next, we'll compile the Java 9 version as follows:

```
$ javac --release 9 -d out/9 java9/src/packt.mylib/module-info.java
java9/src/packt.mylib/packt/mylib/PrintList.java
```

There are two Java files this time--`PrintList.java` and `module-info.java`. The complied classes go to the `out/9` directory.

Now that we have the compiled classes, it's time to create a multi-release JAR. Let's first create a JAR file with the base version classes. We also supply the `MANIFEST.MF` file to be included in the JAR:

```
$ jar -cf mylib.jar MANIFEST.MF -C out/base .
```

The `-c` option tells the `jar` tool to create a new JAR, and `f` option is used to specify the JAR file name (here, `mylib.jar`). The `-C` option changes the directory the tool is looking for to `out.base` and lets it compile classes there (as specified by `"."`).

This creates the JAR file and adds the base classes to it. Next, let's add the Java 9 classes:

```
$ jar -uf mylib.jar --release 9 -C out/9 .
```

The `-u` options tells the `jar` tool to update the JAR rather than create one. We are targeting release 9 this time, and including compiled classes in the `out/9` directory.

 You don't have to add all the classes in your JAR file for every version. Try to keep version-specific classes to a minimum. If there are common classes in the base version that the version-specific copy can reuse, you just don't include it here. The platform will fall back to the base folder for classes it doesn't find for that specific version.

Here are the contents of the JAR file that's generated. This is the structure we have already seen:

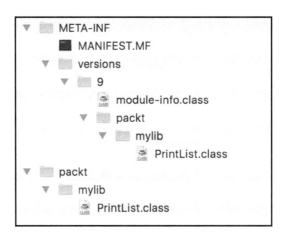

Remember that the multi-release JAR feature was introduced in Java 9. So, you cannot really create version-specific alternatives in your JAR for Java 8 or earlier. Those versions of the platform will not know to read from the META-INF/versions folder. They'd just use the compiled classes in the JAR root folder. This is, however, a good feature to use if you need to create new Java-9-only classes. Since those classes will end up in the META-INF/versions folder, older platforms will ignore them. Once future versions of Java are released, this feature can be used for those versions too. So, you can have a META-INF/versions/10 folder targeting the Java 10 platform, for example.

Summary

In this chapter, we looked at how to migrate a pre-Java 9 application to use the Java 9 modularity features. You learned how to plan the overall migration strategy, and what the ideal end goal of such a migration is. You also learned about a new feature in the platform that lets you handle dependencies and libraries that are not modular--automatic modules. We looked at how automatic modules are named, how they behave, and how we can use them in our migration process.

You then learned how to approach migrating libraries. We looked at some factors to consider when migrating the library code, as well as the multi-release JAR feature that lets us create single JARs that target multiple Java platform versions.

In the next and final chapter, we'll wrap things up by looking at two important aspects that Java developers commonly deal with--build tooling and unit testing. We will understand how they work in the context of a modular Java application.

12
Using Build Tools and Testing Java Modules

In the previous chapter, we looked at several strategies and approaches to migrate an existing Java code base to Java 9. In this chapter, we'll wrap up our journey of Java 9 modularity by looking at two important topics that you are very likely to encounter, irrespective of whether you are migrating a legacy code base or creating a new modular application from scratch. They are build tool integration and unit testing.

Here's what we'll cover in this chapter:

- Integrating Java 9 modules with the Maven build process
- Working with a multi-module Java 9 Maven project
- Writing unit test cases for Java 9 modules using JUnit
- Handling new access issues and challenges with testing in Java 9

Considering that build systems and unit testing are extremely common and important parts of a modern Java developer's workflow, it may seem odd that we are tackling both these topics in the final chapter of this book. This is for a good reason. Understanding and working with these concepts requires an understanding of a lot of the topics we've covered in the last few chapters. Now that you have explored concepts such as open modules in Chapter 9, *Module Design Patterns and Strategies*, and automatic modules in Chapter 11, *Migrating Your Code to Java 9*, you are all set to tackle this chapter with ease!

Integrating with Apache Maven

Two of the build systems that are very commonly used in the Java landscape are Apache Maven and Gradle. When you are working on an enterprise Java application, it's very likely that you'll have to deal with one of these two options. In this book so far, we've been working with the command line to get the compiler and runtime to execute. However, that's rarely a reasonable thing to do in a complex project. So, what does it take to use such a build system in a Java 9 modular application?

 At the time of writing this, Maven has a workable integration with Java 9, while Gradle is still in active development. Thus, we'll only be covering Apache Maven integration in this book. It's only a matter of time before the Java tooling ecosystem catches up to the modularity changes in Java 9, so it shouldn't be surprising to see better integration and an overall experience of using these tools with Java 9 over time.

Let's examine the way you can create a Maven project that contains and builds a Java 9 modular application.

A Maven refresher

This chapter assumes you are familiar with at least the basic concepts of Maven, but here is a quick refresher. Maven is, among other things, a project build tool. It is based on convention and provides a formal structure to organize your code, name your artifacts, and establish dependencies on other projects. This may sound very similar to what we've been doing with Java 9 modularity, but it isn't. Unlike the Java platform module system, Maven is concerned with building (or assembling) your artifacts, and not verifying compile time or runtime accuracy.

When you create a Maven artifact, you assign *coordinates* to it: the group name, the artifact name, and the version. You specify this in a file called pom.xml. This file also lets you specify dependencies on other Maven artifacts so that when the build process runs, Maven can fetch the necessary dependencies and make them available to the Java compiler or runtime.

Using Maven with Java 9 modules

When you bring Java 9 modules into the picture, you can see that there are two parallel concepts of modules here: the Maven concept of an artifact with the definition in `pom.xml` and the Java platform concept of a module with the module definition in `module-info.java`. However, these two work surprisingly well when you collapse the two and have each Maven project containing one Java 9 module.

Consider the following folder structure of a single Maven project. The code is in the `lib` folder. It is a typical Maven project. It has a `pom.xml` descriptor that contains the Maven coordinates for this artifact. However, it also has the module-info.java in the `src/main/java` folder that sets it up as a Java 9 module!

```
lib
├── pom.xml
└── src
    └── main
        └── java
            ├── com
            │   └── packt
            │       └── lib
            │           └── Lib.java
            └── module-info.java
```

With this approach, the idea is to create a Maven artifact for each Java 9 module. This means that you'll need to come up with two separate names:

- The coordinates for the Maven artifact--comprising of group name and artifact name
- The name of the Java 9 module

Now, when it comes to establishing dependencies between two of these modules, you will need to specify dependencies in two places. Let's say, for example, that you have two Maven Java 9 projects called **A** and **B**. In order to specify that A is dependent on B, you need to do the following:

- Add a `<dependency>` tag in the Maven `pom.xml` file of A specifying the Maven coordinates of B
- Add a `requires` declaration in the `module-info.java` file of A specifying the module name of B

The advantage of this approach is that Maven takes care of fetching the necessary artifacts and placing them in the module path. Then, the Java platform module system has everything it needs when the compiler or runtime executes! Note that this doesn't work if you miss either one of these two dependency configurations. If you forget to specify the Maven dependency, Maven will not fetch the artifact and place it in the module path. If you forget to add the requires declaration in `module-info.java`, your code cannot access the types in the dependency, even though Maven has made it available in the module path.

While this works great for one or two modules, this can also get tricky to manage when you are dealing with an application consisting of multiple modules. In such situations, we can leverage the multi-module project feature of Maven to better organize multiple Maven + Java 9 modules.

Working on a multi-module Java 9 Maven project

Let's look at a sample Maven multi-module project. Let's say we want to build two Java modules: `packt.main` and `packt.lib`. The `packt.lib` module contains a library class `Lib` with a method called `sampleMethod`, and the `packt.main` module contains a class `App` with a main method calling `sampleMethod` from `Lib`. Thus, `packt.main` has to read `packt.lib`, as shown here:

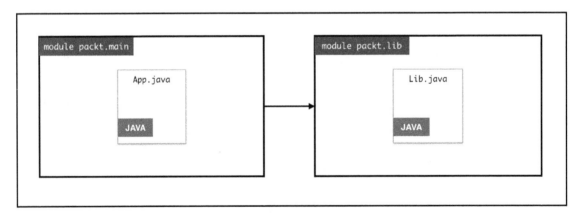

You've already learned that you should have one Maven project corresponding to each Java module. However, in order to ease the development, and to leverage the concept of a multi-module project in Maven, we can instead create a parent root Maven artifact. Now, both the modules of our application can be Maven child projects, as shown here:

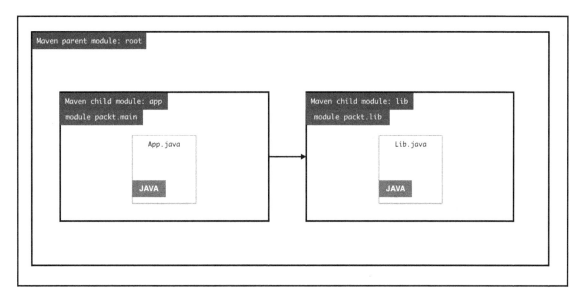

The code is available in the `12-build-tools-and-testing/01-maven-integration` folder. There is a root Maven module at the root directory. This module acts as a parent module. This is just a Maven container to facilitate the build process. We don't really need a corresponding Java module for this. Within the root folder are two child Maven projects `main` and `lib`.

Here, its `pom.xml` at the root (truncated for brevity):

```xml
<project ...>
 <modelVersion>4.0.0</modelVersion>
 <groupId>com.packt</groupId>
 <artifactId>root</artifactId>
 <packaging>pom</packaging>
 <version>1.0-SNAPSHOT</version>
 <name>root</name>
 <modules>
   <module>main</module>
   <module>lib</module>
 </modules>
 ...
</project>
```

The packaging node in the XML specifies the pom value, indicating that this is a parent pom. It has two module declarations indicating the two Maven child modules that it is a parent to. Don't be confused by the use of the term modules here. We are talking about Maven modules, not Java 9 modules.

Within each child module, main and lib, it's just like we've seen so far. They are standard Maven projects, but with the `module-info.java` file in the `src/main/java` location making them Java 9 modules.

The following screenshot shows the complete folders structure:

```
root
├── lib
│   ├── pom.xml
│   └── src
│       └── main
│           └── java
│               ├── com
│               │   └── packt
│               │       └── lib
│               │           └── Lib.java
│               └── module-info.java
├── main
│   ├── pom.xml
│   └── src
│       └── main
│           └── java
│               ├── com
│               │   └── packt
│               │       └── App.java
│               └── module-info.java
└── pom.xml
```

Since the main project is using a type from the lib project, both the Maven and Java dependencies are configured.

Here's the main project's `pom.xml` file specifying the dependency:

```
<dependency>
  <groupId>com.packt</groupId>
  <artifactId>lib</artifactId>
  <version>1.0-SNAPSHOT</version>
</dependency>
```

And here's its `module-info.java` file:

```
module packt.main {
  requires packt.lib;
}
```

Building the multi-module project

Before we build, make sure you have the latest version of Maven installed in your path. Running the following command should give you the Maven version that's installed on your machine:

```
$ mvn -v
  Apache Maven 3.5.0 (ff8f5e7444045639af65f6095c62210b5713f426;
  2017-04-03T12:39:06-07:00)
```

If you don't see this output, you'll need to download Apache Maven from `https://maven. apache.org` and add the `bin` folder on the download to your operating system's `PATH` variable.

Let's try to build this project. There are inclusions in the root project's `pom.xml` to make this ready to be built on Java 9. Following is the Maven compiler plugin used to set the Java version to 9:

```
<plugin>
 <groupId>org.apache.maven.plugins</groupId>
 <artifactId>maven-compiler-plugin</artifactId>
 <version>3.6.2</version>
 <configuration>
   <release>9</release>
 </configuration>
</plugin>
```

With this, you should be able to run Maven's build command and have the Java 9 compiler compile our classes. Switch to the `12-build-tools-and-testing/01-maven-integration/root` directory and run the following command:

```
$ mvn clean install
```

The output below, truncated for readability, indicates that all the modules have been compiled:

```
[INFO] Reactor Summary:
[INFO]
[INFO] root ....................................... SUCCESS [  0.379 s]
[INFO] lib ........................................ SUCCESS [  3.646 s]
[INFO] main ....................................... SUCCESS [  0.195 s]
[INFO] ------------------------------------------------------------
[INFO] BUILD SUCCESS
```

Executing the multi-module project

In order to execute the class with the `main` method as a Maven lifecycle, we use the `exec-maven-plugin`. This is also possible thanks to the configuration in the root project's `pom.xml` file. Here's the listing that specifies this configuration:

```
<plugin>
    <groupId>org.codehaus.mojo</groupId>
    <artifactId>exec-maven-plugin</artifactId>
    <version>1.6.0</version>
    <executions>
      <execution>
        <goals>
          <goal>exec</goal>
        </goals>
      </execution>
    </executions>
    <configuration>
      <executable>${JAVA_HOME}/bin/java</executable>
      <arguments>
        <argument>--module-path</argument>
        <modulepath/>
        <argument>--module</argument>
        <argument>packt.main/com.packt.App</argument>
      </arguments>
    </configuration>
</plugin>
```

As is typical with Maven configuration, this looks verbose. However, what's interesting for us is the configuration section. We are configuring the `java` command, so you have the executable path here mapped from `$JAVA_HOME`. We are also passing in the two arguments we should be very familiar with now--the `--module-path` argument indicating where the compiled modules are, and the `--module` indicating what's the module and class containing the main method.

Note that for the `--module-path` argument, we aren't specifying the path manually. This is because Maven is compiling the modules for us, so we want Maven itself to supply us with the path where it has placed the compiled classes. That is done using the special `<modulepath />` tag. We'll discuss the module path in Maven in a bit more detail in the following section.

Switch to the `12-build-tools-and-testing/01-maven-integration/root/main` directory and run the following command to call the `exec` plugin:

```
$ mvn exec:exec
```

Here's the truncated output:

```
[INFO] Scanning for projects...
[INFO]
[INFO] ------------------------------------------------------------------------
----
[INFO] Building main 1.0-SNAPSHOT
[INFO] ------------------------------------------------------------------------
----
[INFO]
[INFO] --- exec-maven-plugin:1.6.0:exec (default-cli) @ main ---
Library method called!
...
```

The `Library method called!` line is the output of the `main` method calling the library method and printing the message to the console.

Understanding the exec plugin's module path

While there are several advantages to using Maven this way, one significant advantage is how easy it becomes to manage the directories during the compile and build step. When we ran `javac` manually, we always had to manually specify the *output* directory where all the compiled classes would go. When we ran `java`, we had to make sure the module path contained the output location of classes, as well as any dependent modules and libraries. Maven takes that work away from us. Thanks to the `<modulepath/>` line that we added as the module path argument to `exec-maven-plugin`, Maven automatically constructs the module path for us. Here's what Maven adds to the module path:

- It automatically includes the build location of the project. We ran the plugin on the `main` project. Maven makes sure the compiled classes from `main` are available in the module path.
- It automatically makes sure the dependencies are in the module path as well. In the `main` project's `pom.xml`, we specified a dependency on `lib`. Maven acknowledges the dependency and automatically includes the complied `lib` module into the module path!

- It automatically includes dependencies that aren't Java 9 modules too! Let's say your `pom.xml` file specifies a dependency on a third-party library that isn't migrated to Java 9 yet. Maven automatically adds those jars to the module path as well. Guess what happens when you add a pre-Java 9 JAR into the module path? They become automatic modules! Your modules can use the `requires` syntax to depend on them, just like any Java 9 module. Thus, your workflow becomes extremely simple and consistent when dealing with dependencies, be it Java 9 or older.

Unit testing modules with Java 9

The readability and accessibility constraints pose new and interesting problems when it comes to testing in Java 9. Let's look back at the way we've always been unit testing code in Java. Here are two common practices:

- The unit test code typically resides in a separate source folder that is added to the classpath. This is to separate the test code from the actual application code and to also make it easy to exclude the test folder when building an application for deployment.
- The unit test classes typically share the same package as the class under test. This is to make sure the test classes can access the package-private members of the classes under test, even though they are in a completely different location.

These two design decisions work well when classes are in the classpath, because we know that the physical location of the classes in the classpath doesn't matter. However, all that is changing with Java 9! Here's how:

- In Java 9, the test code could face access restrictions due to strong encapsulation. Your Java 9 classes under test are in a module. So, the only way to access all the types in your module from your test classes is to put your test classes in the same module as well! This is not ideal because, when you build and ship a Java module, the entire contents go with it. The only other option is to keep your test classes outside the module and only test the classes that are *exported*.
- If you keep your tests in a separate folder and in a separate module, you cannot have your test classes share the same package as the classes under test. This will cause the split package problem since the same package exists in both the application module and the test module. Thus, you cannot access and test package-private members

Considering these challenges, one way to work around them is as follows:

- Create a separate test module for every module you need to test.
- Write test cases that test the exported module interface.
- If you need to write tests for any internal types that aren't exported by the module, use `--add-exports` overrides during test execution. Yes, `--add-exports` isn't a good idea for application code, but it's a reasonable workaround for testing.

Testing a Java 9 module

Let's examine how this works by testing the `packt.sortutil` from the sample address book viewer application. The code is available at the `12-build-tools-and-testing/02-testing` location. The `src` folder contains the `packt.sortutil` module--the module under test.

To test this, we can create a new test module: `packt.sortutil.test`. A good convention to follow is to name the test modules with the name of the module being tested followed by `.test`. Here's the module definition for `packt.sortutil.test`:

```
module packt.sortutil.test {
    requires packt.sortutil;
}
```

By declaring the dependency on the module, you can access its exported types and test them through code. Here's a sample class in the test module that verifies that the output is accurate:

```
package packt.util.test;
public class SortUtilTestMain {
  public static void main(String[] args) {
    SortUtil sortUtil = new SortUtil();
    List out = sortUtil.sortList(Arrays.asList("b", "a", "c"));
    assert out.size() == 3;
    assert "a".equals(out.get(0));
    assert "b".equals(out.get(1));
    assert "c".equals(out.get(2));
  }
}
```

Compiling and running the code with assertions enabled (the −ea argument) tells us that our tests have passed:

```
$ javac -d out --module-source-path src --module
  packt.sortutil,packt.sortutil.test
$ java -ea --module-path out:lib --module
  packt.sortutil.test/packt.util.test.SortUtilTestMain
```

You should not see any output, which indicates all assertions have successfully passed.

Integrating with JUnit

While writing classes with main methods can get the job done with unit testing, we can do better. You typically write tests in Java using a framework such as JUnit. JUnit is a complete testing framework with handy life cycle hooks and annotations that you can use to write tests easily. Let's look at converting our test module to use JUnit.

Here are the steps:

1. Get the JUnit jars. You can either download them from the JUnit website (http://junit.org/junit4/) or download them from Maven Central. It also has a dependency on the hamcrest core JAR file, so download that too. Place the JARs in a lib folder. We intend to add this location to the module path. The downloaded JAR files are available in the lib folder at 12−build−tools−and−testing/02−testing/src/packt.sortutil.test.

2. Use the JUnit annotations in your test code. Here's the new SortUtilTest written as a JUnit test:

```java
public class SortUtilTest {
  private SortUtil sortUtil;
  @Before public void setUp() {
    sortUtil = new SortUtil();
  }
  @Test
  public void testReturnsSameSize() {
    List out = sortUtil.sortList(Arrays.asList("b", "a", "c"));
    SortUtil sortUtil = new SortUtil();
    assert out.size() == 3;
  }
  @Test
  public void sortsList() {
    List out = sortUtil.sortList(Arrays.asList("b", "a", "c"));
    assert "a".equals(out.get(0));
    assert "b".equals(out.get(1));
```

```
        assert "c".equals(out.get(2));
    }
}
```

3. Specify that the test module has a dependency on the JUnit library. Since the JUnit JAR will be added to the classpath, it will be treated as an automatic module. So, to establish dependency, you'll need to figure out what the automatic module name will be from the JAR file name. The JAR file downloaded is called `junit-4.12.jar`. Stripping off the `.jar` extension and the version number, we'll end up with the automatic module--name – `junit`.

4. Declare the test module as `open`. The way JUnit works is by scanning the annotations on your classes to figure out what to do. So, it needs access to the test classes in your test module. You can either export the necessary packages or declare them as open. I prefer the latter, since we only need to enable reflective access to JUnit.

Here's the updated module definition of the `packt.sortutil.test` module:

```
open module packt.sortutil.test {
    requires packt.sortutil;
    requires junit;
}
```

Let's compile and run the test to see what the behavior is:

```
$ javac -d out --module-source-path src --module-path lib --module
  packt.sortutil,packt.sortutil.test
```

The only change this time is the addition of the lib directory as the module path. This lets the Java platform treat the JUnit JAR as an automatic module, which is what we need. This should succeed without any errors.

What happens if we run this now? We are running the JUnit test runner class, so that's what we need to specify in the core JUnit runner class `JUnitCore` (in the automatic module `junit`) as value to the `--module` argument to Java. Following that is the fully qualified name of the class under test--`SortUtilTest`. Here's what the command looks like:

```
$ java --module-path out:lib --module junit/org.junit.runner.JUnitCore
  packt.util.test.SortUtilTest
```

Will it work? It will not! Here's the error you should see:

```
JUnit version 4.12.E
Time: 0.001
There was 1 failure:
1) initializationError(org.junit.runner.JUnitCommandLineParseResult)
java.lang.IllegalArgumentException: Could not find class
[packt.util.test.SortUtilTest]
```

Turns out Java is unable to find the `SortUtilTest` class. Why is that? The compiled module is available in the out directory that we've passed to the `--module-path` option! There's a reason why it does not see the class.

Think back to the module resolution discussion in Chapter 8, *Understanding Linking and Using jlink*. The module resolution is a traversal of dependent modules originating from the starting point--the module you specify in the `--module` argument. Since the starting point here is the JUnit automatic module, the module resolution process never resolves the application or test modules. This is because the JUnit automatic module does not read our modules! The way to solve this problem and have the runtime see our modules is using the `--add-modules` option. Passing our test module using this option should result in the execution completing successfully:

```
$ java --module-path out:lib --add-modules packt.sortutil.test --module
junit/org.junit.runner.JUnitCore packt.util.test.SortUtilTest
JUnit version 4.12
..
Time: 0.005

OK (2 tests)
```

Note that we did not have to add the `packt.sortutil` module to the `--add-modules` option. Just the test module sufficed. This is because the test module has an explicit dependency on `packt.sortutil` through the requires declaration, and so the module resolution process now picks it up automatically!

Wrapping up

With this, we come to the end of our exploration of Java 9 modularity together. You now have a good understanding of Java 9 modularity and more importantly, how to use the feature and the related concepts in your code. This is certainly an exciting new addition to the Java language, and we, as developers, have both the ability and the responsibility to use these features wisely and well.

While this is the end of the book, I hope you are excited and well equipped to continue your journey into learning about and building awesome modular applications in Java.

Summary

In this chapter, we covered two important aspects of Java programming that play a significant role in most real-world Java applications--build systems and testing. We looked at how we can use Maven to structure our projects and align Maven's multi-module project concepts with Java 9 modular applications. We examined how such an application looks like, and learned how to compile and execute the application through Maven lifecycle processes. We then learned about how testing can be incorporated into a Java modular application. We looked at some of the challenges with testing that result from some constraints that Java modularity introduces to the language and how to work around them. We then created a JUnit test case and leveraged the JUnit framework to execute a module test case.

Index